The Reference Shelf®

Reproductive Rights

The Reference Shelf
Volume 96 • Number 5
H.W. Wilson
a Division of EBSCO Information Services, Inc.

Published by
GREY HOUSE PUBLISHING
Amenia, New York
2024

The Reference Shelf

Cover photo: istock

The books in this series contain reprints of articles, excerpts from books, addresses on current issues, and studies of social trends in the United States and other countries. There are six separately bound numbers in each volume, all of which are usually published in the same calendar year. Numbers one through five are each devoted to a single subject, providing background information and discussion from various points of view and concluding with an index and comprehensive bibliography that lists books, pamphlets, and articles on the subject. The final number of each volume is a collection of recent speeches. Books in the series may be purchased individually or on subscription.

Copyright © 2024 by Grey House Publishing, Inc. All rights reserved. No part of this work may be used or reproduced in any manner whatsoever or transmitted in any form or by any means, electronic or mechanical, including photocopying, recording, or any information storage and retrieval system, without written permission from the copyright owner. For subscription information and permissions requests, contact Grey House Publishing, 4919 Route 22, PO Box 56, Amenia, NY 12501.

∞ The paper used in these volumes conforms to the American National Standard for Permanence of Paper for Printed Library Materials, Z39.48 1992 (R2009).

Publisher's Cataloging-in-Publication Data
(Prepared by Parlew Associates, LLC)

Names: Grey House Publishing, Inc., compiler.
Title: Reproductive rights / [compiled by Grey House Publishing].
Other Titles: Reference shelf ; v. 96, no. 5.
Description: Amenia, NY : Grey House Publishing, 2024. | Includes bibliographic references and index. | Includes b&w and color photos and illustrations.
Identifiers: ISBN 9781637008980 (v.96, no. 5) | ISBN 978167008935 (volume set)
Subjects: LCSH: Reproductive rights – United States. | Abortion – Law and legislation – United States. | Contraception – United States. | Maternal health services – United States. | Medical care – Political aspects – United States. | Fertilization in vitro, Human – Political aspects – United States. | BISAC: HEALTH & FITNESS / Women's Health. | POLITICAL SCIENCE / Public Policy / Health Care. | LAW / Health.
Classification: LCC HQ766.R47 2024 | DDC 323.3/4--dc23

Printed in Canada

Contents

Preface ix

1

The Abortion Battle

Access to Reproductive Care 3
Abortion in the US: What You Need to Know 9
Isabel V. Sawhill and Kai Smith, *Brookings Institution*, May 29, 2024

For Both Sides: Abortion Policy 2 Years After
   Dobbs Decision Hinges on November 17
Jennifer Shutt, *Missouri Independent*, June 24, 2024

The Criminalization of Abortion and Surveillance of Women in a
   Post-*Dobbs* World 21
Jolynn Dellinger and Stephanie K. Pell, *Brookings Institution*, April 18, 2024

U.S. Supreme Court Allows Access to Abortion Pill,
   Unanimously Rejecting Texas Challenge 27
Eleanor Klibanoff and Karen Brooks Harper, *The Texas Tribune,* June 13, 2024

How Missouri Helps Abortion Opponents Divert State Taxes to
   Crisis Pregnancy Centers 30
Jeremy Kohler, *ProPublica*, June 6, 2022

The Abortion Debate Is Headed to the Ballot Box:
   Here's Where Voters Will Decide 34
NPR, May 28, 2024

Tracking Abortion Bans Across the Country 39
Allison McCann and Amy Schoenfeld Walker, *New York Times,* July 1, 2024

2

The Politics of Reproductive Health

Health Care and the Government 47
Surprise: American Voters Actually Largely Agree on Many Issues,
   Including Topics Like Abortion, Immigration, and Wealth Inequality 53
Dante Chinni and Ari Pinkus, *The Conversation*, July 10, 2024

Abortion and the 2024 Election: There Is No Easy Way Out for Republicans 57
Elaine Kamarck, *Brookings Institution*, April 17, 2024

Inside Ziklag, the Secret Organization of Wealthy Christians Trying to
   Sway the Election and Change the Country 61
Andy Kroll and Nick Surgey, *ProPublica*, July 14, 2024

Supreme Court's Blow to Federal Agencies' Power
  Will Likely Weaken Abortion Rights—3 Issues to Watch   69
Jessica L. Waters, *The Conversation*, July 17, 2024

Justice Thomas: SCOTUS "Should Reconsider" Contraception,
  Same-Sex Marriage Rulings   73
Quint Forgey and Josh Gerstein, *Politico*, June 24, 2022

Following Trump's Lead, Republicans Adopt Platform That
  Softens Stance on Abortion   76
Maggie Haberman, Shane Goldmacher, and Jonathan Swan,
  New York Times, July 8, 2024

3

Contraception

Preventing Pregnancies   81
Social Media Will Tell You Birth Control Causes Mental Health Issues,
  Weight Gain, and Infertility: Here Are the Facts   88
Christopher O'Sullivan, *The Conversation*, April 9, 2024

Opinion: Birth Control Access May Get Easier—Here's Why It's Not Enough   91
Lucy Tu and Jocelyn Viterna, *Undark*, February 9, 2023

Contraception in the United States:
  A Closer Look at Experiences, Preferences, and Coverage   95
Brittni Frederiksen, Usha Rajni, Michelle Long, Karen Diep, and Alina Salganicoff,
  KFF, November 3, 2022

Emergency Contraception: Here's What You Probably Don't Know,
  but Should   99
Cathryn Brown, *The Conversation*, August 31, 2023

The GOP Doesn't Want to Talk About Abortion: Harris Wants to Make Them   102
Megan Messerly and Alice Miranda Ollstein, *Politico*, July 24, 2024

4

Assisted Reproduction

Fertility Treatments in the United States   107
Why the Southern Baptists' Vote Opposing IVF
  Could Change National Politics   114
Megan Messerly, *Politico*, June 12, 2024

Alabama Ruling Frozen Embryos Are Equivalent to Living Children
  Has Worrying Implications for IVF   119
Alex Polyakov, *The Conversation*, February 26, 2024

Republicans Can't Be Trusted to Protect IVF 122
Sarah Jones, *New York Magazine*, February 29, 2024

Why IVF Looks Different in the US Than in the Rest of the World 125
Rachel M. Cohen, *Vox*, March 26, 2024

The Connection Between Fertility Treatments and the Overturning of
   Roe v. Wade 131
Fiorella Valdesolo, *Vogue*, January 27, 2023

How IVF Is Complicating Republicans Abortion Messaging 136
Lexie Shapitl, *NPR*, March 16, 2024

5

Maternal Health

Women's Reproductive Health 143
Abortion Bans Are Changing What It Means to Be Young in America 149
Julie Maslowsky, *The Conversation*, June 17, 2024

What to Know About the Roiling Debate over U.S. Maternal Mortality Rates 153
Robin Fields, *ProPublica*, April 5, 2024

A Rare Disease That Underscores the Importance of Abortion Access 158
Doug Johnson, *Undark*, September 26, 2022

The End of *Roe* Is Having a Chilling Effect on Pregnancy 163
Lauren Leader, *Politico*, September 13, 2023

What Overturning *Roe v. Wade* Means Psychologically for Teens
   Who Could Get Pregnant 166
Kimberly Zapata, *Parents*, July 21, 2022

More U.S. Women Are Avoiding Unwanted or Mistimed Pregnancies 170
Claire Cain Miller, *New York Times,* May 3, 2023

Bibliography 173
Websites 177
Index 181

Preface

Reproductive Rights and the Right to Privacy

The landmark cases of *Roe v. Wade* and *Griswold v. Connecticut* prohibited states and the federal government from passing laws that prohibited abortion or barred access to contraception, respectively. In both cases, supporters of safe, legal abortion services and of contraception laid out evidence from physicians and public health experts providing that access to abortion and access to contraception improved women's health and children's health. This was one of the cornerstones of the issue in both cases, but lawyers and those giving testimony also based their arguments on the idea that women had a right to bodily autonomy and privacy in making decisions about their health care. Increasingly, members of the Republican Party, beholden to the views of a small but powerful minority, views of a small but powerful minority are asking to courts to eliminate this right for American women.

Freedom from the Government

There is no explicitly stated "right to privacy" in the American Constitution, but generations of legal and constitutional scholars have interpreted various parts of the Constitution as indirectly demanding this right for citizens of the United States. It was actually in the case of *Griswold v. Connecticut* (1965), which guaranteed Americans the right to access contraception, that the court formally established the idea that a general right to privacy could be *inferred* from various sections of the Constitution.

In the *Griswold* case, a law in Connecticut, known as the General Statutes (established in 1958) stated,

> Any person who uses any drug, medicinal article or instrument for the purpose of preventing conception shall be fined not less than fifty dollars or imprisoned not less than sixty days nor more than one year or be both fined and imprisoned.

And then stated, so that the state would also have the power to threaten physicians who might help patients to obtain contraception, further stated:

> Any person who assists, abets, counsels, causes, hires or commands another to commit any offense may be prosecuted and punished as if he were the principal offender.

In the court, critics of the law argued that the law gave the government the power to regulate private behavior among married people, interfering in decisions that were personal, intimate, and consensual. The question was, essentially, whether the US government had the right to declare that all sexual acts must be reproductive, or whether decisions about how and when to utilize sexuality were private decisions that belonged to the individual.

In this landmark decision, the majority stated,

> The First Amendment has a penumbra where privacy is protected from governmental intrusion. While it is not expressly included in the First Amendment, its existence is necessary in making the express guarantees fully meaningful.[1]

A "penumbra" is the area that is partially illuminated when light passes over a solid object. A hazy section of partially lit space that surrounds the darker shadow. What the justices in the *Griswold* case meant, is that laws can be found in the shadows of the Constitution, and in the way that their overlapping meanings cast illumination on implied or suggested rights that are not specifically stated. This is an important aspect of constitutional law, as many of the rights and protections that Americans enjoy are extracted from the penumbra rather than explicitly stated. There have been legal scholars who argue against such reasoning, and who believe that the only rights protected by the Constitution are those explicitly stated, but most Americans, right or left wing, have benefitted from the freedom of the courts to interpolate meaning from what are otherwise largely the statements made by men at a time when American life and American society bore little resemblance to the modern world.[2]

The court's ruling in the *Griswold* case became the basis for their ruling in *Roe v. Wade*, in which the justices decided that the decision about whether to have an abortion was a private decision, involving a pregnant woman, her family, and her physician, and not a matter that should be dictated by the government. Many different aspects of reproductive health care depend on the idea that women have a right to privacy in making health-care decisions, because there is a dedicated group of ultraconservatives who believe that the proper role for a government is to enforce moral guidelines as they see them.

What's more, the constitutional right to privacy inferred from the penumbra is what protects American sexual and romantic liberties. There were, not long ago in American society, laws to made it illegal to have any nonreproductive sex, classified as "sodomy" in US legal terminology, which is a direct reference to Biblical mythology. These laws allowed the government to prohibit private, consensual sexual intimacy between adults and they were justified by the argument that only certain kinds of sex, between certain classes of people, was morally acceptable. Likewise, laws once prohibited people of different races from having sex, living together, having children, or getting married. Laws until *very* recently, criminalized same-sex sexual relationships. The protection of sexual autonomy and privacy is dependent on the idea that free adult Americans have a right to privacy in their personal lives and a right to be free from governmental interference in matters that concern only them and those with whom they are intimately related. The penumbra of privacy rights also therefore guarantees a right to privacy in the home, it establishes a legal sanctity for a family to be autonomous so long as their lives do not interfere in the lives of others. There are few legal principles more important to protecting what most Americans believe to be fundamental freedoms of citizenship.

To see how legal experts inferred this right to privacy, it is helpful to understand a little more about several key laws in the bill of rights.

The First Amendment states,

> Congress shall make no law respecting an establishment of religion, or prohibiting the free exercise thereof; or abridging the freedom of speech, or of the press; or the right of the people peaceably to assemble, and to petition the Government for a redress of grievances.[3]

From the First Amendment, jurists pointed to the "freedom of assembly," which essentially means that a person cannot be prohibited by their government from forming and joining with other groups of citizens. This primary right is meant to prevent the government from limiting the power of the citizenry as authoritarian governments often do, but making certain kinds of groups illegal, and thus reducing the collective power of the people to challenge governmental oppression.

The Third Amendment states,

> No Soldier shall, in time of peace be quartered in any house, without the consent of the Owner, nor in time of war, but in a manner to be prescribed by law.[4]

The Third Amendment is a cornerstone of private property, essentially stating that the government does not have the right to claim private property, even during wartime, unless the owners of the property have, in some other legal manner, relinquished their right to property. But this freedom also implies a freedom to privacy in the home, suggesting that the government may not intrude on the sanctity of the home unless there is some compelling and legal reason to do so.

The Fourth Amendment states,

> The right of the people to be secure in their persons, houses, papers, and effects, against unreasonable searches and seizures, shall not be violated, and no Warrants shall issue, but upon probable cause, supported by Oath or affirmation, and particularly describing the place to be searched, and the persons or things to be seized.[5]

This Amendment essentially says that the agents of the state do not have the right to seize or even to search a person's property without legitimate cause. It further holds that there is a legal process thorough which the state may claim the power to search or seize property or personal items and that unless this process is followed, the state is in violation of the citizen's rights. Like the Third Amendment, the Fourth Amendment implies a right to privacy in the home, a sanctity of a person's private space that is legally protected under the Constitution.

The Fifth Amendment states,

> No person shall be held to answer for a capital, or otherwise infamous crime, unless on a presentment or indictment of a Grand Jury, except in cases arising in the land or naval forces, or in the Militia, when in actual service in time of War or public danger; nor shall any person be subject for the same offence to be twice put in jeopardy of life

or limb; nor shall be compelled in any criminal case to be a witness against himself, nor be deprived of life, liberty, or property, without due process of law; nor shall private property be taken for public use, without just compensation.[6]

Often simplified as the "right to remain silent," the Fifth Amendment states that the government has no constitutional right to force a person to incriminate themselves. Many of the crimes involving privacy involve behavior that occurs in private, and this amendment has been taken to mean that the government cannot compel an individual to admit to any act that the person undertakes in private, even if the state deems such an act illegal.

The Ninth Amendment states,

The enumeration in the Constitution, of certain rights, shall not be construed to deny or disparage others retained by the people.[7]

The Ninth Amendment refutes the idea that only the laws explicitly created by the founders of the United States are valid. The founders knew that the foundations of American law they had created were insufficient even to address the vagaries of need at their time, much less for the future of the nation, and thus included, in the initial ten amendments of the Bill of Rights, an explicit statement of this fact, and recognition that the Constitution expressly allowed citizens to claim additional rights not already put forward.

The final step on the privacy journey moves beyond the Bill of Rights for the first time, to what is perhaps one of the single most important amendments to the Constitution ever created, the Fourteenth Amendment. The Fourteenth Amendment was established in 1868, in the wake of the Civil War and it was meant to address some of the failings of the American system of law and politics that had become painfully obvious in the civil collapse of the nation. The Fourteenth Amendment was essential to the process of ending slavery and establishing that African Americans were due full citizenship, and it was one of the three basic amendments that were used to expressly prohibit slavery on the constitutional level.

Colloquially known as the "equal protection" amendment, the Fourteenth Amendment essentially states that no state has the power to "deprive any person of life, liberty, or property, without due process of law; nor deny to any person within its jurisdiction the equal protection of the laws."[8]

In the text of the law, the authors refer to "liberty." What exactly does this mean? The term appears in both the Fifth and Fourteenth Amendments of the Constitution, and in the Declaration of Independence, where it is stated that,

We hold these truths to be self-evident, that all men are created equal, that they are endowed by their Creator with certain unalienable Rights, that among these are Life, Liberty and the pursuit of Happiness.[9]

Liberty is thus established as a fundamental right, one that Jefferson and the other framers saw as "unalienable" and that had been endowed by their God to all people. The courts have interpreted liberty as meaning freedom from arbitrary or unreasonable restraint. This means restraint not only of the body, but of thought and will.

Liberty thus means to freedom to behave as one believes is right, unless in the course of doing so, the rights of others are violated.

These fundamental constitutional principles speak to the idea that an American citizen is free to think and to do as they choose and to associate with whomever they wish in whatever manner they chose. However, precedent and law also hold that these rights are "alienable" when behavior infringes on the rights of others. Thus, a person is free to listen to whatever music they choose, but if they listen to this music at an extremely loud volume, such behavior may not be protected by the principles of legal privacy, because the way in which the person has chosen to engage in a personal act, has now interfered to the rights of others to also experience that behavior.

The Right to Sexual Privacy

American people believe in a right to privacy, and this belief transcends any political or class barrier. Polls find that, in general, nearly all Americans, with few exceptions, express general support for the basic idea that American citizenship infers some right to privacy from government intrusion into their lives. On more specific issues, opinions may vary, but support for protected privacy remains strong across partisan lines. For instance, when asked whether the federal government should pass a law guaranteeing the protection of private data in online transactions, 83 percent of voters agreed, including more than 80 percent of conservatives, who are more willing, in general, to believe that the right to privacy should be limited.[10]

In the Digital Age, discussions about privacy often focus on digital privacy, because the economy has shifted to one in which private data from consumers is a commodity that is controlled and sold by corporations. What's more, social media has become a way of life for many Americans and, as this reality has come to fruition, personal information is being essentially given to corporations that operate social media resources, and these companies claim part ownership over this data, which they then sell to companies, who create targeted advertisement. The overall goal is to maximize consumerism and consumer desire, but this shift in America's economic reality has raised serious concerns about privacy. This obscures some of the more primary functions that privacy protections play in American lives, because these protections are also extremely relevant and important to the autonomy and freedom of individuals to live as they see fit. Privacy protections relate to parental choice and rights, to individual and artistic expression, and to gender and sexual identity.

Sexual privacy is a term that refers to a person's privacy in their sexual life and it is an increasingly important concept in American law. In the twenty-first century, violations of sexual privacy have become increasingly common. Writing about this issue in the *Yale Law Journal* in 2019, Danielle K. Citron argued,

> The barriers that protect information about our intimate lives are under assault. Networked technologies are exploited to surveil and expose individuals' naked bodies and intimate activities. Home devices are used to spy on intimates and ex-intimates. Hidden

cameras film people in bedrooms and restrooms, and "up their skirts" without permission. People are coerced into sharing nude images and making sex videos under threat of public disclosure. Sexually explicit images are posted online without their subjects' permission. Technology enables the creation of hyper-realistic "deep fake" sex videos that insert people's faces into pornography.

At the heart of each of these abuses is an invasion of sexual privacy—the social norms (behaviors, expectations, and decisions) that govern access to, and information about, individuals' intimate lives. Sexual privacy concerns the concealment of naked bodies and intimate activities including, but not limited to, sexual intercourse. It involves personal decisions about intimate life, such as whether to entrust others with information about one's sexuality or gender, or whether to expose one's body to others. As I am using the term, sexual privacy is both descriptive and normative. It concerns how the social norms surrounding individuals' intimate lives are currently experienced and how they should be experienced. Sexual privacy sits at the apex of privacy values because of its importance to sexual agency, intimacy, and equality. We are free only insofar as we can manage the boundaries around our bodies and intimate activities.

With sexual privacy, we can experiment with our bodies, our sexuality, and our gender. We can author our intimate lives and be seen as whole human beings rather than as just our intimate parts or innermost sexual fantasies.[11]

The kind of privacy that Citron is focused on, are external invasions of privacy by abusers who would seek to use or misuse a person's sexual identity or characteristics for selfish means, but her arguments about the primacy of privacy speaks to the fundamental freedoms that Americans embrace on the broad scale and that few would see erased. The freedom to form relationships and to make individual decisions about one's sexual identity and behavior is not only central to American identity, but to human identity. Over the many years that conservatives tried to prohibit expressions of sexuality that violated their narrow concept of morally acceptable sexual life, it did not stop people from doing so. Americans continued to engage in nonreproductive sex, in sex acts with no potential reproductive consequence, to utilize contraception even when it was illegal and deemed a violation of divine will, and to have sexual and intimate relationships with those with whom they were told they could not. Even the most famous framer of America's most fundamental laws, Thomas Jefferson, had interracial sexual relationships, despite the prevailing taboos and alleged immorality of such behavior.

And sexual privacy also extends, as the court found in the *Griswold* case, into the realm of reproductive privacy. In the *Griswold* case, the court ruled that the state had no constitutional standing to interfere with the intimate, private decisions that couples made about their reproductive futures, nor to decide whether a person's sexual activities must have the potential to be reproductive. This gets at the heart of the reproductive rights debate, because the debate is essentially about whether or not we should empower the state to compel a person to align with their views on sexuality. Recent studies show that the vast majority of Americans, whether identifying as liberal or conservative, or Republican or Democrat or Independent, support the legal right to contraception as established in *Griswold*. Less than 10 percent of Americans see any need at all to limit access to this basic technology of reproductive control and yet proposals to limit access have been put forward in state legislatures, and even mentioned by individuals at the federal level. None of this represents a popular mandate or the will of the American people, it is a concerted effort, by a group of ultraconservative Christians to make their fundamentalist view of sexuality and reproduction law, and by doing so they also signify that they feel adherence to their highly specific view of morality and sexuality is more important than the personal privacy of American citizens and their capability to manage their own reproductive and sexual lives.

This effort to legally enforce conservative morality is not new in America. In the Colonial Era, and for many years after, the laws of America were shaped by far-right conservatives who believed that their view of morality and human behavior was the only acceptable view, and who saw no problem with instituting authoritarian policies that dictated how a person was allowed to behave in terms of their gender, sexuality, and reproduction. This is echoed also by "Sharia," a series of Islamic laws that base legal policies on biblical Islamic scripture and so can be used to mandate adherence to conservative Islamic gender and sexual roles and reproductive behavior.

To be clear, establishing laws that mandate adherence to perceptions on sexuality, gender, or reproduction that are based on religious principles is a violation of the First Amendment guarantees on religious freedom, which mean not only that Americans are free to practice their religion, but also that Americans are free from being forced to practice another religion. The most recent data suggests that around 63 percent of Americans identify as Christian. Within this group, a smaller percentage are Evangelical Christians or Roman Catholics, the two religious groups most closely associated with the goal of enforcing religious belief through the law. Around three out of every ten Americans are "religiously unaffiliated," meaning that they follow no organized religion. In every measure, recruitment by evangelical Christians, Catholics, and other dominant religions has fallen over the past century and continues to fall. If current trends continue, Christians will constitute less than half of the American population within the next forty years.[12]

The decline in Christianity and the grim outlook for the future of conservative fundamentalism is part of the reason that conservatives are engaged so passionately in the current campaign to erode reproductive freedoms and autonomy. Faced with the reality that they no longer have populist support and are unlikely to attain it given their failure to build support for their views over the decades, conservatives have embraced the idea that the can use the law to *force* Americans to adopt their moral views. They then leverage their influence over the Republican Party, which is dependent on their voting power to win elections, to make these ideas mainstream despite lacking the public support to justify this. Were any of the major reproductive rights issues to be decided by referendum, Americans would choose to protect the rights and their privacy. The conservative activists who are pursuing this agenda know this, and so they are fighting also to prevent the American people from having the opportunity to vote on these issues directly, to prevent the American people from exercising democratic influence over these important issues.

Reproductive Autonomy

Of all the major issues in the reproductive rights debate, abortion rights are the most controversial and also the one on which Americans are most divided. This is because Americans are conflicted about at which stage of development a fetus should be considered a "person," and therefore about what kinds of protections should be afforded to a fetus as an independent life.

Few Americans favor absolute freedom to perform abortions at any point along the developmental cycle of a fetus, but there are also only a very small number of Americans, 10 to 15 percent, who believe that abortion in all its forms should be banned. Most Americans fall in the middle, to greater or lesser degrees, but a full 63 percent of Americans agree that abortion should be legal in all or most cases. Around 36 percent of Americans believe that abortion should be illegal in all or most cases.[13]

The next most controversial arena of the reproductive rights debate concerns medical procedures like in vitro fertilization (IVF) that form part of the science of assisted reproduction. These technologies are controversial because Americans are conflicted about whether or not an "embryo," which is a mass of cells that can potentially, in the right situation, become a fetus, which can then, again only potentially, become a person. Protecting fetuses as living beings has far less support than the antiabortion movement, with fewer than 10 percent of Americans believing that IVF has any significant moral implications.

The next most controversial issue is contraception, which concerns the availability of drugs and other technologies to control reproduction. On this issue, Americans are far more united across partisan lines, because few are willing to view oocytes as beings and so do not feel that sperm and unfertilized eggs require protection. There are a small number of Americans who believe that using contraception encourages immorality or interferes with divine plans. This group is so small that their views have little democratic merit. However, because of the Republican Party's dependence on ultraconservative single-issue voting blocks, challenges to contraception have also been proposed in several states.

All of these big-picture issues describe a field with many other related issues important to health care and public welfare. Reproductive rights are inextricably linked to maternal health, women's health, and child welfare and cannot be separated. All of the legal changes that have come to the fore in this new era of reproductive rights challenges have had serious and damaging consequences to American lives and threaten the lives and welfare of future generations as well.

Often, in the reproductive rights debate, Americans are encouraged to think of the issue as one involving the protection of life. Antiabortion activists position themselves as protectors of the "unborn" and believers in the sanctity of life, but demonstrate this claimed commitment in few other arenas of American life other than through the effort to enact prohibitions on consensual behavior related to reproduction and sexuality. It is therefore important to understand that the kinds of laws being proposed and enacted, are not just about the potential lives of potential children, but are also about the degree to which American citizens can exercise private decisions about their own lives and their own bodies.

Reproductive rights are based on the idea that American people have the right to decide their own religious and moral beliefs and how these beliefs intersect with their lives. Antiabortion activists suggest that pregnant individuals sacrifice their autonomy, because the potential life of the fetus supersedes the pregnant person's claim to autonomy and control over their own body. They argue that such decisions are no longer "private" and that the state has the right and power to compel the woman to utilize her body to carry a pregnancy to term, because the state has the right to protect the potential rights of potential people. How Americans feel about this issue comes down, on some level, to where Americans perceive the line between the pregnant person and the developing life of a fetus, but also reflects how Americans prioritize individual freedom and responsibility versus the right of the state to compel or force behaviors. On issues like contraception and IVF, the argument that the state has the right to intercede has little support, because the arguments are not compelling and depend, entirely, on a view of the primacy of reproductive potential that is not widely embraced.

As one learns more about reproductive rights and the current debate, it is important therefore to remember that it is not just reproductive freedom that is being questioned, but also whether or not Americans have a right to liberty in the form of privacy, or whether this right is alienable towards the goal of mandating one of many potential views on reproductive morality.

Works Used

"14th Amendment." Legal Information Institute (LII). *Cornell Law School*, www.law.cornell.edu/constitution/amendmentxiv.

Citron, Danielle K. "Sexual Privacy." *Yale Law Journal*, 2019.

"Declaration of Independence: A Transcription." *National Archives*, www.archives.gov/founding-docs/declaration-transcript.

"Freedom of Religion, Speech, Press, Assembly, and Petition." *Constitution Center*, constitutioncenter.org/the-constitution/amendments/amendment-i.

"Grand Jury, Double Jeopardy, Self-Incrimination, Due Process, Takings." *Constitution Center*, constitutioncenter.org/the-constitution/amendments/amendment-v.

Iannacci, Nicandro. "Recalling the Supreme Court's Historic Statement on Contraception and Privacy." *Constitution Center*, 7 June 2019, constitutioncenter.org/blog/contraception-marriage-and-the-right-to-privacy.

"Modeling the Future of Religion in America." *Pew Research Center*, 13 Sept. 2022, www.pewresearch.org/religion/2022/09/13/modeling-the-future-of-religion-in-america/.

"Non-Enumerated Rights Retained by People." *Constitution Center*, constitutioncenter.org/the-constitution/amendments/amendment-ix.

"Privacy." Legal Information Institute (LII). *Cornell Law School*, www.law.cornell.edu/wex/privacy.

"Public Opinion on Abortion." *Pew Research Center*, 13 May 2024, www.pewresearch.org/religion/fact-sheet/public-opinion-on-abortion/.

"Public Opinion on Privacy." *Electronic Privacy Information Center (EPIC)*, archive.epic.org/privacy/survey/.

"Quartering of Soldiers." *Constitution Center*, constitutioncenter.org/the-constitution/amendments/amendment-iii.

"Search and Seizure." *Constitution Center*, constitutioncenter.org/the-constitution/amendments/amendment-iv.

Notes

1. Iannacci, "Recalling the Supreme Court's Historic Statement on Contraception and Privacy."
2. "Privacy," *Cornell Law School*.
3. "Freedom of Religion, Speech, Press, Assembly, and Petition," *Constitution Center*.
4. "Quartering of Soldiers," *Constitution Center*.
5. "Search and Seizure," *Constitution Center*.
6. "Grand Jury, Double Jeopardy, Self-Incrimination, Due Process, Takings," *Constitution Center*.
7. "Non-Enumerated Rights Retained by People," *Constitution Center*.
8. "14th Amendment," *Cornell Law School*.
9. "Declaration of Independence: A Transcription," *National Archives*.
10. "Public Opinion on Privacy," *Electronic Privacy Information Center (EPIC)*.
11. Citron, "Sexual Privacy."
12. "Modeling the Future of Religion in America," *Pew Research Center*.
13. "Public Opinion on Abortion," *Pew Research Center*.

1
The Abortion Battle

Image by *Ms.* magazine, CC BY-SA 4.0, via Wikipedia.

Abortion has always been a divisive issue in the United States, as this prescient cover of the 2013 winter issue of *Ms.* magazine makes evident.

Access to Reproductive Care

The United States Supreme Court ruling in the case of *Dobbs v. Jackson Women's Health Organization* overruled the case of *Roe v. Wade*, which had, for fifty years, prohibited states from outright prohibitions on abortion. In the ruling, Justice Samuel Alito quoted Justice Byron R. White, who filed a dissent in the original *Roe* case, in which White accused the court of using "raw judicial power" to strike down a state's ban on abortion (in that case the state of Texas). White essentially accused his associates on the court of engaging in "judicial activism," which occurs when jurists utilize the law to pursue a political goal, rather than merely acting as interpreters of the law bound to recognize precedent. Alito argued, in the *Dobbs* case, that "it is time to heed the Constitution and return the issue of abortion to the people's elected representatives." In other words, states were now free to prohibit abortion, and many did so. Some states, in fact, had "trigger laws" in place just in case a moment like this came. As soon as *Roe* verdict was overturned, these laws went into effect, prohibiting or restricting access to abortion in those states.

Writing for the *American Constitution Society*, Alan B. Morrison, the Lerner Family Associate Dean for Public Interest and Public Service Law at George Washington University Law School, argues that it is the Roberts's court that has been "activist" in its interpretations of constitutional precedent. In a review of all of the high-profile cases in the Roberts's Court's history, and found that "The Roberts Court has failed to follow the premises of *Dobbs* and has been an activist court when it suits the goals of the Republican Party, but not otherwise."[1] In his book *Supermajority*, Brennan Center President Michael Waldman argued that "The *Dobbs* ruling on abortion overturned a fundamental right for the first time in this country's history, a protection for women over a half century. It puts at risk all other privacy rights as well."[2]

Abortion Rates and Pregnancy Rates

Abortion rates in the United States have been in decline since the 1980s. Anti-abortion activists have argued that this is because states have fought against *Roe*, instituting restrictions and withdrawing federal support from clinics that provide abortion services, thus making it more difficult for women to have abortions. According to these activists, the decline in abortion rates since 1980 shows that this campaign against abortion access, which includes protests outside abortion clinics and, for some, threats and attacks against women seeking abortion or physicians providing abortion, has been a success, but the data does not support this perception. Abortion declined also in states with liberal reproductive laws, where abortion access has remained strong despite conservative activism. Data indicates that access to contraception is the key to understanding much of the decline from 1980 through the 2010s. The availability of long-term contraception, like intrauterine devices (IUDs) and implants, likely played a role as well as the shift in public attitudes about oral contraceptives. Women had been empowered to take a more active role in managing their reproductive lives, and this resulted in fewer unplanned pregnancies.[3]

The continued decline, between 2010 and 2020 is more difficult to explain, but is likely cultural. Pregnancy rates dropped by 9 percent between 2010 and 2019, while unintended pregnancy rates declined by more than 15 percent during this same period. Pregnancies ending in abortion fell by 17 percent during this same period. Pregnancy rates for teens (under age nineteen) declined by 52 percent over this period.[4] Fewer pregnancies, fewer unplanned pregnancies, and fewer teen pregnancies all reflect the continuing normalization of contraception, the influence of cultural pressures promoting the idea of postponing pregnancy and childbirth, increasing affluence among some subsets of the population, and a higher level of agency among American women to engage in family planning, despite ongoing conservative efforts to limit access to family planning information, knowledge about sex and anatomy, and contraception.

Prior to the end of *Roe*, conservative activists had successfully restricted abortion access in many states. Studies show that the number of abortion providers, nationwide, had declined by nearly half from the 1980s to the 2020s, in part because of state laws that placed extreme limitations on abortion services. In 2020, one in ten women seeking an abortion needed to travel across state lines to receive care.[5] Antiabortion activists believe that the *Dobbs* decision will lead to a further decline in abortion, and early evidence suggested that, in fact, that abortion rates have remained steady and increased slightly across the country. While it is still estimated that 5 percent of women who would seek abortion care were unable to receive that care because of state laws following *Dobbs*.[6]

It is worth noting, as well, that this refers only to abortions in the formal medical system, that is, those that are recorded by health-care organizations. In 2023, medical authorities recorded the highest number of abortions in a decade, and an increase of more than 11 percent from 2020, which already saw a major rise in abortion rates, in part linked to COVID-19. Data also showed that self-managed abortions rose sharply after *Dobbs*, and many of these are not recorded and so do not figure into estimates on abortion.[7] Fortunately, thanks to the availability of effective medication, self-managed abortion in the 2020s is not as often life-threatening as it was in the years pre-*Roe*, but the rise in the population of women without access to medical guidance or who fear legal reprisal if their self-managed abortions become public, is believed by abortion rights activists to represent a significant threat to women's health across the country.

Among the most controversial issues in the abortion debate has been the availability of medication abortion and specifically the pill mifepristone, commonly called "the abortion pill." Access to this medication has been challenged at the state level but has not resulted in absolute bans. The Supreme Court ruled that there was no constitutional basis for challenging Food and Drug Administration (FDA) approval of the medication and subsequent FDA actions that increased access to mifepristone. However, antiabortion activists continue to challenge the availability of the drug in separate state cases. Studies have shown a marked increase in use of mifepristone since the *Dobbs* decision, as part of either physician-managed or self-managed abortion care, and this is why medication abortion is considered, by antiabortion activists, a primary political issue, but public opinion remains strongly aligned with the perspective that access to the drug should remain legal.

Abortion and Public Opinion

The legal battle over abortion access, at the level of the Supreme Court, featured frequent mentions to individual and state liberties. In other words, the justices who ruled in favor of overturning *Roe* argued that the people should decide this issue within their own more limited communities, the artificial conglomerations of populations united into "states." However, turning the issue over to populist influence does not, on the broader level, serve the interests of antiabortion activists. Public opinion on abortion has fluctuated over the decades, but has remained relatively stable for some time. Around 63 percent of Americans believe that abortion should be legal in all or most cases, while around 36 percent believe that abortion should be illegal in all or most cases. Support for legal abortion is unsurprisingly higher among women than men, higher among those with higher levels of educational achievement. The proportion of people who feel that abortion should be illegal in most cases falls by more than 10 percent among those who achieve a college education, and 6 percent for those who obtain "some college" education.[8]

Overall, studies show that almost no Americans have an absolutist view on abortion. Most Americans are against very late-stage abortions and few Americans oppose very early stage abortions, or abortions of pregnancies resulting from rape, incest, or child abuse, or in cases where a woman's life is threatened by abortion complications. Even among the 36 percent who believe that abortion should be illegal in all or most cases, only about 10 percent of Americans support total abortion bans, of the type that have been enacted in some cases following the *Dobbs* decision. This holds true even when pollsters speak to people in states where severe abortion restrictions have been enacted. Even in these states, therefore, the severe abortion restrictions are not a reflection of public opinion or the people's will.[9]

If the American people were to hold a public referendum asking if abortion should be legal, across the board, or illegal, across the board, abortion would remain legal in the United States. The antiabortion movement does not have and is unlikely to gain majority support. The shift, in the abortion rights debate, from the federal to the state level, has proven this. In 2022, six states had ballot measures regarding abortion. Following the *Dobbs* decision, twenty-five states have enacted extreme bans on abortion. Since *Dobbs*, abortion has been on the ballot in seven states. Each time that voters have been given the freedom to vote on abortion directly, voters have chosen to protect access to legal abortion. Opponents of abortion access are aware that they do not have majority support and have resorted to trying to block abortion measures from appearing on state ballots, undermining the claim that the abortion issue is a populist issue. As of 2024, no state has held a public referendum on abortion where residents of the state chose to prohibit all abortions.[10]

Given that few Americans support absolute abortion bans and the fact that this extreme approach to the issue has yet to be validated by public support even in red states where conservative voters dominate legislators, raises questions about how states end up passing extreme abortion restrictions. The reasons for this are complex, but, essentially it is because voters are not being given the opportunity to vote on this issue directly. Conservative politicians campaign on a variety of issues and few Americans have made abortion their top voting priority, especially in the years leading up to the fall of *Roe*. This might be changing, as polls in 2023 and 2024 indicate that, for progressives, abortion is increasingly a top voting issue, with one in eight claiming abortion as their leading issue in the leadup to the 2024 elections. Gallup poll found that a record 32 percent of Americans say they would only vote for a candidate who shares their view on abortion.[11] Even with this shift, eight in ten Americans see some other issue as more important than abortion when voting, and this is how many conservative states end up electing individuals whose influence on the abortion issue conflicts with the views held by a majority of people in their state. This has allowed extremist anti-abortion activists to claim an outsized influence in conservative politics. Politicians who enact extremist abortion laws in conservative states face little in the way of backlash, because a majority of conservative voters are not voting on that issue primarily. Whether or not this changes in red states as extreme abortion bans take effect remains to be seen.

Misinformation and False Narratives

Another of the more controversial issues in the abortion rights debate has been the establishment of "crisis pregnancy centers," or "CPCs," which are facilities that market themselves to women and families as reproductive health-care clinics, but are actually engaged in an effort to discourage women from seeking abortion and, in some cases, other forms of family planning. As of 2024, these CPCs are unregulated and many do not hire medically trained staff members. The facilities are not required to adhere to the Health Insurance Portability and Accountability Act (HIPAA) guidelines on patient confidentiality and many are funded, directly or indirectly, by activist antiabortion organizations.

According to a study by the Center for Countering Digital Hate, 71 percent of CPCs use deceptive strategies and have been linked to the spread of false information about abortion and contraception. Studies of these manipulative facilities have uncovered staff members claiming that abortion is linked with mental illness and breast cancer, claims demonstrably proven false by scientific inquiry. Further, 38 percent do not state in their marketing materials, directly, that they do not provide abortions and engage in other manipulative practices, such as linking their online pages to keywords like "abortion clinic," and manipulating data to appear in searches for abortion care despite not providing that kind of care. Further, critics have argued that many CPCs should not be legally allowed to represent themselves as medical facilities despite having no staff members who are medically trained and licensed.[12]

These kinds of manipulative practices, utilizing misinformation and engaging in coercion and manipulation, are common in situations where those promoting a minority view lack substantive data to promote their case. Likewise, the American debate over gun safety has been marred by illegitimate data purporting links between gun ownership and reductions in crime rates, links that are easily disproven by data. Antiabortion activists have also been willing to promote misinformation about the ballot measures brought to state legislatures on the abortion issue. In some states, activists have spread false claims about the ballot measures indicating that passage would create economic burdens or would force all taxpayers to fund abortions. In other cases, activist legislators have illegitimately purged voters or engaged in other kinds of illegitimate tactics in an effort to provide an advantage to the minority perspective on this issue. Defenders of these tactics have argued that the ends justify the means and that such manipulation saves lives, but critics argue activists abandon any moral high ground they would seek to claim when they use lies and false claims to achieve their goals by fear and manipulation.

Certain Republican Party politicians have stated that they would seek to see a national, federal abortion ban put into effect, since the Supreme Court has now ruled that such a law would be within constitutional limits. What this means, is that abortion access is under threat and that even states in which citizens have voted to keep access to abortion-related care legal are faced with a rise of a far-right groups interested in restricting these rights for all Americans regardless of their beliefs.

Works Used

"Abortion Policy in the Absence of Roe." *Guttmacher Institute*, 24 Apr. 2023, www.guttmacher.org/state-policy/explore/abortion-policy-absence-roe.

Brenan, Megan, and Sydia Saad. "Record Share of U.S. Electorate Is Pro-Choice and Voting on It." *Gallup*, 13 June 2024, news.gallup.com/poll/645836/record-share-electorate-pro-choice-voting.aspx.

"Crisis Pregnancy Centers." *ACOG*, www.acog.org/advocacy/abortion-is-essential/trending-issues/issue-brief-crisis-pregnancy-centers.

Horowitch, Rose. "*Dobb's* Confounding Effect on Abortion Rates." *The Atlantic*, 26 Oct. 2023, www.theatlantic.com/politics/archive/2023/10/post-roe-national-abortion-rates/675778/.

Maddow-Zimet, Isaac, and Kathryn Kost. "Even Before Roe Was Overturned, Nearly One in 10 People Obtaining an Abortion Traveled Across State Lines for Care." *Guttmacher Institute,* July 2022, www.guttmacher.org/article/2022/07/even-roe-was-overturned-nearly-one-10-people-obtaining-abortion-traveled-across.

Morrison, Alan B. "Selective Judicial Activism in the Roberts Court." *American Constitution Society*, www.acslaw.org/analysis/acs-journal/acs-supreme-court-review-sixth-edition/selective-judicial-activism-in-the-roberts-court/#_ftnref1=.

Mulvihill, Geoff, and Linley Sanders. "Few Adults Support Full Abortion Bans, Even in States That Have Them, an AP-NORC Poll Finds." *Associated Press*, 11 July 2023, https://apnews.com/article/abortion-poll-roe-dobbs-ban-opinion-fcfdfc5a799ac3be617d99999e92eabe.

Popovich, Nadja. "Explainer: US Abortion Rates Drop, but Data and Reasons Behind It Are Complex." *The Guardian*, 8 June 2015, https://www.theguardian.com/world/2015/jun/08/us-abortion-down-new-survey.

"Public Opinion on Abortion." *Pew Research Center*, 13 May 2024, www.pewresearch.org/religion/fact-sheet/public-opinion-on-abortion/.

Rice, Andrea. "Self-Managed Abortions Rose Sharply After Roe's Reversal, Study Finds." *Healthline*, 25 Mar. 2024, www.healthline.com/health-news/self-managed-abortions-increasing-post-roe.

"U.S. Pregnancy Rates Drop During Last Decade." *CDC*, 12 Apr. 2023, www.cdc.gov/nchs/pressroom/nchs_press_releases/2023/20230412.htm.

Waldman, Michael. *The Supermajority: How the Supreme Court Divided America*. Simon & Schuster, 2023.

Notes

1. Morrison, "Selective Judicial Activism in the Roberts Court."
2. Waldman, *The Supermajority: How the Supreme Court Divided America*.
3. Popovich, "Explainer: US Abortion Rates Drop, But Data and Reasons Behind It Are Complex."
4. "U.S. Pregnancy Rates Drop During Last Decade," *CDC*.
5. Maddow-Zimet and Kost, "Even Before Roe Was Overturned, Nearly One in 10 People Obtaining an Abortion Traveled Across State Lines for Care."
6. Horowitch, "*Dobb's* Confounding Effect on Abortion Rates."
7. Rice, "Self-Managed Abortions Rose Sharply After Roe's Reversal, Study Finds."
8. "Public Opinion on Abortion," *Pew Research Center*.
9. Mulvihill and Sanders, "Few US Adults Support Full Abortion Bans, Even in States That Have Them, an AP-NORC Poll Finds."
10. "Abortion Policy in the Absence of Roe," *Guttmacher Institute*.
11. Brenan and Saad, "Record Share of U.S. Electorate is Pro-Choice and Voting on It."
12. "Crisis Pregnancy Centers," *ACOG*.

Abortion in the US: What You Need to Know

By Isabel V. Sawhill and Kai Smith
Brookings Institution, May 29, 2024

Key takeaways:

- One in every four women will have an abortion in their lifetime.
- The vast majority of abortions (about 95%) are the result of unintended pregnancies.
- Most abortion patients are in their twenties (61%), Black or Latino (59%), low-income (72%), unmarried (86%), between six and twelve weeks pregnant (73%), and already have given birth to one or more children (55%).
- Despite state bans, U.S. abortion totals increased in the first full year after the Supreme Court overturned *Roe v. Wade*.

Introduction

Two years after the Supreme Court overturned *Roe v. Wade*, abortion remains one of the most hotly contested issues in American politics. The abortion landscape has become highly fractured, with some states implementing abortion bans and restrictions and others increasing protections and access. The Supreme Court heard two more cases on abortion this term and will likely release those decisions in June. Beyond the Supreme Court, pro-choice and pro-life advocates are fiercely battling it out in the voting booths, state legislatures, and courts. If the 2022 midterm elections are any indication, abortion will be one of the most influential issues of the 2024 election. So what are the basic facts about abortion in America? This primer is designed to tell you most of what you need to know.

What Are the Different Types of Abortion?

There are two main types of abortion: procedural abortions and medication abortions. Procedural abortions (also called in-clinic or surgical abortions) are provided by health care professionals in a clinical setting. Medication abortions (also called medical abortions or the abortion pill) typically involve the oral ingestion of two drugs in succession, mifepristone and misoprostol.

Credit line: From *Brookings Institution*, May 29 © 2024. Reprinted with permission. All rights reserved.

Most women discover they are pregnant in the first five to six weeks of pregnancy, but about a third of women do not learn they are pregnant until they are beyond six weeks of gestation.[1] Women with unintended pregnancies detect their pregnancies later than women with intended pregnancies, between six and seven weeks of gestation on average. Even if a woman discovers she is pregnant relatively early, for many it takes time to decide what to do and how to arrange for an abortion if that is her preference.

Why Do Women Have Abortions?

The vast majority of abortions (about 95%) are the result of unintended pregnancies. That includes pregnancies that are mistimed as well as those that are unwanted.

Women's reasons for not wanting a child—or not wanting one now—include finances, partner-related issues, the need to focus on other children, and interference with future education or work opportunities.

In short, if there were fewer unintended pregnancies, there would be fewer abortions.

How Common Are Abortions?

One in every four women will have an abortion in their lifetime.

About two in every five pregnancies are unintended (40% in 2015). Roughly the same share of these unintended pregnancies end in abortion (42% in 2011). About one in every five pregnancies are aborted (21% in 2020).

How Have Abortion Totals Changed Over Time?

The number of abortions occurring in the U.S. jumped up after the *Roe v. Wade* decision in 1973. After peaking in 1990, the number of abortions declined steadily for two and a half decades until reaching its lowest point since 1973 in 2017.[2] Possible contributing factors explaining this long-term decline include delays in sexual activity amongst young people, improvements in the use of effective contraception, and overall declines in pregnancy rates, including those that are unintended. In addition, state restrictions which became more prevalent beginning in 2011 prevented at least some individuals in certain states from having abortions.

In 2018 (four years before the Supreme Court overturned *Roe v. Wade*), the number of abortions in the U.S. began to increase. The causes of this uptick are not yet fully understood, but researchers have identified multiple potential contributing factors. These include greater coverage of abortions under Medicaid that made abortions more affordable in certain states, regulations issued by the Trump administration in 2019 which decreased the size of the Title X network and therefore reduced the availability of contraception to low-income individuals, and increased financial support from privately-financed abortion funds to help pay for the costs associated with getting an abortion.

Another contributing factor, whose importance bears emphasizing, is the surging popularity of medication abortions.

The use of medication abortions has increased steadily since becoming available in the U.S. in 2000. However, in 2016, the FDA increased the gestational limit for the use of mifepristone from seven to ten weeks and thereby doubled the share of abortion patients eligible for medication abortions from 37% to 75%.

Later, during the COVID-19 pandemic, the FDA revised its policy in 2021 so that clinicians are no longer required to dispense medication abortion pills in person. Patients can now have medication abortion pills mailed to their homes after conducting remote consultations with clinicians via telehealth. In January 2023, the FDA issued another change which allows retail pharmacies like CVS and Walgreens to dispense medication abortion pills to patients with a prescription. Previously only doctors, clinics, or some mail-order pharmacies could dispense abortion pills.

Although access varies widely by state, medication abortions are now the most commonly used abortion method in the U.S. and account for nearly two-thirds of all abortions (63% in 2023).[3]

This is why the Supreme Court's upcoming decision in the Mifepristone case (*FDA v. Alliance for Hippocratic Medicine*) is so consequential. Among other issues, at stake is whether access to medication abortion will be sharply curtailed and whether regulations regarding medication abortions will revert to pre-2016 rules when abortion pills were not authorized for use after seven weeks of pregnancy and could not be prescribed via telemedicine, sent to abortion patients by mail, or dispensed by retail pharmacies.

Who Has Abortions?

Most abortion patients are in their twenties (61%), Black or Latino (59%), low-income (72%), unmarried (86%), and between six and twelve weeks pregnant (73%).[4]

The majority of abortion patients have already given birth to one or more children (55%) and have not previously had an abortion (57%).[5] Among abortion patients twenty years old or older, most had attended at least some college (63%). The vast majority of abortions occur during the first trimester of pregnancy (91%). So-called "late-term abortions" performed at or after 21 weeks of pregnancy are very rare and represent less than 1% of all abortions in the U.S.

The abortion rate per 1,000 women of reproductive age is disproportionately high for certain population groups. Among women living in poverty, for example, the abortion rate was 36.6 abortions per 1,000 women of reproductive age in 2014, compared to 14.6 abortions per 1,000 women among all women of reproductive age.

How Much Does an Abortion Cost?

The cost of an abortion varies depending on what kind of abortion is administered, how far along the patient is in their pregnancy, where the patient lives, where the patient is seeking an abortion, and whether health insurance or financial assistance is available. In 2021, the median self-pay cost for abortion services was $625 for a procedural abortion in the first trimester of pregnancy and $568 for a medication abortion.

Since 1977, the Hyde Amendment has banned the use of federal funds to pay for abortions except in cases of rape, incest, or life endangerment. Today, among the 36 states that have not banned abortion, fewer than half (17 as of March 2024) allow the use of state Medicaid funds to pay for abortions.[6] Many insurance plans do not cover abortions, often due to state limitations.

> **Many states with abortion bans do not include exceptions in cases where the health of the pregnant person is at risk, the pregnancy is the result of rape or incest, or there is a fatal fetal anomaly.**

Most abortion patients pay for abortions out of pocket (53%). State Medicaid funding is the second-most-commonly used method of payment (30%), followed by financial assistance (15%) and private insurance (13%).[7]

Whether state law allows state Medicaid funds to cover abortions has a very large impact on the difficulty of paying for abortions and the methods used by women to pay for them. In the year before the *Dobbs* Supreme Court decision, 50% of women residing in states where state Medicaid funds did not cover abortion reported it was very or somewhat difficult to pay for their abortions, compared to only 17% of women residing in states where abortions were covered.

How Has the Supreme Court Handled Abortion?

In *Roe v. Wade* (1973), the Supreme Court established that states could not ban abortions before fetal viability, the point at which a fetus can survive outside the womb. Under the three-trimester framework established by *Roe*, states were not allowed to ban abortions during the first two trimesters of pregnancy but were allowed to regulate or prohibit abortions in the third trimester, except in cases where abortions were necessary to protect the life or health of a pregnant person. The Court ruled that the fundamental right to have an abortion is included in the right to privacy implicit in the "liberty" guarantee of the Due Process Clause of the Fourteenth Amendment.

Since it was decided, *Roe v. Wade* has faced legal criticism. Notwithstanding these critiques, the Court upheld *Roe* multiple times over the next half-century including in *Planned Parenthood v. Casey* (1992). But after former President Trump appointed three new Justices to the Supreme Court, a new conservative supermajority overturned *Roe v. Wade* in *Dobbs v. Jackson Women's Health Organization* (2022) and established that there is no Constitutional right to have an abortion.

In his *Dobbs* majority opinion, Justice Alito concluded "*Roe* was egregiously wrong from the start." Writing for the majority, he underscored that "[t]he Constitution makes no reference to abortion," and while he recognized there are constitutional rights not expressly enumerated in the Constitution, he concluded the right to have an abortion is not one of them. Justice Alito reasoned that the only legitimate rights not explicitly stated in the Constitution are those "deeply rooted in the nation's history and traditions," and he found no evidence of this for abortion.

Because the Court determined there is no Constitutional right to abortion, it allowed the Mississippi state law which banned abortion after 15 weeks of pregnancy with limited exceptions to go into effect. The Court ruled that states have the authority to restrict access to abortion or ban it completely and that the power to regulate or prohibit abortions would be "returned to the people and their elected representatives."

The Court's three liberal Justices criticized the majority's decision in a withering joint dissent. The dissenting Justices argued the right to abortion established in *Roe* and upheld in *Casey* is necessary to respect the autonomy and equality of women and prevent the government from controlling "a woman's body or the course of a woman's life." They lamented "one result of today's decision is certain: the curtailment of women's rights, and of their status as free and equal citizens."

How Did the States Respond to the Overturning of *Roe v. Wade*?

Since *Roe v. Wade* was overturned, many states have implemented abortion bans or restrictions, while others have added protections and expanded access. The abortion landscape in America is now fractured and highly variegated.

As of May 2024, abortion is banned completely in almost all circumstances in 14 states. In 7 states, abortion is banned at or before 18 weeks of gestation. Many states with abortion bans do not include exceptions in cases where the health of the pregnant person is at risk, the pregnancy is the result of rape or incest, or there is a fatal fetal anomaly.

Access to abortion varies widely even among states without bans since many states have restrictions such as waiting periods, gestational limits, or parental consent laws making it more difficult to get an abortion.

Many state bans and restrictions are still being litigated in court. The interjurisdictional issues and legal questions arising from the post-*Dobbs* abortion landscape have not been fully resolved.

Despite the Supreme Court's stated intention in *Dobbs* to leave the abortion issue to elected officials, the Court will likely hear more cases on abortion in the near future. This term, in addition to the case about Mifepristone, the Court will decide in *Moyle v. United States* whether a federal law called the Emergency Medical Treatment and Labor Act (EMTLA) can require hospitals in states with abortion bans to perform abortions in emergency situations that demand "stabilizing treatment" for the health of pregnant patients.

What Are the Trends in Abortion Statistics Post-*Dobbs*?

In 2023, the first full year since the *Dobbs* Supreme Court decision, states with abortion bans experienced sharp declines in the number of abortions occurring within their borders. But these declines were outweighed by increases in abortion totals in states where abortion remained legal. Nearly all states without bans witnessed increases in 2023. Taken together, abortions in non-ban states increased by 26% in 2023 compared to 2020 levels.

As a result, the nationwide abortion statistics from 2023 represent the highest total number (1,037,000 abortions) and abortion rate (15.9 abortions per 1,000 women of reproductive age) in the U.S. in over a decade. The 2023 U.S. total represents an 11% increase from 2020 levels.

It's unclear why, despite *Dobbs*, abortions have continued to rise. It may be because of the increased use of medication abortions, especially after the FDA liberalized regulations related to telehealth and in-person visits. In addition, multiple states where abortion remains legal have implemented shield laws and other new protections for abortion patients and providers, increased insurance coverage, or otherwise expanded access. Abortion funds provided greater financial and practical assistance. Interstate travel for abortions doubled after the *Dobbs* decision.

In short, the impacts of *Dobbs* are being felt unevenly. Although most women who want abortions are still able to obtain them, a significant minority are instead carrying their pregnancies to term. In the first six months of 2023, state abortion bans led between one-fifth and one-fourth of women living in ban states who may have otherwise gotten an abortion not to have one.

Young, low-income, and minority women will be most affected by state bans and restrictions because they are disproportionately likely to have unintended pregnancies and less able to overcome economic and logistical barriers involved in travelling across state lines or receiving medication abortion pills through out-of-state networks.

What Are the Effects of Expanding or Restricting Abortion Access on Women and Their Families?

Effects of abortion restrictions on women

Abortion bans jeopardize the lives and health of women. The impacts on their health can be especially troublesome. Pregnancies can go wrong for many reasons—fetal abnormalities, complications of a miscarriage, ectopic pregnancies—and without access to emergency care, some women could face serious threats to their own health and future ability to bear children. Abortion restrictions can place doctors in difficult situations and undermine women's health care.

Although medication abortions are safe and effective, abortion bans could also increase the number of women who use unsafe methods to induce self-managed abortions, thereby endangering their own health or even their lives. State abortion legalizations in the years before *Roe* reduced maternal mortality among non-white women by 30–40%.

Enforcement of state laws that restricted access to abortion in the years before *Dobbs* has even been associated with increases in intimate partner violence-related homicides of women and girls.

In addition, lack of access to abortion leads to worse economic outcomes for women. After a conservative group suggested that such effects have not been well documented, a group of economists filed an amicus brief to the Supreme Court in the *Dobbs* case, noting that in recent years methods for establishing the causal effects of abortion have shown that they do affect women's life trajectories. Although there has been some difficulty in separating the effects of access to abortion from access to the Pill or other forms of birth control, an extensive literature shows that reducing unintended pregnancies increases educational attainment, labor force participation, earnings, and occupational prestige for women. These trends are especially pronounced for Black women.

One example that focuses solely on abortion is the Turnaway study, in which researchers compared the outcomes for women who were denied abortions on the basis of just being a little beyond the gestational cutoff for eligibility to the outcomes of otherwise similar women who were just under that cutoff. The study along with subsequent related research has shown that women who are denied abortions are nearly four times more likely to be living in poverty six months after being denied an abortion, a difference that persists through four years after denial. They are also more likely to be unemployed, rely on public assistance, and experience financial distress such as bankruptcies, evictions and court judgements.

Finally, increased access to abortion results in lower rates of single and teen parenthood. State abortion legalizations in the years before *Roe* reduced the number of teen mothers by 34%. The effects were especially large for Black teens.

Effects of abortion restrictions on children

Along with contraception, access to abortion reduces unplanned births. That means fewer children dying in infancy, growing up in poverty, needing welfare, and living with a single parent. One study suggests that if all currently mistimed births were aligned with the timing preferred by their mothers, children's college graduation rates would increase by about 8 percentage points (a 36% increase), and their lifetime incomes would increase by roughly $52,000.

Despite this evidence that the denial of abortions to women who want them would be harmful to women and to children once born, those who are pro-life argue that these costs are well worth the price to save the lives of the unborn. As of April 2024, 36% of Americans believe abortion should be illegal in all (8%) or most (28%) cases, while 63% of Americans believe abortion should be legal in all (25%) or most (28%) cases.

Looking Ahead

The abortion landscape in America is continually evolving. Whereas pro-choice advocates will seek to expand access and add additional protections for abortion patients and providers, opponents of abortion will continue to criminalize abortions and further restrict availability.

Abortion will be one of the top issues of the 2024 elections in November. Democratic candidates in particular believe abortion is a winning issue for them and will broadcast their pro-choice stance on the campaign trail. Some evidence suggests the overturning of *Roe* has galvanized a new class of abortion-rights voters. Multiple states will have abortion referenda on the ballot.

The Supreme Court's *Dobbs* decision will not prevent women and other citizens from affecting the legislative process by voting, organizing, influencing public opinion, or running for office. What they do with that power in November remains to be seen.

Print Citations

CMS: Sawhill, Isabel V., and Kai Smith. "Abortion in the US: What You Need to Know." In *The Reference Shelf: Reproductive Rights,* edited by Micah L. Issitt, 9-16. Amenia, NY: Grey House Publishing, 2024.

MLA: Sawhill, Isabel V., and Kai Smith. "Abortion in the US: What You Need to Know." *The Reference Shelf: Reproductive Rights,* edited by Micah L. Issitt, Grey House Publishing, 2024, pp. 9-16.

APA: Sawhill, I. V., & Smith K. (2024). Abortion in the US: What you need to know. In M. L. Issitt (Ed.), *The reference shelf: Reproductive rights* (pp. 9-16). Amenia, NY: Grey House Publishing. (Original work published 2024)

For Both Sides: Abortion Policy 2 Years After *Dobbs* Decision Hinges on November

By Jennifer Shutt
Missouri Independent, June 24, 2024

WASHINGTON—Exactly two years after the U.S. Supreme Court overturned the constitutional right to an abortion, the battles rage among both advocates and lawmakers over the future of reproductive rights at the state and federal levels.

Anti-abortion groups that have achieved considerable success in deep-red parts of the country are working to sway voters away from approving ballot questions in more than a dozen states this November that could bolster protections for abortion. Several will be decided in states that will have an outsized role in determining control of Congress and the White House.

Abortion opponents are also preparing a game plan to implement if former President Donald Trump regains the Oval Office, a prospect that could lead to sweeping executive actions on abortion access as well as at least one more conservative Supreme Court justice.

Reproductive rights organizations are honing in on the numerous ballot questions as a crucial way to remove decisions from the hands of lawmakers, especially in purple or conservative-leaning states.

Abortion rights supporters are also trying to shore up support for Democrats in key races for the U.S. House and Senate as well as hoping to keep President Joe Biden in office for another four years.

$100 Million to Be Spent by Abortion Rights Advocates

Both sides plan to spend millions to win over voters.

The Center for Reproductive Rights, National Women's Law Center, American Civil Liberties Union and several other organizations announced Monday they're putting at least $100 million toward building "a long-term federal strategy to codify the right to abortion, including lobbying efforts, grassroots organizing, public education, and comprehensive communication strategies to mobilize support and enact change."

"Anti-abortion lawmakers have already banned or severely restricted abortion in 21 states with devastating consequences, and they won't stop until they can force a nationwide ban on abortion and push care out of reach entirely, even in states that have protected abortion access," they wrote.

Credit line: From *Missouri Independent*, June 24 © 2024. Reprinted with permission. All rights reserved.

Susan B. Anthony Pro-Life America and PAC Women Speak Out announced they would dedicate $92 million to make contact with at least 10 million voters in the swing states of Arizona, Georgia, Montana, North Carolina, Pennsylvania, Wisconsin, Michigan and Ohio.

> **Ballot referendums are shaping up to be the more fruitful battleground for those supportive of abortion access.**

SBA President Marjorie Dannenfelser wrote in a statement released Monday that there "is still much work ahead to ensure that every mother and child is supported and protected."

"Meanwhile we are just one election cycle away from having every gain for life ripped away," Dannenfelser wrote. "Joe Biden and the Democrats are hell-bent on banning protections for unborn children, spreading fear and lies, and forcing all-trimester abortion any time for any reason—even when babies can feel pain—as national law."

Democrats have tried repeatedly to enact protections for abortion access, contraception and in vitro fertilization in Congress—both when they had unified control of government following the fall of *Roe* in 2022 in *Dobbs v. Jackson Women's Health Organization*, and during divided government.

None of Democrats' bills have garnered the support needed to move past the Senate's 60-vote legislative filibuster.

In addition to calling on Congress to restore the protections that existed under *Roe*, the Biden administration is attempting to defend abortion and other reproductive rights through executive actions as well as in front of the Supreme Court.

Abortion Pill, Emergency Care

Earlier this year, Solicitor General Elizabeth Prelogar argued two cases on abortion access.

The first case, brought by four anti-abortion medical organizations and four anti-abortion doctors, addressed access to mifepristone, one of two pharmaceuticals used in medication abortions.

The justices unanimously ruled earlier this month that the groups didn't have standing to bring the case in the first place, though they didn't address any other aspects of the case.

The second case, yet undecided, has to do with when doctors can provide abortions as emergency medical care under the Emergency Medical Treatment and Active Labor Act or EMTALA.

Assistant to the President and Director of the Gender Policy Council Jennifer Klein said on a call with reporters Monday that there's not much the Biden administration will be able to do if the justices side with Idaho in the case.

"If the court rejects our current interpretation, our options on emergency medical care are likely to be limited," Klein said.

U.S. Health and Human Services Secretary Xavier Becerra in July 2022, shortly after the *Dobbs* ruling came out, released a letter saying that EMTALA protected health care providers who use abortion as stabilizing care.

The letter stated that "if a physician believes that a pregnant patient presenting at an emergency department, including certain labor and delivery departments, is experiencing an emergency medical condition as defined by EMTALA, and that abortion is the stabilizing treatment necessary to resolve that condition, the physician must provide that treatment."

"And when a state law prohibits abortion and does not include an exception for the life and health of the pregnant person—or draws the exception more narrowly than EMTALA's emergency medical condition definition—that state law is preempted," Becerra wrote.

The Centers for Medicare & Medicaid Services recently established a new portal that is supposed to make it easier for people to file complaints under EMTALA if they're denied an emergency abortion.

Comstock Act Repeal

Klein also said on the call the White House will likely support a bill introduced last week in Congress to repeal sections of the Comstock Act, an 1873 anti-obscenity law, that could be used to bar the mailing of medication abortion during a future GOP administration.

"We support all actions by Democrats in Congress to protect reproductive freedom, including this one," Klein said, after noting the interagency process for determining whether the Biden administration will support the bill was still ongoing.

The legislation, however, is unlikely to pass in a Congress with a Republican-controlled House and a Democratic majority in the Senate. And divided government appears likely to continue during the next four years, regardless of which presidential candidate wins in November.

Ballot Questions in States

Outside of court cases and executive actions, ballot referendums are shaping up to be the more fruitful battleground for those supportive of abortion access, though anti-abortion groups are hoping to make some headway this fall.

Advocates in Arizona, Arkansas, Colorado, Florida, Iowa, Maine, Maryland, Missouri, Montana, Nebraska, Nevada, Pennsylvania and South Dakota have either secured questions for the November ballot or are in the process of doing so, according to the health news publication *KFF*.

Residents in California, Kansas, Kentucky, Michigan, Vermont and Ohio have all previously decided to bolster or add protection for abortion access in the two years since the Supreme Court ruling was released.

Polling from the Pew Research Center conducted earlier this year shows that 63% of Americans support abortion access being legal in all or most cases, while 36% say it should be illegal in most or all cases.

The polling shows that Democrats and Republicans hold views in both directions, with 41% of Republicans and 85% of Democrats saying it should be legal in most or all cases, while 57% of Republicans and 14% of Democrats say it should be illegal in most or all cases.

The issue, as well as Biden and Trump's records on abortion, are likely to be a central part of the first presidential debate on Thursday, just three days after the two-year anniversary of the *Dobbs* ruling.

Print Citations

CMS: Shutt, Jennifer. "For Both Sides: Abortion Policy 2 Years After *Dobbs* Decision Hinges on November." In *The Reference Shelf: Reproductive Rights,* edited by Micah L. Issitt, 17-20. Amenia, NY: Grey House Publishing, 2024.

MLA: Shutt, Jennifer. "For Both Sides: Abortion Policy 2 Years After *Dobbs* Decision Hinges on November." *The Reference Shelf: Reproductive Rights,* edited by Micah L. Issitt, Grey House Publishing, 2024, pp. 17-20.

APA: Shutt, J. (2024). For both sides: Abortion policy 2 years after *Dobbs* decision hinges on November. In M. L. Issitt (Ed.), *The reference shelf: Reproductive rights* (pp. 17-20). Amenia, NY: Grey House Publishing. (Original work published 2024)

The Criminalization of Abortion and Surveillance of Women in a Post-*Dobbs* World

By Jolynn Dellinger and Stephanie K. Pell
Brookings Institution, April 18, 2024

- The authors' new article, "Body of Evidence," explores how some states are criminalizing abortion; the way medication abortion is disrupting abortion bans; the threat of prosecution faced by women who self-manage abortions with medication; and the ways modern surveillance technologies enable law enforcement investigations of abortion crimes.

- Medication abortion, which is approved by the FDA for terminating a pregnancy of up 10 weeks, accounts for 63% of abortions in the United States but currently faces a challenge before the Supreme Court.

- Meanwhile, as an array of modern technologies enable the investigation of abortion-related crimes, some states are subjecting women to the threat of prosecution for self-managing abortions.

On February 16, the Alabama Supreme Court held that frozen embryos were "children" under Alabama's Wrongful Death of a Minor Act. While this was a decision about in vitro fertilization (IVF), Alabama's recognition of embryos as persons is simply a logical extension of the anti-abortion movement's long-time commitment to the notion of fetal personhood, an idea now animating the post-*Dobbs* criminalization of reproductive care. A number of state legislatures have already granted personhood status to fertilized eggs or unborn children in utero at any stage of development.

Consistent with the anti-abortion movement's goal of a nationwide recognition of fetal personhood, the criminalization of abortion is a tool for preventing abortions from ever occurring. In our new article, "Bodies of Evidence: The Criminalization of Abortion and Surveillance of Women in a Post-*Dobbs* World," we explore: how ban states are criminalizing abortion; the way medication abortion is disrupting abortion bans; the threat of prosecution faced by women who self-manage abortions with medication; and the ways modern surveillance technologies enable law enforcement investigations of abortion crimes.

Credit line: From *Brookings Institution*, April 18 © 2024. Reprinted with permission. All rights reserved.

The criminalization of abortion is one of several strategies endorsed by the anti-abortion movement and adopted in states attempting to enforce abortion bans and defend them against circumvention by medication abortion.

Medication abortion, a two-pill regimen involving mifepristone and misoprostol, is approved by the FDA for terminating a pregnancy up to 10 weeks. While the FDA approved the use of mifepristone in 2000, the revolutionary promise of medication abortion—where a woman can receive the medication in the mail, then safely self-manage an abortion in the privacy of her own home—was not realized until the FDA permanently lifted the in-person dispensing requirement in 2021. Not surprisingly, research from the Guttmacher Institute indicates that medication abortion now accounts for 63% of abortions in the United States, up from 53% in 2020.

Because of medication abortion, pregnant people living in states that ban or severely restrict abortions have access to a form of abortion care that was not available pre-*Roe*. Today, pills can be moved across state lines, doctors in abortion-protective states can offer telehealth care to women in ban states, and organizations like Aid Access can mail abortion medication from overseas. It is no longer necessary for all women in ban states to travel out of state to access abortion care.

The anti-abortion movement is, of course, aware of the ways in which medication abortion can thwart abortion bans and is attacking the problem on a number of fronts. In one response to this threat, a group of anti-abortion doctors brought a lawsuit challenging both the FDA's original approval of mifepristone in 2000 and subsequent actions in 2016 and 2021 to improve access to and availability of the drug. The goal of the lawsuit is to remove mifepristone from the U.S. market, a result that would drastically reduce access to medication abortion for all women in the United States, regardless of the state in which they live. The Fifth Circuit granted partial relief to the doctors, landing the case in front of the Supreme Court after the government's petition for writ of certiorari was granted. The Court heard oral arguments on March 26.

While it is unwise to predict how the Court will rule on any case, a majority of justices during the oral argument seemed to express some skepticism that the doctors who brought the suit had the necessary legal standing to seek the requested relief. The Court could thus dispose of the case without ever reaching its merits.

Even if the challenge to the FDA's treatment of mifepristone is unsuccessful, however, the case presented an opportunity for the plaintiffs to bring attention to another of the movement's strategies—one that was raised on three separate occasions during the oral argument by Justices Alito and Thomas. This strategy concerns the Comstock Act, a federal obscenity law from 1873, virtually dormant but still on the books, that criminalizes the mailing of "[e]very article, instrument, substance, drug, medicine, or thing which is advertised or described in a manner calculated to lead another to use or apply it for producing abortion."

A literal interpretation of this law would, at a minimum, make the mailing of any kind of abortifacient unlawful, essentially resulting in a nationwide ban on medication abortion. While the Department of Justice under the Biden administration interprets the Comstock Act narrowly, the Justice Department under a Trump administration is free to reject that interpretation. To achieve a nationwide abortion ban, the anti-abortion movement doesn't need Congress or even the courts—it only needs Donald Trump to be elected. And while Congress could certainly repeal the Comstock Act, that is not an outcome anyone should expect in the near future.

> **The criminalization of abortion necessarily involves the surveillance of women.**

As the anti-abortion movement pursues these strategies, another more familiar tactic for preventing women from self-managing abortion with medication is also available: the prosecution of women and those that may assist them. Although providers have historically been the primary targets of abortion laws, women have been investigated and prosecuted for pregnancy-related conduct and a variety of pregnancy outcomes, even during the *Roe* era. And, in 2016, when candidate Donald Trump was asked whether he thought women who sought an illegal abortion should face criminal punishment, he answered in the affirmative—"there has to be some sort of punishment."

Some state officials, politicians, and movement leaders claim that no one intends to prosecute pregnant women for abortion crimes. Others, emboldened by the demise of *Roe*, have suggested that criminal punishment of pregnant women who seek or obtain abortions is logical, morally justifiable, and required to end abortion.

As we explore in our article, a number of current states' laws—including personhood laws—provide prosecutors with the tools to investigate and prosecute women who self-manage abortion using medication and those that assist them. The decision whether to do so will generally turn on a prosecutor's interpretation of these laws, many of which do not *explicitly* exempt women from prosecution, and his or her exercise of prosecutorial discretion.

Georgia, for example, has passed a personhood law. Its "Living Infants Fairness and Equality" Act (LIFE Act) bans abortion after six weeks, a time at which most women don't even know they are pregnant, and states that "[i]t shall be the policy of the state of Georgia to recognize unborn children as natural persons." It defines "natural person" as "any human being, including an unborn child," and defines "unborn child" as "a member of the species of Homo sapiens at any stage of development who is carried in the womb." By including "unborn child" in the definition of natural person, the LIFE Act raises the *possibility* that a woman who obtains or self-manages an abortion after six weeks could be charged with murder.

In Georgia, a person commits murder "when he unlawfully and with malice aforethought, either express or implied, causes the death of another human being." No exemptions from prosecution are provided in the LIFE Act. While our article identifies some ambiguity surrounding whether a woman having or self-managing an abortion could be prosecuted for murder under Georgia's LIFE Act, Douglas County District Attorney Ryan Leonard previously indicated that women in Georgia "should prepare for the possibility that they could be criminally prosecuted for having an abortion. . . . If you look at it from a purely legal standpoint, if you take the life of another human being, it's murder." This prosecutor's statement is an example of a threat of prosecution, where a public official purposefully wields fear and uncertainty to enforce an abortion ban.

Meanwhile, an April 1 ruling by the Florida Supreme Court enabled a six-week abortion ban to take effect by May 1, replacing the current law, which bans abortion after 15 weeks. In Florida, "*[a]ny person* who willfully performs, or actively participates in, a termination of pregnancy in violation" of the law before or during viability "commits a felony of the third degree, punishable" by a term of imprisonment not exceeding five years and fines. There is no exemption for pregnant women. The broad "any person" language subjects women who self-manage abortion through medication to the threat of investigation and prosecution.[1] Recognizing this possibility, Florida legislators proposed H.B.111 in October 2023, a bill that explicitly exempts pregnant women from prosecution for terminating their pregnancies: "This paragraph does not apply to the pregnant woman who terminates the pregnancy." The bill died in subcommittee in March of this year.

Florida's six-week ban features the same broad language prohibiting "any person" from engaging in the proscribed conduct. Accordingly, women will continue to be at risk of investigation and prosecution under the new law. There were 84,052 abortions in Florida last year, an increase of 2,000 abortions from 2022. More than 7,000 of those women came to Florida from other states. With the imposition of the six-week ban, the use of medication abortion will undoubtedly spike. Women continue to have abortions even when they are illegal.

Georgia and Florida are just two examples of states with laws that subject women to the threat of prosecution for self-managing abortions. There are also a range of laws "related to fetal remains, child abuse, felony assault or assault of an unborn child, practicing medicine without a license, or homicide and murder" that don't even mention or outlaw abortion, but which have been used to investigate and prosecute people for conduct related to the alleged termination of their own pregnancies, even while *Roe* was the law of the land.

In the post-*Dobbs* world, prosecutors who choose to investigate women for self-managing abortions have an array of modern surveillance technologies at their disposal. In our article, we present three hypothetical scenarios involving law enforcement investigations of a single mom, a college student, and a high school student based on alleged self-managed abortions. In each of the scenarios, we attempt to illustrate what is possible based on current law and technology. We are not suggesting that these exact scenarios have occurred or will occur. But aspects of these fact patterns are consistent with cases described in If/When/How's 2023 report documenting the ways in which women were investigated and prosecuted for conduct pertaining to self-managed abortions between 2000 and 2020, prior to the fall of *Roe*.

Whether abortion laws target providers, aiders and abettors, or women themselves, the criminalization of abortion necessarily involves the surveillance of women. Women's bodies are often the so-called scene of the crime, and their personal data will, more likely than not, be evidence of the crime. The modern digital environment only amplifies the scope and harm of that surveillance. Communications with friends and family, internet searches, websites visited, purchases made, data shared with mobile apps, location, and other data generated in the course of everyday life become evidence that can be used in prosecutions against women and those that assist them in obtaining abortions.

We offer no single, silver bullet solution for the threat of surveillance and prosecution women face in a post-*Dobbs* world. But there are some intermediate measures that can mitigate this threat. As our research demonstrates, state laws criminalizing abortion are, on the whole, a confusing morass. They often do not unambiguously preclude the prosecution of women. Confusing statutory language coupled with the unpredictability of prosecutorial discretion creates uncertainty— which in turn curtails women's liberty, compromises their privacy interests, and puts their health at risk. State legislators, especially those who claim that there is no intention to prosecute women, should ensure that laws clearly and explicitly exempt women from prosecution.

Another avenue that holds some promise for disrupting the threat is specifically tied to the state of Delaware, where many big platforms and technology companies are incorporated. Delaware, we argue, should join California and Washington in passing a data shield law that includes provisions specifically designed to prevent companies from turning over data sought by law enforcement organizations from ban states that are investigating abortion crimes. Such a shield law could provide one significant hurdle to law enforcement attempts to investigate and prosecute women who have abortions and those that assist them. As the chosen state of incorporation for many tech companies holding data relevant to the investigation of abortion crimes, Delaware has a unique opportunity to engage in threat mitigation.

Note

1. Notably, a provision in Section 390.0111 that specifically bans partial birth abortion includes explicit language exempting women from prosecution for such procedures: "A woman upon whom a partial-birth abortion is performed may not be prosecuted under this section for a conspiracy to violate the provisions of this section." *Id.* § 5(b). No other language in the statute exempts women from prosecution for abortion in any other circumstances.

Print Citations

CMS: Dellinger, Jolynn, and Stephanie K. Pell. "The Criminalization of Abortion and Surveillance of Women in a Post-*Dobbs* World." In *The Reference Shelf: Reproductive Rights*, edited by Micah L. Issitt, 21-26. Amenia, NY: Grey House Publishing, 2024.

MLA: Dellinger, Jolynn, and Stephanie K. Pell. "The Criminalization of Abortion and Surveillance of Women in a Post-*Dobbs* World." *The Reference Shelf: Reproductive Rights*, edited by Micah L. Issitt, Grey House Publishing, 2024 pp. 21-26.

APA: Dellinger, J., & Pell, S. K. (2024). The criminalization of abortion and surveillance of women in a post-*Dobbs* world. In M. L. Issitt (Ed.), *The reference shelf: Reproductive rights* (pp. 21-26). Amenia, NY: Grey House Publishing. (Original work published 2024)

U.S. Supreme Court Allows Access to Abortion Pill, Unanimously Rejecting Texas Challenge

By Eleanor Klibanoff and Karen Brooks Harper
The Texas Tribune, June 13, 2024

Mifepristone, a common abortion inducing medication, will remain on the market without additional restrictions after the U.S. Supreme Court unanimously rejected an anti-abortion group's challenge to the drug's approval.

In the high court's first abortion-related ruling since it overturned *Roe v. Wade* in 2022, the nine justices ruled to change nothing about the drug's legal status. The ruling is a rebuke to the 5th U.S. Circuit Court of Appeals and District Judge Matthew Kacsmaryk of Amarillo. The opinion was written by Justice Brett Kavanaugh, with a concurring opinion by Justice Clarence Thomas.

Medication abortion, typically performed with a combination of mifepristone and misoprostol, is the most common abortion method in the United States. In the nearly 25 years since it was first approved by the U.S. Food and Drug Administration, mifepristone has been conclusively shown to be safe and effective.

This case originated in Amarillo, where only one anti-abortion judge hears almost all cases, and then went to the conservative 5th Circuit in New Orleans, which upheld most of the ruling. The Supreme Court stepped in at that point and allowed mifepristone to remain on the market while the case proceeded.

With abortion all but banned in more than a dozen states, these medications have become a key part of the strategy to help people continue to access the procedure—and, as a result, a major focus for anti-abortion groups.

This ruling comes as a relief to abortion providers and advocates, but also pharmaceutical companies, who had expressed concern about the precedent of allowing a judge to overturn a long-standing drug approval.

The Mifepristone Challenge from Texas

Mifepristone was first approved in 2000 to be used alongside misoprostol to terminate a pregnancy up to seven weeks. The medication is also commonly used to pass fetal tissue after a miscarriage.

Almost immediately, anti-abortion groups began challenging the drug's approval, starting with a citizen petition in 2002. The FDA did not respond to the petition until 2016, rejecting it the same day it announced new guidelines allowing the

---

Credit line: From the *Texas Tribune*, June 13 © 2024. Reprinted with permission. All rights reserved.

medication to be used through 10 weeks of pregnancy.

In 2019, the FDA approved a generic version of mifepristone, and later began allowing the drug to be prescribed through telehealth, dispensed at retail pharmacies and sent through the mail.

Medication abortion is the most common abortion method in the United States.

In November 2022, the Alliance for Hippocratic Medicine, an anti-abortion medical group, filed a lawsuit arguing that the original 2000 drug approval was improper and should be reversed, alongside all the recent changes. The group filed the lawsuit in Amarillo, where all cases are heard by U.S. District Judge Matthew Kacsmaryk, a former religious liberty lawyer who previously litigated against abortion and contraception access before he was appointed to the bench by President Donald Trump.

In a ruling laced with anti-abortion rhetoric, Kacsmaryk ruled that the FDA's approval of mifepristone was improper and should be revoked.

"The Court does not second-guess FDA's decision-making lightly," Kacsmaryk wrote. "But here, FDA acquiesced on its legitimate safety concerns—in violation of its statutory duty—based on plainly unsound reasoning and studies that did not support its conclusions."

Kacsmaryk gave the U.S. Department of Justice five days to appeal the ruling before it went into effect, which it did. The 5th Circuit ruled that the drug could remain on the market, but reinstated the restrictions that were in place before 2016. The Supreme Court stepped in at that point and ruled that nothing about mifepristone's approval would change until the case was resolved.

In late March, the Supreme Court heard arguments about whether the drug's status should remain unchanged—or whether it should revert back to the pre-2016 restrictions, when it could only be used up to seven weeks of pregnancy, and not prescribed via telehealth or sent through the mail. The hearing also focused on whether the anti-abortion doctors who brought the lawsuit had legal standing to file their lawsuit.

"Rolling back FDA's changes would unnecessarily restrict access to mifepristone with no safety justification," U.S. Solicitor General Elizabeth Prelogar argued. "Some women could be forced to undergo more invasive surgical abortions. Others might not be able to access the drug at all. And all of this would happen at the request of plaintiffs who have no certain injury of their own. The Court should reject that profoundly inequitable result."

The Ruling

In his opinion on Thursday, Kavanaugh wrote that the plaintiffs can't sue simply because they might "desire to make a drug less available for others."

The ruling notes that the plaintiffs bringing the lawsuit do not, in fact, use or prescribe mifepristone and are not required by the FDA to do so—and therefore they are unaffected by its accessibility in the market.

"Federal law fully protects doctors against being required to provide abortions or other medical treatment against their consciences—and therefore breaks any chain of causation between FDA's relaxed regulation of mifepristone and any asserted conscience injuries to the doctors," the ruling reads.

On a broader scale, doctors do not and should not have the power to change federal public health policy and allowing the lawsuit to succeed would set a dangerous precedent, the ruling reads.

"Allowing doctors or other healthcare providers to challenge general safety regulations as unlawfully lax would be an unprecedented and limitless approach and would allow doctors to sue in federal court to challenge almost any policy affecting public health," it reads.

The ruling also leaves open the possibility that another plaintiff, including one who could show direct injury or a "sufficient likelihood of future injury" could successfully bring the case in the future.

"But in this case—even assuming for the sake of argument that FDA's 2016 and 2021 changes to mifepristone's conditions of use cause more pregnant women to require emergency abortions and that some women would likely seek treatment from these plaintiff doctors—the plaintiff doctors have not shown that they could be forced to participate in an abortion or provide abortion-related medical treatment over their conscience objections," the ruling reads.

Print Citations

CMS: Klibanoff, Eleanor, and Karen Brooks Harper. "U.S. Supreme Court Allows Access to Abortion Pill, Unanimously Rejecting Texas Challenge." In *The Reference Shelf: Reproductive Rights,* edited by Micah L. Issitt, 27-29. Amenia, NY: Grey House Publishing, 2024.

MLA: Klibanoff, Eleanor, and Karen Brooks Harper. "U.S. Supreme Court Allows Access to Abortion Pill, Unanimously Rejecting Texas Challenge." *The Reference Shelf: Reproductive Rights,* edited by Micah L. Issitt, Grey House Publishing, 2024, pp. 27-29.

APA: Klibanoff, E., & Harper, K. B. (2024). U.S. Supreme Court allows access to abortion pill, unanimously rejecting Texas challenge. In M. L. Issitt (Ed.), *The reference shelf: Reproductive rights* (pp. 27-29). Amenia, NY: Grey House Publishing. (Original work published 2024)

How Missouri Helps Abortion Opponents Divert State Taxes to Crisis Pregnancy Centers

By Jeremy Kohler
ProPublica, June 6, 2022

In the final days of Missouri's legislative session in May 2019, lawmakers turned their focus to a bill that would outlaw abortion in the state if the U.S. Supreme Court were to overturn *Roe v. Wade*.

The abortion ban passed by the legislature and signed by Gov. Mike Parson remains in limbo, at least for now. A leaked draft opinion suggests the high court is preparing to overturn the landmark 1973 ruling, which would trigger bans in Missouri and about a dozen other states.

But another piece of the same Missouri bill that has garnered far less attention has already taken effect. It has funneled millions of tax dollars to fight abortion, and it may well move tens of millions of dollars more to that battle—a drain on state revenues that legislative oversight officials failed to forecast.

That provision beefed up tax credits for Missouri taxpayers who donate money to pregnancy resource centers, or crisis pregnancy centers. Abortion foes praise the nonprofit centers for supporting women and presenting alternatives to ending pregnancies, but supporters of abortion say the facilities mislead women by appearing to offer clinical services and unbiased advice.

An analysis by *ProPublica* found the measure is proving costly for the state. Until an expansion took effect last year, Missouri residents who donated to the centers were able to claim a credit of 50% for their donations, meaning for every $1,000 in donations, a taxpayer's bill dropped by $500. The law increased the credit to 70% in 2021, further shifting the cost of those contributions to the state.

Because the centers are nonprofit, donors can deduct the remaining $300 of a $1,000 donation from their federal income taxes. (A deduction is worth less than a credit because it only reduces taxable income. A credit reduces dollar-for-dollar what a person owes in taxes.) Ultimately, a donor can end up recouping close to 80% of their gift in credits and deductions.

Lawmakers also removed the limit to how many pregnancy resource tax credits the state could issue in a given year starting in July 2021. And they removed the program's previous end date of 2024; the tax credit program will continue unless the law is changed.

Credit line: From *ProPublica*, June 6 © 2022. Reprinted with permission. All rights reserved.

The cost analysis of the bill, authored by nonpartisan legislative oversight directors, concluded the changes would carry a nominal cost to taxpayers. Increasing the tax credit to 70% from 50% meant the same donations that resulted in $3.5 million in tax credits a year—the maximum for the program before the increase took effect—would now result in $4.9 million, a jump of $1.4 million a year. But that was only if donations did not increase.

The authors acknowledged that without a cap, the impact could be greater if the increased tax credit led to more giving. And that's exactly what happened. In the quarter ending March 31, the state authorized more than $7 million in pregnancy resource tax credits, more than three times higher than in any previous quarter.

Pregnancy Resource Tax Credits See a Huge Jump in 2022

Bigger tax incentives for giving to the crisis pregnancy centers brought out more donors than in previous years.

"We definitely did see an increase in big donations," said Deb Beussink, assistant director of Birthright of Cape Girardeau, one of the 76 pregnancy resource centers across the state authorized to participate in the program.

"And these were from donors who had already been donating well to us," she added. "But they wanted to take advantage of that tax credit, so they enlarged their donation."

Until recently, Missouri has been the only state to issue tax credits for donations to pregnancy resource centers. In April, Mississippi Gov. Tate Reeves signed into law a program offering a maximum of $3.5 million per year in tax credits. Ohio considered a similar measure, but it did not advance.

Missouri's tax credits for pregnancy resource centers come on top of the record $8 million in funding for the centers that lawmakers allocated for the fiscal year starting July 1. Those funds go to centers for the social services they provide. Missouri has long been one of the nation's leading suppliers of tax dollars for pregnancy resource centers. An Associated Press analysis this year estimated the state had issued more than $44 million to centers since 2010, third most of any state behind Texas and Pennsylvania.

The tax credit's impact on state revenues, and the potential for that impact to deepen, has one Missouri budget analyst concerned.

"It does make me nervous," said Amy Blouin, the president and CEO of the Missouri Budget Project, a nonpartisan, nonprofit group that studies the state's spending and public policy decisions.

Legislators and advocates on both sides of the abortion debate said they were surprised by the increase in the tax credits that were issued. Even the bill's sponsor in the state Senate said he was unaware of the $7 million in tax credits for one quarter. "I would have expected that for an annual number," said Sen. Andrew Koenig, a Republican from St. Louis' western suburbs.

Taxpayers can only redeem tax credits up to the amount of their tax bill, but what's left over can be used the next year. Businesses also can take advantage. The maximum tax credit per taxpayer per year is $50,000.

The recipients of Missouri's pregnancy resource tax credits are confidential—unlike other types of state tax credits that are reported on the Missouri Accountability Portal.

> **Crisis pregnancy centers or pregnancy resource centers are unregulated, unlicensed fronts.**

Kyle Rieman, who was the oversight director and lead author of the cost analysis of the tax credit expansion, said lawmakers gave his staff only an hour to analyze the financial impact before they voted. And he said state agencies provided him with little data to help make an estimate of more than the program's minimum cost.

"It pretty much didn't matter what the cost was," he said in a text, "they were going to pass the bill."

But Koenig said he provided Rieman's office with the tax credit proposal weeks before the vote and asked for—and received—a confidential financial analysis. He said that if the research had pointed to major costs ahead, "it could give pause."

Rieman said such requests are common but "not official or required, so they are not a priority."

The analysis sent to legislators before the vote said Rieman's staff wanted more information to update their analysis. But Parson signed the measure before Rieman could publish a more complete review.

The final analysis, published nearly a month after the governor's signature, still did not fully explore the potential cost. It said the Department of Social Services, which issues the tax credit, indicated there would be "no fiscal impact" on the agency. Asked how there could be none, a Social Services spokesperson told *ProPublica* that the department meant the program did not affect its own budget and the "impact is on the state's general revenue."

Rieman said the Office of Administration, which coordinates management of the state, did not provide information about how much the program's cost could exceed the minimum estimate or consider the costs of removing the program's end date. The office did not respond to questions from *ProPublica*.

Rieman said the experience was "a clear example of a policy that was passed by the General Assembly and Governor without any real public process or consideration of what the fiscal impact would be to the state."

A spokesperson for Parson did not respond to *ProPublica's* questions.

Koenig said he did not consider the amount of revenue diverted for the pregnancy resource tax credit to be significant next to the state's $48 billion budget.

"If we're going to put this ban on abortions in place, I wanted to make sure we support women who are going to be having these babies, and the way to do that was increasing the pregnancy resource tax credit," Koenig said.

Mallory Schwarz, the executive director of Pro-Choice Missouri, said abortion foes knew exactly what they were doing when they expanded the tax credit.

"Crisis pregnancy centers or pregnancy resource centers are unregulated, unlicensed fronts designed to look like legitimate medical clinics, run by people who are anti-abortion, and intentionally mislead and coerce pregnant people to try to scare them out of having abortions or delay their care to the point where they can no longer have an abortion," she said. "But at the same time, we're lining the pockets of these pregnancy centers and incentivizing (people) to give against their own self-interest and their own well-being."

Jill Schupp, a Democratic senator from St. Louis County who voted against the bill, said she was "shocked" by the amount of tax credits being issued: "These numbers are huge." While the budget is flush with federal stimulus, she said, the cost "might not look like it's hurting other programs. But that will change."

And even a Republican who voted for the bill said the new numbers are concerning. "I wasn't aware it was that much money. You just brought it to my attention," said Rep. John Wiemann, a St. Charles County Republican. "If it's outside what the fiscal note said, someone needs to explain why it's that high."

Print Citations

CMS: Kohler, Jeremy. "How Missouri Helps Abortion Opponents Divert State Taxes to Crisis Pregnancy Centers." In *The Reference Shelf: Reproductive Rights,* edited by Micah L. Issitt, 30-33. Amenia, NY: Grey House Publishing, 2024.

MLA: Kohler, Jeremy. "How Missouri Helps Abortion Opponents Divert State Taxes to Crisis Pregnancy Centers." *The Reference Shelf: Reproductive Rights,* edited by Micah L. Issitt, Grey House Publishing, 2024, pp. 30-33.

APA: Kohler, J. (2024). How Missouri helps abortion opponents divert state taxes to crisis pregnancy centers. In M. L. Issitt (Ed.), *The reference shelf: Reproductive rights* (pp. 30-33). Amenia, NY: Grey House Publishing. (Original work published 2022)

The Abortion Debate Is Headed to the Ballot Box: Here's Where Voters Will Decide

NPR, May 28, 2024

Since the U.S. Supreme Court overturned the federal right to abortion in 2022, states have had the final say on abortion rights. And now abortion-rights supporters across the United States seek to maneuver around Republican-led legislatures and go straight to voters.

This year, voters in up to 11 states could face abortion-rights amendments. Several states that outlaw most abortions could see those bans reversed if the ballot measures pass: Arkansas, Florida, Missouri, Nebraska and South Dakota.

Voters have already backed abortion rights at the ballot box in at least six states since the reversal of *Roe v. Wade,* including conservative-leaning Kentucky and Kansas.

Getting amendments on the ballot takes legwork, gathering tens or hundreds of thousands of signatures. Then, there could be court challenges.

The statewide up-or-down votes could motivate more voters to the polls, shaping the race for president, the battle for which party controls Congress and, in Arizona for example, which party runs the legislature.

NPR is tracking the amendment campaigns taking place across the country and will update the developments through November.

Colorado

Colorado doesn't restrict abortion at any time during pregnancy. That has led to the state becoming a regional hub for abortion access.

Coloradans did use the ballot to impose one limit in 1984, when they passed a constitutional amendment banning public funding for abortions.

Now, abortion-rights advocates have gotten a proposed amendment on the ballot to guarantee a right to abortion in the state constitution, which would prohibit any laws impeding that right.

The amendment would also remove that current constitutional ban against public funding for abortions—in Medicaid or state employee health plans. The initiative is similar to the state law passed in 2022. It would need 55% of the vote to get into the constitution.

Credit line: From *NPR*, May 28 © 2024. Reprinted with permission. All rights reserved.

Florida

Florida is the most populous state where abortion-rights advocates already have enough signatures and the official approval to put a question on the ballot this November. The state will ask voters whether to protect abortion in the state constitution up to the point of fetal viability—usually about 24 weeks of pregnancy—or, in all cases, to protect the life of the pregnant person.

The state's six-week abortion ban, which has exceptions for rare circumstances, went into effect in May, further energizing voters on both sides of the issue to come out in November. And Florida requires 60% approval to pass the amendment, a level no other state has met since *Roe v. Wade*'s reversal in 2022.

Maryland

Since taking office in 2023, Democratic Gov. Wes Moore has billed Maryland as a "sanctuary state" for reproductive rights. Moore's administration stockpiled mifepristone—one of two drugs used in medication abortion—when federal court cases threatened the drug's future, and it has put money into training more health care workers in reproductive care.

In November, Maryland voters will decide on an amendment that would enshrine reproductive rights in the state constitution. The amendment would protect "the ability to make and effectuate decisions to prevent, continue, or end one's own pregnancy." The referendum needs a simple majority to pass and is expected to meet that threshold.

Meanwhile, during the legislative session this year, Maryland lawmakers put money aside to help facilities that provide abortions improve security.

New York

The proposed amendment that could enshrine abortion rights into the New York state constitution doesn't mention the word "abortion." The legislature placed on the November ballot a sweeping equal rights amendment banning discrimination based on race, gender, age and other categories including, "pregnancy, pregnancy outcomes, and reproductive healthcare and autonomy."

Movement toward the ballot proposal started in response to the U.S. Supreme Court overturning *Roe vs. Wade* in 2022. Some Republicans oppose it saying it codifies abortion rights in the state constitution—which seems to be the intent.

It survived an initial court challenge and was restored to the fall ballot in June, but opponents could still appeal.

New York already allows abortion until fetal viability—around 24 weeks of pregnancy—and has laws protecting reproductive healthcare providers. But there are no such laws—or an equal rights amendment—in the constitution.

South Dakota

South Dakota voters will weigh in on a ballot measure that could enshrine abortion protections into the state constitution. Reproductive rights group Dakotans for Health submitted 55,000 signatures in support of the proposal.

After the *Dobbs* decision ended the federal right to abortion, an already-in-place South Dakota law went into effect banning all abortions except to save the life of the mother—though critics say that this exception remains undefined.

The proposed amendment would allow abortions in the first trimester, add more restrictions in the second and prohibit abortions in the third trimester, with some exceptions.

Some abortion-rights groups say the amendment is too weak, while an anti-abortion group has called it "extreme."

Arizona

Arizona took a confusing turn this spring when a court ruled that a near-total ban on abortions, from a law that had been dormant for decades, could be enforced again. But the Legislature and courts have nullified that law, and the state's ban on abortions after the 15th week of pregnancy is still in effect.

Now a proposed constitutional amendment would protect abortion rights until the point of fetal viability, or around 24 weeks. The ballot measure would also allow exceptions later in pregnancy when health risks are involved.

Organizers submitted more than 820,00 signatures in support of the amendment in early July. They're now being verified by the Arizona secretary of state.

Arkansas

Arkansas' ban on abortion is one of the most restrictive in the country, making an exception only to save the life of the mother. In early July, reproductive rights group Arkansans for Limited Government submitted more than 101,000 signatures in support of an amendment for abortion access.

The petition still has to be verified by the Arkansas secretary of state in order for it to appear on the ballot in November.

If approved, the amendment would protect abortions through the 18th week of pregnancy.

Some abortion-rights groups, like Planned Parenthood, have backed off supporting the effort, saying it doesn't go far enough to make abortion more accessible.

Missouri

Missouri's abortion-rights advocates have collected far more than enough signatures to place a constitutional amendment protecting abortion on the 2024 ballot. The measure would undo the state's law banning all abortions, except to save the life of the pregnant person, and replace it with language making abortion legal up to the point of fetal viability.

The ballot initiative is receiving significant financial support from out-of-state groups, as well as more volunteer support than any other proposed amendment in the state.

To curb the amendment effort, Republican lawmakers tried to get a separate ballot measure to voters that would have made it more difficult to amend the state constitution. However, using the longest filibuster in state history, Democrats overpowered that attempt.

> **Voters have already backed abortion rights at the ballot box in at least six states since the reversal of *Roe v. Wade*, including conservative-leaning Kentucky and Kansas.**

Montana

The proposed ballot measure in Montana would add language protecting abortion access up until fetal viability—around 24 weeks of pregnancy—to the state constitution during a referendum in November.

In late June, the initiative's supporters submitted more than 117,000 signatures in support of the proposal, far more than the 60,000 signatures required to qualify for the ballot. The Montana secretary of state is working to verify the petition.

Abortion remains legal and accessible in the state. That's even though Republican lawmakers have passed several restrictive abortion laws at the request of GOP Gov. Greg Gianforte in recent years. Abortion rights are protected under state judicial precedent.

In 1999, the Montana Supreme Court ruled that the state's constitutional right to privacy protects access to abortion until the point of viability. The court has reaffirmed the ruling in recent years.

Nebraska

In 2023, the Legislature banned abortion after 12 weeks of pregnancy, down from 20 weeks previously. There are exceptions for rape, incest and the life of the pregnant patient. Medicaid and private health insurance plans are banned from covering most abortions.

Now two competing amendment drives are aiming for November. Abortion-rights groups propose asking voters whether they want to guarantee abortion access until fetal viability—usually around 24 weeks of pregnancy—and when needed to "protect the life or health of the pregnant patient." Meanwhile, another group has started a petition drive to place the state's 12-week ban into the constitution.

Both groups said they cleared the requirement of collecting more than 123,000 signatures from registered voters to appear on the ballot. The Nebraska secretary of state is working to verify the signatures.

If both efforts make it onto the ballot and pass, whichever initiative gets more votes will go into the constitution.

Nevada

Under a state law approved by voters in 1990, abortion is legal in Nevada within the first 24 weeks of pregnancy. Abortion-rights advocates want to put that in the state constitution with an amendment guaranteeing abortion access up until fetal viability, which is usually about 24 weeks.

In late June, the Nevada Secretary of State said the issue met all requirements to appear on the ballot. For the amendment to take effect, voters would have to approve the initiative twice, once in 2024 and again in 2026.

Polling has consistently shown that roughly two-thirds of Nevadans believe access to abortion should be legal in "all or most cases."

Nevada Democrats believe protecting abortion access mobilized voters during the 2022 midterm elections, and they plan to make the issue central to their cause this year, with a U.S. Senate seat and congressional seats at stake.

Print Citations

CMS: NPR. "The Abortion Debate Is Headed to the Ballot Box: Here's Where Voters Will Decide." In *The Reference Shelf: Reproductive Rights,* edited by Micah L. Issitt, 34-38. Amenia, NY: Grey House Publishing, 2024.

MLA: NPR. "The Abortion Debate Is Headed to the Ballot Box: Here's Where Voters Will Decide." *The Reference Shelf: Reproductive Rights,* edited by Micah L. Issitt, Grey House Publishing, 2024, pp. 34-38.

APA: NPR. (2024). The abortion debate is headed to the ballot box: Here's where voters will decide. In M. L. Issitt (Ed.), *The reference shelf: Reproductive rights* (pp. 34-38). Amenia, NY: Grey House Publishing. (Original work published 2024)

Tracking Abortion Bans Across the Country

By Allison McCann and Amy Schoenfeld Walker
New York Times, July 1, 2024

Twenty-one states ban abortion or restrict the procedure earlier in pregnancy than the standard set by *Roe v. Wade*, which governed reproductive rights for nearly half a century until the Supreme Court overturned the decision in 2022.

In some states, the fight over abortion access is still taking place in courtrooms, where advocates have sued to block bans and restrictions. Other states have moved to expand access to abortion by adding legal protections.

Latest Updates

- The Iowa Supreme Court ruled that the state's six-week abortion ban can soon be enforced while a lawsuit against it proceeds.
- A U.S. Supreme Court ruling will temporarily allow emergency abortions in Idaho when a woman's health is at risk. Lower courts must still decide whether the state's abortion ban violates a federal law requiring emergency care for any patient.
- The court earlier upheld access to a widely available abortion pill, rejecting a bid from anti-abortion groups to undo federal approval of the medication.

The *New York Times* is tracking abortion laws in each state after the Supreme Court's decision in *Dobbs v. Jackson Women's Health Organization*, which ended the constitutional right to an abortion.

Where Abortion Is Legal

In a few states that have enacted bans or restrictions, abortion remains legal for now as courts determine whether these laws can take effect. Abortion is legal in the rest of the country, and many states have added new protections since *Dobbs*.

> **The fight over abortion access is still taking place in courtrooms.**

Credit line: From the *New York Times*, July 1 © 2024. Reprinted with permission. All rights reserved.

State details

More details on the current status of abortion in each state are below.

STATE	STATUS OF ABORTION	LEGAL UNTIL	MORE DETAILS
Alabama	Banned	—	Abortion is banned in almost all circumstances.
Arkansas	Banned	—	Abortion is banned in almost all circumstances.
Idaho	Banned	—	Abortion is banned in almost all circumstances, and the Idaho Supreme Court ruled in 2023 that there is no constitutional right to an abortion in the state. A U.S. Supreme Court ruling will allow access to emergency abortions while lower courts decide if the state's ban violates a federal law requiring emergency care for any patient.
Indiana	Banned	—	Abortion is banned in almost all circumstances. In 2023, the Indiana Supreme Court ruled that the state Constitution does not include a right to abortion except in dire situations. A separate challenge to the ban by residents who argue that it violates their religious rights is ongoing.
Kentucky	Banned	—	Abortion is banned in almost all circumstances. In 2022, voters rejected a ballot measure that would have amended the state Constitution to say it did not contain the right to an abortion.
Louisiana	Banned	—	Abortion is banned in almost all circumstances.
Mississippi	Banned	—	Abortion is banned in almost all circumstances.
Missouri	Banned	—	Abortion is banned in almost all circumstances.
North Dakota	Banned	—	Abortion is banned in almost all circumstances.
Oklahoma	Banned	—	Abortion is banned in almost all circumstances.
South Dakota	Banned	—	Abortion is banned in almost all circumstances. Voters will decide in November whether to enact a constitutional amendment that prohibits regulation of abortion in the first trimester.
Tennessee	Banned	—	Abortion is banned in almost all circumstances.
Texas	Banned	—	Abortion is banned in almost all circumstances. Private citizens can sue abortion providers and those who assist patients who are seeking an abortion after about six weeks of pregnancy.
West Virginia	Banned	—	Abortion is banned in almost all circumstances.
Florida	Gestational limit	6 weeks	Abortion is banned after about six weeks of pregnancy. The Florida Supreme Court ruled in 2024 that the state Constitution's privacy protections do not extend to abortion. Voters will decide in November whether to enshrine a right to abortion in the state Constitution.

STATE	STATUS OF ABORTION	LEGAL UNTIL	MORE DETAILS
Georgia	Gestational limit	6 weeks	Abortion is banned after about six weeks of pregnancy. In 2023, the State Supreme Court reversed a lower court's ruling that the ban was void. The lower court must still weigh whether the ban violates the state's Constitution.
South Carolina	Gestational limit	6 weeks	Abortion is banned after about six weeks of pregnancy. The South Carolina Supreme Court upheld the ban in 2023, finding that the state Constitution's privacy protections do not extend to abortion.
Nebraska	Gestational limit	12 weeks	Abortion is banned after 12 weeks of pregnancy.
North Carolina	Gestational limit	12 weeks	Abortion is banned after 12 weeks of pregnancy.
Arizona	Gestational limit	15 weeks	Abortion is banned after 15 weeks of pregnancy. The legislature repealed a law from 1864 that would have placed a near-total ban on abortions.
Utah	Gestational limit	18 weeks	Abortion is banned after 18 weeks of pregnancy. A judge has temporarily blocked a law that would have halted most abortions by requiring the procedure to be performed in hospitals. Another ban on most abortions was indefinitely blocked, and the State Supreme Court is expected to rule on it in 2024.
Iowa	Ban blocked	22 weeks	The Iowa Supreme Court ruled in June that the state's six-week abortion ban can soon be enforced while a lawsuit against it proceeds. It will take at least 21 days for the case to go back to the district court, during which time abortion will remain legal.
Montana	Ban blocked	Viability	The Montana Supreme Court has ruled that the state Constitution protects the right to an abortion. A ban on the most commonly used procedure in the second trimester and several other restrictions have been blocked by a court.
Wyoming	Ban blocked	Viability	A judge has temporarily blocked a ban on most abortions and another law that explicitly bans the use of abortion pills. A separate ban on most abortions remains indefinitely blocked.
Alaska	Legal	No limit	The State Supreme Court has recognized a right to "reproductive choice" under the state Constitution.
Kansas	Legal	22 weeks	The State Supreme Court ruled in 2019 that a pregnant woman's right to personal autonomy is protected in the state Constitution, and in 2022, Kansans rejected a ballot measure that would have removed the right to abortion from the state Constitution.

STATE	STATUS OF ABORTION	LEGAL UNTIL	MORE DETAILS
New Hampshire	Legal	24 weeks	Abortion is not expressly protected by state law.
Ohio	Legal	22 weeks	Voters enshrined abortion protections in the state Constitution in 2023. Courts are still deciding how the amendment affects existing abortion restrictions, such as waiting periods and consent requirements.
Virginia	Legal	Viability	Abortion is not expressly protected by state law.
Wisconsin	Legal	22 weeks	In late 2023, a Wisconsin judge ruled that an 1849 law widely interpreted as a ban did not apply to abortion. The case may come before the State Supreme Court, which has a liberal majority.
Washington, D.C.	Legal with new protections	No limit	Local law protects abortion throughout pregnancy and shields providers and patients from laws in other jurisdictions.
California	Legal with new protections	Viability	The California Supreme Court has recognized a right to abortion and voters explicitly enshrined abortion protections in the state Constitution in 2022. State law protects abortion and shields patients and providers from laws in other states.
Colorado	Legal with new protections	No limit	State law protects abortion and shields those seeking or providing the procedure in Colorado from laws in other states. Voters will decide in November if the state Constitution should provide a right to an abortion.
Connecticut	Legal with new protections	Viability	State law protects abortion and shields those seeking or providing abortions in Connecticut from laws in other states.
Delaware	Legal with new protections	Viability	State law protects abortion and shields those seeking or providing abortions in Delaware from laws in other states.
Hawaii	Legal with new protections	Viability	State law protects abortion and shields those seeking or providing abortions in Hawaii from laws in other states.
Illinois	Legal with new protections	Viability	The State Supreme Court has recognized abortion protections under the state Constitution. State law protects the procedure and shields those seeking or providing abortions in Illinois from laws in other states.
Maine	Legal with new protections	Viability	State law protects abortion and shields those seeking or providing abortions in Maine from laws in other states. A 2023 law allows an abortion past the point of fetal viability if a doctor decides it is medically necessary.

STATE	STATUS OF ABORTION	LEGAL UNTIL	MORE DETAILS
Maryland	Legal with new protections	Viability	State law protects abortion and shields those seeking or providing abortions in Maryland from laws in other states. Voters will decide in November whether the state Constitution should establish a right to reproductive freedom.
Massachusetts	Legal with new protections	24 weeks	The Massachusetts Supreme Judicial Court has recognized the right to abortion under the state Constitution. A law shields those seeking or providing abortions in Massachusetts from laws in other states, regardless of the patient's location.
Michigan	Legal with new protections	Viability	Voters enshrined abortion protections in the state Constitution in 2022. State law protects abortion and an executive order shields those seeking or providing abortions in Michigan from laws in other states.
Minnesota	Legal with new protections	No limit	The State Supreme Court has recognized the right to abortion under the state Constitution. State law protects a right to reproductive care and shields those seeking or providing abortions in Minnesota from laws in other states.
Nevada	Legal with new protections	24 weeks	State law protects abortion and shields those seeking or providing abortions in Nevada from laws in other states. Voters will decide in November if the state Constitution should provide a right to an abortion.
New Jersey	Legal with new protections	No limit	The New Jersey Supreme Court has recognized the right to abortion under the state Constitution. State law protects abortion throughout pregnancy and shields those seeking or providing abortions in New Jersey from laws in other states.
New Mexico	Legal with new protections	No limit	State law shields those seeking or providing abortions in New Mexico from laws in other states.
New York	Legal with new protections	Viability	State law protects abortion and shields patients and providers from laws in other states. Voters will decide in November whether there should be equal protection for reproductive health care and autonomy under the state's bill of rights.
Oregon	Legal with new protections	No limit	State law protects abortion throughout pregnancy and shields those seeking or providing abortions in Oregon from laws in other states.
Pennsylvania	Legal with new protections	24 weeks	An executive order shields those seeking or providing abortions in Pennsylvania from laws in other states.

STATE	STATUS OF ABORTION	LEGAL UNTIL	MORE DETAILS
Rhode Island	Legal with new protections	Viability	State law protects abortion and an executive order shields those seeking or providing abortions in Rhode Island from laws in other states.
Vermont	Legal with new protections	No limit	Voters enshrined abortion protections in the state Constitution in 2022. State law protects abortion throughout pregnancy and shields those seeking or providing abortions in Vermont from laws in other states, including those using medication abortion.
Washington	Legal with new protections	Viability	State law protects abortion and shields those seeking or providing abortions in Washington from laws in other states.

Note: Weeks of pregnancy are counted since the last menstrual period.

Print Citations

CMS: McCann, Allison, and Amy Schoenfeld Walker. "Tracking Abortion Bans Across the Country." In *The Reference Shelf: Reproductive Rights*, edited by Micah L. Issitt, 39-44. Amenia, NY: Grey House Publishing, 2024.

MLA: McCann, Allison, and Amy Schoenfeld Walker. "Tracking Abortion Bans Across the Country." *The Reference Shelf: Reproductive Rights*, edited by Micah L. Issitt, Grey House Publishing, 2024, pp. 39-44.

APA: McCann, A., & Walker, A. S. (2024). Tracking abortion bans across the country. In M. L. Issitt (Ed.), *The reference shelf: Reproductive rights* (pp. 39-44). Amenia, NY: Grey House Publishing. (Original work published 2024)

2
The Politics of Reproductive Health

Photo by Legoktm, CC BY-SA 4.0, via Wikipedia.

Pro-abortion protestors arrived in Foley Square hours after the leak of the Supreme Court draft that indicated that *Roe v. Wade* would be overturned.

Health Care and the Government

The American political system is, in many ways, deeply flawed and Americans know that this is the case. In a 2023 study by Pew Research, only 4 percent of Americans said that the political system works extremely or very well. A majority, 63 percent, claimed to have little or no confidence in the future of the US political system. Views of Congress, the US Supreme Court, and the political parties are in many ways historically negative. Around 27 percent of Americans believe that the system have little faith at all in American politics.[1]

One of the reasons that Americans are so broadly dissatisfied with their political system is that few Americans actually feel represented at the highest levels of the system. Much of the focus in politics is placed on the federal level, which Americans have been trained to believe is the acme of the American political system, the most important elections that have the most direct influence. The presidential race is the biggest political contest in American political culture, receiving international coverage, and even then, only around an average of 37 percent of Americans of voting age participate in elections. The 2020 election, the largest political contest in many years, coming amidst an international pandemic and after the presidency of one of the lowest-rated and most reviled politicians in American history, still only attracted 66 percent of eligible voters. More than three in ten Americans did not vote, even in an election that was perhaps the most famous in the world at that time.[2]

At the state and municipal levels turnout can be extremely low. In 2019, the city of Philadelphia elected a mayor with just 27 percent eligible voters casting a vote. In Chicago, that same year, just 35 percent of eligible voters voted in the election.[3] Local and state elections are, in many very specific ways, more important than federal elections in terms of how the laws directly shape people's lives. The Supreme Court's *Dobbs* decision, for instance, now means that it is voters in states that decide whether or not abortion will be legal in their state. Local elections also determine the level of state support for issues like contraception, sex education, family planning, maternity care, and policies on sexual and domestic abuse. Yet, few Americans make local elections a priority, in part because they have been conditioned to see these races as relatively unimportant.

A Destructive Pattern

Low levels of citizen engagement with politics is a self-perpetuating cycle. Year after year, Americans perceive their country as getting worse and perceive their politicians as unable or unwilling to do anything about this perceived decline. Whether or not America is actually in a state of decline is a complex question related to many different issues in American culture, but whether or not this perception is reality, the perception of a failing or failed state encourages voter apathy, especially at the state level where races receive far less in terms of promotion.

The aggressively "online" nature of political campaigning, and the focus on fundraising over promotion of substantive policy proposals, is another part of this destructive cycle. Super political action committees (PACs) and PACs collecting funding for candidate races utilize misleading "polls" and "questionnaire" and sometimes issue false claims in an effort to attract donations, using fear and threats of crumbling democratic institutions to maximize economic political action, but this feeds into the perception that politicians are greedy, corrupt, and that economic influence matters more than political ideals or ideas.

Because voters have low levels of engagement and because they focus on the high-profile federal contests and not on lower level races, few Americans feel that their laws and policies reflect them. Studies actually show that Americans agree on many issues, such as that teachers in America should get more pay, on which 73 percent of Americans agree, or that there should be rent control laws to protect tenants, which draws some 61 percent of support in polls. Majorities also agree that public spending on housing should be increased, that the government should forgive medical debt, that inflation is a major problem, that social welfare programs are a benefit rather than a detriment, that it should be legal to record police. Even on reproductive issues, there is far more agreement than policies would make it seem is the case. A strong majority of Americans believe that abortion should be legal in all or most cases, and only 10 to 15 percent of Americans believe in the kind of absolute abortion bans that have been passed in twenty-one states.[4]

Even though a majority of Americans agree on many key issues, policies do not reflect this consensus. Policies do not align with public opinion and this is because minority voting blocks, who are highly motivated but also often represent views outside of the majority view, have an outsized influence in American politics. In the arena of reproductive rights, this is extremely clear. The absolute abortion bans put into place in many states in no way reflect public opinion, even within those states, but reflect the views of a small, deeply engaged, and economically powerful minority that exerts an enormous influence on Republican Party policy in red states. Candidates put forward policies to keep *these* voters engaged, ignoring consensus or even acting directly against consensus in favor of catering to the views of these extremely engaged voting groups.

The power that these groups exert is high because among them are many single-issue voters, for whom one issue dominates above all. The abortion issue is one of those issues that attracts many single-issue voters, voters who are willing to ignore or even forgive policies that contrast with their other views, because they deem the abortion issue to be more important. There are likewise, on the opposite side, voters who see environmental protection as a single-issue, or elderly voters who view Medicare as the most important issue. Individuals who vote single-mindedly thus have more political potency than voters who must weigh a variety of issues.

The Two-Party Illusion

The fact that policies do not reflect public opinion also comes down to political distillation. In a two-party system, Americans are ultimately forced to choose between two major candidates, with the possible addition of several fringe candidates whose chances of victory are nil and whose candidacies are often political stunts staged to send messages to the major parties or to detract support from one or the other of the two leading candidates so as to shift the balance of voters in the other party's favor. What this means is that a variety of complex issues must be distilled into a single choice, a selection between two positions. For every potential voter, this means that this choice is a compromise in values. There are many Democratic voters, for instance, who are more politically aligned with radical left values, but who are not represented by candidates in the United States, as the Democratic Party is forced to aim their political strategies and policy proposals, for the *middle* of their potential voting block. A radical leftist voter, in the United States, does not have the option of voting, at least at the federal level, for a politician who actually represents their views on many important issues, but must settle for a more moderate Democratic candidate with the ability to appeal to more moderate liberals and progressives who fear more extreme progressive changes. The artificial distillation of politics into two-party options therefore means that few Americans actually feel that their political system, at least at its highest levels, reflects who they are and what they would like to see happen in their world.

This distillation is another reason that Americans perceive their system as dysfunctional and see little progress coming out of the political system. For instance, repeated polls have shown that Americans, as a whole, overwhelmingly approve of sex education in American schools. A 2018 poll found that 89 percent of voters believed that sex education should be taught in middle school, and 98 percent believed it was important to teach sex education in high school. Further, American overwhelmingly oppose sex education based on the "abstinence only" sex education system proposed by Conservative Christian activists, where the major focus is simply on teaching children to avoid sex rather than providing more comprehensive information about sex and sexuality.[5]

Despite this overwhelming support, just over half of adolescents received the minimum level of sex education recommended by the US Department of Health. Studies have even shown that despite an *increase* in support for sex education in the years since 1995, fewer students have been able to access sex education programs between 1995 and 2019. Whereas, in 1995, 81 percent of males and 87 percent of females learned about birth control methods, this percentage decreased to only 63 percent of males and 64 percent of females by 2019.[6] Given the level of parental and public support for comprehensive sex education, it might seem difficult to understand why so few students receive even the minimal level of information deemed important by experts in the field.

The reason is that local legislators are receiving far more influence from small, ultraconservative groups than from the public as a whole. For many Americans, sex education is not a voting priority, but there are a small number of Americans who believe that American sexual morality can be preserved by restricting access to information about sex. These highly motivated individuals might embrace opposition to sex education along with opposition to contraception, to abortion, and to any other measures that reduce the likelihood of Christian children being born into their societies. Because this group is dedicated and committed to voting, and because the rest of the population does not make sex education a top priority, states respond to the wishes of these far-right activists, restricting funding for sex education or emphasizing only moralistic abstinence based sex "education," despite the many studies showing that this approach is not at all effective in combating rates of sexual intercourse, unwanted pregnancy, or sexually transmitted disease (STD) transmission.[7]

Engagement and Reproductive Health Issues

Many other issues in the realm of reproductive health are influenced by the same kinds of political situation. As mentioned, a full 63 percent of Americans want abortion to remain legal in all or most cases, and only 10 to 15 percent would support absolute abortion bans, and yet absolute abortion bans exist in many states. This is because the laws in these states have not been decided by public referendum, but by politicians who have responded to far-right activist groups and provided them with outsized influence in making political decisions. Unless a higher proportion of the voting public comes to view the abortion issue is a top voting priority, these smaller groups of dedicated voters dominate in this issue.

While abortion is an issue that is majorly in flux in the United States, public opinion on contraception is far more easily understood. Polls show that over 80 percent of all Americans believe that birth control should be legal in all or most cases. In fact, on the issue of condoms, a FiveThirtyEight poll even found *stronger* support, among Republicans (92 vs. 91 percent) for keeping condoms legal. Likewise, on birth control pills and intrauterine devices (IUDs) more than 90 percent of Republicans and Democrats believe that these kinds of contraception methods should remain legal.[8]

Less than 5 percent of Americans would support a measure to ban access to birth control and yet conservative politicians have voiced support for banning birth control. In the ultrared state of Missouri, for instance, a bill proposed by conservative politicians included a state ban on IUDs. This was a small measure stuck into a bill that also targeted abortion and this is how small groups of ideological extremists manage to make their minority views mainstream. Voters in Missouri might have supported restrictions on abortion access, but, based on polling, this does not mean that even a significant minority of Missouri voters would've approved of restrictions on birth control devices like IUDs. Sticking this provision within the bill, however, gives conservative politicians a way to market themselves to extremists within that 5 to 7 percent of Republicans who would like to see contraception limited, often because they believe that higher-birth rates will contribute to the political power of their population going forward.[9]

Low Engagement Is Intentional

Public opinion polls indicate that public opinion on many issues related to reproductive rights, including contraception, abortion, sex education, maternal health care, etc., Americans tend to align more closely with liberal or progressive values. This is an example, therefore, of a situation in which conservative leaders who are interested in promoting far-right views as policies in these arenas, are working *against* mainstream public opinion. This helps to explain why the conservative movement has, over the years, worked to limit voting rights and access. Numerous studies have shown that conservatives do better when voter turnout is low, because they can rely on a small but dedicated population of voters who will vote on far-right issues like absolute abortion bans, banning contraception, etc.

This is not always true at the federal level. When it came to the 2020 presidential election, for instance, high-voter turnout was especially important for Republicans, because they needed to absolutely maximize votes in order to overcome a broad public opinion problem. They did not overcome this disadvantage and lost the presidential election, but higher turnout is necessary for high-profile conservative candidates. At the lower levels, lower-voter turnout and limiting voting among lower-income citizens, voters of color, and voters in other minority groups, favors conservative candidates and this is why the conservative movement favors voter restrictions and efforts to make voting more complicated and difficult. As voting becomes more difficult, only more dedicated voters will engage in the process, and this gives a remarkable advantage to far-right politicians, who are absolutely dependent on voter engagement among single-issue conservative voters and so cater to these voters by proposing policies that do not align with public opinion overall and even fail to align with Republican public opinion, but align specifically with the minority voting blocks that conservatives depend on for political success.

Works Used

Farrar, Lauren. "Sex Education in America: The Good, the Bad, the Ugly." *KQED*, 16 Sept. 2020, www.kqed.org/education/534518/sex-education-in-america-the-good-the-bad-the-ugly.

Janfaza, Rachel. "The Nuanced Push for American Sex Education." *Harvard Political Review*, 24 Jan. 2020, harvardpolitics.com/american-sex-education/.

Martin, Jennifer. "50 Surprising Things Americans Actually Agree On." *CBS News*, 27 Sept. 2022, www.cbsnews.com/pictures/surprising-things-americans-actually-agree-on/.

Ollove, Michael. "Some States Already Are Targeting Birth Control." *Stateline*, 19 May 2022, stateline.org/2022/05/19/some-states-already-are-targeting-birth-control/.

Skelley, Geoffrey, and Holly Fuong. "How Americans Feel About Contraception." FiveThirtyEight, 12 July 2022, fivethirtyeight.com/features/abortion-birth-control-poll/.

"Turnout in the United States." *Fairvote*, fairvote.org/resources/voter-turnout/.

"US Adolescents' Receipt of Formal Sex Education." *Guttmacher Institute*, Feb. 2022, www.guttmacher.org/fact-sheet/adolescents-teens-receipt-sex-education-united-states?gad_source=1&gclid=CjwKCAjwnqK1BhBvEiwAi7o0Xw-8jEk2O-R7g1cB4l8eeHKy9nM0e8SwFEjdnmk64TYx_i5DZ5TgDRoCPP4QAvD_BwE#gad_source=1.

"Views of the U.S. Political System, the Federal Government and Federal-State Relations." *Pew Research Center*, 19 Sept. 2023.

"Voter Turnout, 2018–2022." *Pew Research Center*, 12 July 2023, www.pewresearch.org/politics/2023/07/12/voter-turnout-2018-2022/.

Notes

1. "Views of the U.S. Political System, the Federal Government and Federal State Relations," *PEW Research Center*.
2. "Voter Turnout, 2018–2022," *Pew Research Center*.
3. "Turnout in the United States," *Fairvote*.
4. Martin, "50 Surprising Things That Americans Actually Agree On."
5. Janfaza, "The Nuanced Push for American Sex Education."
6. "US Adolescents' Receipt of Formal Sex Education," *Guttmacher Institute*.
7. Farrar, "Sex Education in America: The Good, the Bad, the Ugly."
8. Skelley and Fuong, "How Americans Feel About Abortion and Contraception."
9. Ollove, "Some States Already Are Targeting Birth Control."

Surprise: American Voters Actually Largely Agree on Many Issues, Including Topics Like Abortion, Immigration, and Wealth Inequality

By Dante Chinni and Ari Pinkus
The Conversation, July 10, 2024

As the presidential election campaign heats up, media coverage suggests Americans are hopelessly divided and headed for a difficult fall—perhaps also a tense January.

But that isn't the whole story, according to reporting and poll results from the American Communities Project, a journalism and research effort we lead that is based at Michigan State University that analyzes the country by looking at 15 different community types.

In fact, on issues and policies where government has a serious role—such matters as taxes, immigration, the state of the economy and even abortion—a 2023 survey from the American Communities Project, or the ACP, found a great deal of agreement in the 15 community types we examine.

But when the topic turned to "culture war" issues (religion, gender identity, guns, family values), the differences were deep.

That divide between talking about "policy" and talking about "culture"—between arguing about "what we want" versus "who we are"—is having a hugely divisive impact on the nation. And if politics and governing are going to get more productive, Americans need to find a way to move past the issues around cultural identity.

Broad Agreement on Policy

We saw the policy/culture difference in our 2023 survey.

The 15 community types in the ACP are very different from one another demographically, geographically and politically. The deeply rural, largely white community type we call "Aging Farmlands"—small rural counties spread across the Great Plains—gave 79% of their vote to Donald Trump in 2020. The densely populated and diverse group we call "Big Cities"—counties home to most of the nation's 50 largest cities—gave 66% of their vote to Joe Biden.

And yet, on a range of questions concerning policy or the state of the nation, there was wide agreement.

For instance, in every one of the community types, more than 60% of those surveyed said they thought "the American economy is rigged to advantage the rich and the powerful." On the statement "The U.S. government should cut social programs in order to lower taxes," no more than 38% agreed in any community—a question we dug into with voters in Florida in a voter roundtable discussion.

> **Obtaining an abortion should be a decision made by a woman in consultation with her doctor, without the government's involvement.**

Even on the thorny issue of abortion there was agreement around the statement "Obtaining an abortion should be a decision made by a woman in consultation with her doctor, without the government's involvement." More than 50% in every community type agreed. Many polls show high levels of support for keeping abortion legal, but the agreement across the different ACP types was surprising to us.

To be clear, the areas of agreement didn't all favor Democratic positions. The statement "America would be better off if we let in more immigrants" didn't get to 30% support in any community type. And "Government should take a more active role in policing private-sector behavior" didn't get above 45% support anywhere.

Regardless, for a country that often feels hopelessly divided, that is a lot of agreement on statements that center on government action in one way or another.

Questions of Culture

But when cultural issues were the focus of the poll, the well-known divisions appeared across our communities.

The widest chasm in the survey came on the statement "The right to own a firearm is central to what it means to be an American." Overall, 49% of Americans agreed, but the divides by community type and landscape were stark.

In the rural "Evangelical Hubs," based in the South and Midwest, 71% agreed that owning a gun is central to what it means to be an American, while in the "Aging Farmlands," concentrated in the Central and Great Plains, 73% did. In the "Big Cities" and "Urban Suburbs," outside of cities, the centrality of this right dropped to 30% and 34%, respectively.

There were similar divides around gender identity.

Those surveyed were asked whether they agreed or disagreed with the statement "People should be free to express their gender identity however is best for them." Gender expression was much more accepted in diverse communities, such as "Big Cities" "Urban Suburbs" and rural "Native American Lands," at 61%, 60% and 60%, respectively. In rural blue-collar "Working Class Country" and "Evangelical Hubs," the numbers sat at 37% and 32%, respectively.

Faith and Religion

At the national level, there was something of a coalescing on the importance of faith and religion.

Overall, 58% agreed that "Faith and religion are important parts of American life." But again, there were large differences by community type.

In the "Aging Farmlands," faith and religion's importance reached 77%, in the "Native American Lands," 73%, while in the "Evangelical Hubs," dominated by Christian evangelicals, it was 70%. Comparatively, in the "Big Cities" and "Urban Suburbs," it was 47%, a difference of more than 20 points from these rural communities.

And there were sharp splits on the statement "Traditional structures for families, with a wage-earning father and homemaking mother, best equips children to succeed." The percentages that agreed were highest in the "Native American Lands," at 59%, and in the rural communities of "Christian faith," "LDS Enclaves," at 55%, and "Evangelical Hubs," at 54%. The "Big Cities," "Urban Suburbs" and "College Towns" were at the other end of the spectrum, at 33%, 36% and 36%, respectively.

Political Debate "Hijacked" by Culture Fights

These issues—guns, gender, faith and families—clearly matter deeply to many Americans. But how much do they have to do with politics?

People are going to hold the beliefs they hold on gender or live by their personal ideals about faith and family regardless of who is in the White House. The government realistically cannot police every bedroom and kitchen table in America. The question about guns can be discussed as a matter of the U.S. Supreme Court's constitutional interpretation as much as one's personal belief, but that issue, too, is very personal, as we learned when we talked to people about it in Michigan.

In many ways, these culture fights have hijacked the political debate when there is broader agreement on issues in which government really does play an important role.

Of course, agreeing on the importance of key issues is not the same as agreeing on what should be done about them.

We know from our work talking to people in these different communities that their respective answers on how to handle a "rigged" system or taxation or abortion or immigration would likely be different. But those conversations are about give-and-take and hashing out answers. That's the point of politics and different from the culture fights that dominate our discussions.

In a nation of 330 million people, there will never be easy answers to "who are we?" In fact, the country was designed to largely leave that question open within broad parameters.

But until politics moves on to the more relevant question of "What should we do?" the deadlock and tensions Americans feel in the 2024 election likely aren't going to change.

Print Citations

CMS: Chinni, Dante, and Ari Pinkus. "Surprise: American Voters Actually Largely Agree on Many Issues, Including Topics Like Abortion, Immigration, and Wealth Inequality." In *The Reference Shelf: Reproductive Rights,* edited by Micah L. Issitt, 53-56. Amenia, NY: Grey House Publishing, 2024.

MLA: Chinni, Dante, and Ari Pinkus. "Surprise: American Voters Actually Largely Agree on Many Issues, Including Topics Like Abortion, Immigration, and Wealth Inequality." *The Reference Shelf: Reproductive Rights,* edited by Micah L. Issitt, Grey House Publishing, 2024, pp. 53-56.

APA: Chinni, D., & Pinkus, A. (2024). Surprise: American voters actually largely agree on many issues, including topics like abortion, immigration, and wealth inequality. In M. L. Issitt (Ed.), *The reference shelf: Reproductive rights* (pp. 53-56). Amenia, NY: Grey House Publishing. (Original work published 2024)

Abortion and the 2024 Election: There Is No Easy Way Out for Republicans

By Elaine Kamarck
Brookings Institution, April 17, 2024

- The *Wall Street Journal* came out with a poll showing that abortion was the number one issue—by far—for suburban women voters in swing states.
- The expectation is that at least some, if not most, of the pro-choice voters likely to be mobilized by the abortion issue will help Democrats up and down the ballot.
- There are two swing states, Arizona and Florida, where turnout for the pro-choice referenda could help President Biden.

Republicans are thrashing around trying to get themselves out of the abortion ban they have tried to win for so many decades. Senator Lindsey Graham (R-SC) was the first. In the fall of 2022, just months after the Supreme Court struck down *Roe v. Wade*, he proposed legislation calling for a national abortion ban after 15 weeks. So far, this bill has gone nowhere. Then, in 2023, gubernatorial candidate Glenn Youngkin of Virginia put the 15-week abortion ban at the center of his campaign to help the GOP take full control of the Virginia legislature. Rather than holding one house and picking up the other, he lost both.

Recently, former President Donald Trump—who often brags about appointing the three Supreme Court justices who made possible the repeal of *Roe v. Wade*—offered his own way out of the thicket by applauding the fact that states now can decide the issue for themselves. And in Arizona, the Republican Senate candidate, Kari Lake, is trying to rally the party around the notion of a 15-week ban instead of the 1864 near total ban their court just affirmed, even though she's facing criticism for this on the far right.

Meanwhile, the *Wall Street Journal* came out with a poll showing that abortion was the number one issue—by far—for suburban women voters in swing states.

In each instance (and there will be more) we find Republicans desperately trying to find a position on the issue that makes their base and the other parts of their coalition happy.

It doesn't exist, and here's why—abortion is an integral part of health care for women.

Credit line: From *Brookings Institution*, April 17 © 2024. Reprinted with permission. All rights reserved.

Since 2022, when the Supreme Court eviscerated *Roe* in the *Dobbs* case, we have been undergoing a reluctant national seminar in obstetrics and gynecology. All over the country, legislators—mostly male—are discovering that pregnancy is not simple. Pregnancies go wrong for many reasons, and when they do, the fetus needs to be removed. One of the first to discover this reality was Republican State Representative Neal Collins of South Carolina. He was brought to tears by the story of a South Carolina woman whose water broke just *after* 15 weeks of pregnancy. Obstetrics lesson #1—a fetus can't live after the water breaks. But "lawyers advised doctors that they could not remove the fetus, despite that being the recommended medical course of action." And so, the woman was sent home to miscarry on her own, putting her at risk of losing her uterus and/or getting blood poisoning.

A woman from Austin, Texas had a similar story—one that eventually made its way into a heart-wrenching ad by the Biden campaign. Amanda Zurawski was 18 weeks pregnant when her water broke. Rather than remove the fetus, doctors in Texas sent her home where she miscarried—and developed blood poisoning (sepsis) so severe that she may never get pregnant again. Note that in both cases the medical emergency happened *after* 15 weeks—late miscarriages are more likely to have serious medical effects than early ones. The 15-week idea, popular among Republicans seeking a way out of their quagmire, doesn't conform to medical reality.

Over in Arkansas, a Republican state representative learned that his niece was carrying a fetus who lacked a vital organ, meaning that it would never develop normally and either die in utero or right after birth. Obstetrics lesson #2—severe fetal abnormalities happen. He changed his position on the Arkansas law saying, "Who are we to sit in judgment of these women making a decision between them and their physician and their God above?"

In a case that gained national attention, Kate Cox, a Texas mother of two, was pregnant with her third child when the fetus was diagnosed with a rare condition called Trisomy 18, which usually ends in miscarriage or in the immediate death of the baby. Continuing this doomed pregnancy put Cox at risk of uterine rupture and would make it difficult to carry another child. Obstetrics lesson #3—continuing to carry a doomed pregnancy can jeopardize future pregnancies. And yet the Texas Attorney General blocked an abortion for Cox and threatened to prosecute anyone who took care of her, and the Texas Supreme Court ruled that her condition did not meet the statutory exception for "life-threatening physical condition."

So, she and her husband eventually went to New Mexico for the abortion.

Obstetrics lesson #4—miscarriages are very common, affecting approximately 30% of pregnancies. While many pass without much drama and women heal on their own—others cause complications that require what's known as a D&C for dilation and curettage. This involves scraping bits of pregnancy tissue out of the uterus to avoid infection. When Christina Zielke of Maryland was told that her fetus had no heartbeat, she opted to wait to miscarry naturally.

While waiting, she and her husband traveled to Ohio for a wedding where she began to bleed so heavily that they had to go to an emergency room. A D&C would have stopped the bleeding, but in Ohio, doctors worried that they would be criminally charged under the new abortion laws and sent her home in spite of the fact that she was still bleeding heavily and in spite of the fact that doctors in Maryland had confirmed that her fetus had no heartbeat. Eventually her blood pressure dropped, and she passed out from loss of blood and returned to the hospital where a D&C finally stopped the bleeding.

> **Ever since the Supreme Court decided the *Dobbs* case, analysts have underestimated the size of the pro-choice vote.**

These are but a few of the horror stories that will continue to mount in states with partial or total bans on abortion. As these stories accumulate, the issue will continue to have political punch. We have already seen the victory of pro-choice referenda in deep red conservative states like Kansas, Kentucky, Montana, and Ohio; and in swing states like Michigan and in deep blue states like California and Vermont. In an era where almost everything is viewed through a partisan lens, abortion rights transcend partisanship.

And more referenda are coming in November. The expectation is that at least some, if not most, of the pro-choice voters likely to be mobilized by the abortion issue will help Democrats up and down the ballot. As a result, Democratic campaigns are working hard to make sure the public knows that Republicans are responsible. The following table shows the states that are likely to have referenda in November. States where the referenda are already on the ballot are at the end of the table. Once the deadline occurs for filing signatures, a battle will take place in each state as pro-life groups seek to challenge enough signatures to keep the referenda from getting on the ballot, which is why pro-choice groups are gathering many more signatures than needed.

What is the likely political impact? Judging from what we've seen so far, these referenda are likely to succeed even in the most conservative states. The question is: What is the likely impact on other races? There are two states, Arizona and Florida, where turnout for the pro-choice referenda could help President Biden. Biden won Arizona last time but by a very small margin. Trump won Florida by just over three percentage points, so putting it in Biden's column is tougher but not impossible. Besides the presidential, there are Senate races in Arizona, Nevada, and Maryland that could be affected by the abortion referenda. Arizona and Nevada are competitive races. Maryland should be a Democratic seat given how strong Democrats are there, but the popular ex-governor, a moderate non-Trump Republican, is running for Senate, increasing the odds that a Republican could take the seat. Finally, there are seven competitive House seats that could also be affected by turnout for the abortion referenda—two in Arizona, one in Colorado, one in Nebraska, and three in New York.[1] Deep red states like Arkansas, Missouri, and South Dakota don't have any races that are likely to be so impacted by the abortion referenda that the election outcomes would flip the seats from one party to the other, but any large increase in Democratic-leaning voters could affect races in the future.

Ever since the Supreme Court decided the *Dobbs* case, analysts have underestimated the size of the pro-choice vote. In hindsight, there's no question that it was instrumental in blocking the expected red wave in the 2022 midterms and instrumental in putting both houses of the Virginia legislature in Democratic hands in 2023. Biden's first abortion ads will, no doubt, be followed by others, and Republicans will try to come up with ways of softening their stances—but in the end, this could be the most decisive issue in the election.

Note

1. Arizona congressional districts one and six; Colorado district eight; Nebraska district two; and New York districts four, 17, and 19.

Print Citations

CMS: Kamarck, Elaine. "Abortion and the 2024 Election: There Is No Easy Way Out for Republicans." In *The Reference Shelf: Reproductive Rights,* edited by Micah L. Issitt, 57-60. Amenia, NY: Grey House Publishing, 2024.

MLA: Kamarck, Elaine. "Abortion and the 2024 Election: There Is No Easy Way Out for Republicans." *The Reference Shelf: Reproductive Rights,* edited by Micah L. Issitt, Grey House Publishing, 2024, pp. 57-60.

APA: Kamarck, E. (2024). Abortion and the 2024 election: There is no easy way out for Republicans." In M. L. Issitt (Ed.), *The reference shelf: Reproductive rights* (pp. 57-60). Amenia, NY: Grey House Publishing. (Original work published 2024)

Inside Ziklag, the Secret Organization of Wealthy Christians Trying to Sway the Election and Change the Country

By Andy Kroll and Nick Surgey
ProPublica, July 14, 2024

A network of ultrawealthy Christian donors is spending nearly $12 million to mobilize Republican-leaning voters and purge more than a million people from the rolls in key swing states, aiming to tilt the 2024 election in favor of former President Donald Trump.

These previously unreported plans are the work of a group named Ziklag, a little-known charity whose donors have included some of the wealthiest conservative Christian families in the nation, including the billionaire Uihlein family, who made a fortune in office supplies, the Greens, who run Hobby Lobby, and the Wallers, who own the Jockey apparel corporation. Recipients of Ziklag's largesse include Alliance Defending Freedom, which is the Christian legal group that led the overturning of *Roe v. Wade*, plus the national pro-Trump group Turning Point USA and a constellation of right-of-center advocacy groups.

ProPublica and *Documented* obtained thousands of Ziklag's members-only email newsletters, internal videos, strategy documents and fundraising pitches, none of which has been previously made public. They reveal the group's 2024 plans and its long-term goal to underpin every major sphere of influence in American society with Christianity. In the Bible, the city of Ziklag was where David and his soldiers found refuge during their war with King Saul.

"We are in a spiritual battle and locked in a terrible conflict with the powers of darkness," says a strategy document that lays out Ziklag's 30-year vision to "redirect the trajectory of American culture toward Christ by bringing back Biblical structure, order and truth to our Nation."

Ziklag's 2024 agenda reads like the work of a political organization. It plans to pour money into mobilizing voters in Arizona who are "sympathetic to Republicans" in order to secure "10,640 additional unique votes"—almost the exact margin of President Joe Biden's win there in 2020. The group also intends to use controversial AI software to enable mass challenges to the eligibility of hundreds of thousands of voters in competitive states.

In a recording of a 2023 internal strategy discussion, a Ziklag official stressed that the objective was the same in other swing states. "The goal is to win," the

---

Credit line: From *ProPublica*, July 14 © 2024. Reprinted with permission. All rights reserved.

official said. "If 75,000 people wins the White House, then how do we get 150,000 people so we make sure we win?"

According to the Ziklag files, the group has divided its 2024 activities into three different operations targeting voters in battleground states: Checkmate, focused on funding so-called election integrity groups; Steeplechase, concentrated on using churches and pastors to get out the vote; and Watchtower, aimed at galvanizing voters around the issues of "parental rights" and opposition to transgender rights and policies supporting health care for trans people.

In a member briefing video, one of Ziklag's spiritual advisers outlined a plan to "deliver swing states" by using an anti-transgender message to motivate conservative voters who are exhausted with Trump.

But Ziklag is not a political organization: It is a 501(c)(3) tax-exempt charity, the same legal designation as the United Way or Boys and Girls Club. Such organizations do not have to publicly disclose their funders, and donations are tax deductible. In exchange, they are "absolutely prohibited from directly or indirectly participating in, or intervening in, any political campaign on behalf of (or in opposition to) any candidate for elective public office," according to the IRS.

ProPublica and *Documented* presented the findings of their investigation to six nonpartisan lawyers and legal experts. All expressed concern that Ziklag was testing or violating the law.

The reporting by *ProPublica* and *Documented* "casts serious doubt on this organization's status as a 501(c)(3) organization," said Roger Colinvaux, a professor at Catholic University's Columbus School of Law.

"I think it's across the line without a question," said Lloyd Hitoshi Mayer, a University of Notre Dame law professor.

Ziklag officials did not respond to a detailed list of questions. Martin Nussbaum, an attorney who said he was the group's general counsel, said in a written response that "some of the statements in your email are correct. Others are not," but he then did not respond to a request to specify what was erroneous. The group is seeking to "align" the culture "with Biblical values and the American constitution, and that they will serve the common good," he wrote. Using the official tax name for Ziklag, he wrote that "USATransForm does not endorse candidates for public office." He declined to comment on the group's members.

There are no bright lines or magic words that the IRS might look for when it investigates a charitable organization for engaging in political intervention, said Mayer. Instead, the agency examines the facts and circumstances of a group's activities and makes a conclusion about whether the group violated the law.

The biggest risk for charities that intervene in political campaigns, Mayer said, is loss of their tax-exempt status. Donors' ability to deduct their donations can be a major sell, not to mention it can create "a halo effect" for the group, Mayer added.

"They may be able to get more money this way," he said, adding, "It boils down to tax evasion at the end of the day."

Dominion Over the Seven Mountains

Ziklag has largely escaped scrutiny until now. The group describes itself as a "private, confidential, invitation-only community of high-net-worth Christian families."

According to internal documents, it boasts more than 125 members that include business executives, pastors, media leaders and other prominent conservative Christians. Potential new members, one document says, should have a "concern for culture" demonstrated by past donations to faith-based or political causes, as well as a net worth of $25 million or more. None of the donors responded to requests for comment.

Tax records show rapid growth in the group's finances in recent years. Its annual revenue climbed from $1.3 million in 2018 to $6 million in 2019 and nearly $12 million in 2022, which is the latest filing available.

The group's spending is not on the scale of major conservative funders such as Miriam Adelson or Barre Seid, the electronics magnate who gave $1.6 billion to a group led by conservative legal activist Leonard Leo. But its funding and strategy represent one of the clearest links yet between the Christian right and the "election integrity" movement fueled by Trump's baseless claims about voting fraud. Even several million dollars funding mass challenges to voters in swing counties can make an impact, legal and election experts say.

Ziklag was the brainchild of a Silicon Valley entrepreneur named Ken Eldred. It emerged from a previous organization founded by Eldred called United In Purpose, which aimed to get more Christians active in the civic arena, according to Bill Dallas, the group's former director. United In Purpose generated attention in June 2016 when it organized a major meeting between then-candidate Trump and hundreds of evangelical leaders.

After Trump was elected in 2016, Eldred had an idea, according to Dallas. "He says, 'I want all the wealthy Christian people to come together,'" Dallas recalled in an interview. Eldred told Dallas that he wanted to create a donor network like the one created by Charles and David Koch but for Christians. He proposed naming it David's Mighty Men, Dallas said. Female members balked. Dallas found the passage in Chronicles that references David's soldiers and read that they met in the city of Ziklag, and so they chose the name Ziklag.

The group's stature grew after Trump took office. Vice President Mike Pence appeared at a Ziklag event, as did former Housing and Urban Development Secretary Ben Carson, Sen. Ted Cruz, then-Rep. Mark Meadows and other members of Congress. In its private newsletter, Ziklag claims that a coalition of groups it assembled played "a hugely significant role in the selection, hearings and confirmation process" of Amy Coney Barrett for a Supreme Court seat in late 2020.

Confidential donor networks regularly invest hundreds of millions of dollars into political and charitable groups, from the liberal Democracy Alliance to the Koch-affiliated Stand Together organization on the right. But unlike Ziklag, neither of those organizations is legally set up as a true charity.

Ziklag appears to be the first coordinated effort to get wealthy donors to fund an overtly Christian nationalist agenda, according to historians, legal experts and other people familiar with the group. "It shows that this idea isn't being dismissed as fringe in the way that it might have been in the past," said Mary Ziegler, a legal historian and University of California, Davis law professor.

The Christian nationalism movement has a variety of aims and tenets, according to the Public Religion Research Institute: that the U.S. government "should declare America a Christian nation"; that American laws "should be based on Christian values"; that the U.S. will cease to exist as a nation if it "moves away from our Christian foundations"; that being Christian is essential to being American; and that God has "called Christians to exercise dominion over all areas of American society."

One theology promoted by Christian nationalist leaders is the Seven Mountain Mandate. Each mountain represents a major industry or a sphere of public life: arts and media, business, church, education, family, government, and science and technology. Ziklag's goal, the documents say, is to "take dominion over the Seven Mountains," funding Christian projects or installing devout Christians in leadership positions to reshape each mountain in a godly way.

To address their concerns about education, Ziklag's leaders and allies have focused on the public-school system. In a 2021 Ziklag meeting, Ziklag's education mountain chair, Peter Bohlinger, said that Ziklag's goal "is to take down the education system as we know it today."

The producers of the film "Sound of Freedom," featuring Jim Caviezel as an anti-sex-trafficking activist, screened an early cut of the film at a Ziklag conference and asked for funds, according to Dallas.

The Seven Mountains theology signals a break from Christian fundamentalists such as Jerry Falwell Sr. and Pat Robertson. In the 1980s and '90s, Falwell's Moral Majority focused on working within the democratic process to mobilize evangelical voters and elect politicians with a Christian worldview.

The Seven Mountain theology embraces a different, less democratic approach to gaining power. "If the Moral Majority is about galvanizing the voters, the Seven Mountains is a revolutionary model: You need to conquer these mountains and let change flow down from the top," said Matthew Taylor, a senior scholar at the Institute for Islamic, Christian and Jewish Studies and an expert on Christian nationalism. "It's an outlined program for Christian supremacy."

The Amorphous, Tumultuous Wild West

The Christian right has had compelling spokespeople and fierce commitment to its causes, whether they were ending abortion rights, allowing prayer in schools or displaying the Ten Commandments outside of public buildings. What the movement has often lacked, its leaders argue, is sufficient funding.

"If you look at the right, especially the Christian right, there were always complaints about money," said legal historian Ziegler. "There's a perceived gap of 'We aren't getting the support from big-name, big-dollar donors that we deserve and want and need.'"

That's where Ziklag comes in.

Speaking late last year to an invitation-only gathering of Ziklaggers, as members are known, Charlie Kirk, who leads the pro-Trump Turning Point USA organization, named left-leaning philanthropists who were, in his view, funding the destruction of the nation: MacKenzie Scott, ex-wife of Amazon founder Jeff Bezos; billionaire investor and liberal philanthropist George Soros; and the two founders of Google, Larry Page and Sergey Brin.

"Why are secular people giving more generously than Christians?" Kirk asked, according to a recording of his remarks. "It would be a tragedy," he added, "if people who hate life, hate our country, hate beauty and hate God wanted it more than us."

"Ziklag is the place," Kirk told the donors. "Ziklag is the counter."

Similarly, Pence, in a 2021 appearance at a private Ziklag event, praised the group for its role in "changing lives, and it's advanced the cause, it's advanced the kingdom."

A driving force behind Ziklag's efforts is Lance Wallnau, a prominent Christian evangelist and influencer based in Texas who is described by Ziklag as a "Seven Mountains visionary & advisor." The fiery preacher is one of the most influential figures on the Christian right, experts say, a bridge between Christian nationalism and Trump. He was one of the earliest evangelical leaders to endorse Trump in 2015 and later published a book titled *God's Chaos Candidate: Donald J. Trump and the American Unraveling*.

More than 1 million people follow him on Facebook. He doesn't try to hide his views: "Yes, I am a Christian nationalist," he said during one of his livestreams in 2021. (Wallnau did not respond to requests for comment.)

Wallnau has remained a Trump ally. He called Trump's time in office a "spiritual warfare presidency" and popularized the idea that Trump was a "modern-day Cyrus," referring to the Persian king who defeated the Babylonians and allowed the Jewish people to return to Jerusalem. Wallnau has visited with Trump at the White House and Trump Tower; last November, he livestreamed from a black-tie gala at Mar-a-Lago where Trump spoke.

Wallnau did not come up with the notion that Christians should try to take control of key areas of American society. But he improved on the idea by introducing the concept of the seven mountains and urged Christians to set about conquering them. The concept caught on, said Taylor, because it empowered Christians with a sense of purpose in every sphere of life.

As a preacher in the independent charismatic tradition, a fast-growing offshoot of Pentecostalism that is unaffiliated with any major denomination, Wallnau and his acolytes believe that God speaks to and through modern-day apostles and prophets — a version of Christianity that Taylor, in his forthcoming book *The Violent Take It By Force*, describes as "the amorphous, tumultuous Wild West of the modern church." Wallnau and his ideas lingered at the fringes of American Christianity for years, until the boost from the Trump presidency.

The Ziklag files detail not only what Christians should do to conquer all seven mountains, but also what their goals will be once they've taken the summit. For the government mountain, one key document says that "the biblical role of government is to promote good and punish evil" and that "the word of God and prayer play a significant role in policy decisions."

For the arts and entertainment mountain, goals include that 80% of the movies produced be rated G or PG "with a moral story," and that many people who work in the industry "operate under a biblical/moral worldview." The education section says that homeschooling should be a "fundamental right" and the government "must not favor one form of education over another."

Other internal Ziklag documents voice strong opposition to same-sex marriage and transgender rights. One reads: "transgender acceptance = Final sign before imminent collapse."

Heading into the 2024 election year, Ziklag executive director Drew Hiss warned members in an internal video that "looming above and beyond those seven mountains is this evil force that's been manifesting itself." He described it as "a controlling, evil, diabolical presence, really, with tyranny in mind." That presence was concentrated in the government mountain, he said. If Ziklaggers wanted to save their country from "the powers of darkness," they needed to focus their energies on that government mountain or else none of their work in any other area would succeed.

Operation Checkmate

In the fall of 2023, Wallnau sat in a gray armchair in his TV studio. A large TV screen behind him flashed a single word: "ZIKLAG."

"You almost hate to put it out this clearly," he said as he detailed Ziklag's electoral strategy, "because if somebody else gets ahold of this, they'll freak out."

He was joined on set by Hiss, who had just become the group's new day-to-day leader. The two men were there to record a special message to Ziklag members that laid out the group's ambitious plans for the upcoming election year.

The forces arrayed against Christians were many, according to the confidential video. They were locked in a "spiritual battle," Hiss said, against Democrats who were a "radical left Marxist force." Biden, Wallnau said, was a senile old man and "an empty suit with an agenda that's written and managed by somebody else."

In the files, Ziklag says it plans to give out nearly $12 million to a constellation of groups working on the ground to shift the 2024 electorate in favor of Trump and other Republicans.

A prominent conservative getting money from Ziklag is Cleta Mitchell, a lawyer and Trump ally who joined the January 2021 phone call when then-President Trump asked Georgia's secretary of state to "find" enough votes to flip Georgia in Trump's favor.

Mitchell now leads a network of "election integrity" coalitions in swing states that have spent the last three years advocating for changes to voting rules and how elections are run. According to one internal newsletter, Ziklag was an early funder of Mitchell's post-2020 "election integrity" activism, which voting-rights experts have criticized for stoking unfounded fears about voter fraud and seeking to unfairly remove people from voting rolls. In 2022, Ziklag donated $600,000 to the Conservative Partnership Institute, which in turn funds Mitchell's election-integrity work.

Internal Ziklag documents show that it provided funding to enable Mitchell to set up election integrity infrastructure in Florida, North Carolina and Wisconsin.

Now Mitchell is promoting a tool called EagleAI, which has claimed to use artificial intelligence to automate and speed up the process of challenging ineligible voters. EagleAI is already being used to mount mass challenges to the eligibility of hundreds of thousands of voters in competitive states, and, with Ziklag's help, the group plans to ramp up those efforts.

> **Ziklag says it plans to give out nearly $12 million to a constellation of groups working on the ground to shift the 2024 electorate in favor of Trump and other Republicans.**

According to an internal video, Ziklag plans to invest $800,000 in "EagleAI's clean the rolls project," which would be one of the largest known donations to the group.

Ziklag lists two key objectives for Operation Checkmate: "Secure 10,640 additional unique votes in Arizona (mirroring the 2020 margin of 10,447 votes), and remove up to one million ineligible registrations and around 280,000 ineligible voters in Arizona, Nevada, Georgia, and Wisconsin."

In a recording of an internal Zoom call, Ziklag's Mark Bourgeois stressed the electoral value of targeting Arizona. "I care about Maricopa County," Bourgeois said at one point, referring to Arizona's largest county, which Biden won four years ago. "That's how we win."

For Operation Watchtower, Wallnau explained in a members-only video that transgender policy was a "wedge issue" that could be decisive in turning out voters tired of hearing about Trump.

The left had won the battle over the "homosexual issue," Wallnau said. "But on transgenderism, there's a problem and they know it." He continued: "They're gonna wanna talk about Trump, Trump, Trump. ... Meanwhile, if we talk about 'It's not about Trump. It's about parents and their children, and the state is a threat,'" that could be the "target on the forehead of Goliath."

The Ziklag files describe tactics the group plans to use around parental rights—policies that make it easier for parents to control what's taught in public schools—to turn out conservative voters. In a fundraising video, the group says it plans to underwrite a "messaging and data lab" focused on parental rights that will supply "winning messaging to all our partner groups to create unified focus among all on the right." The goal, the video says, is to make parental rights "the difference-maker in the 2024 election."

According to Wallnau, Ziklag also plans to fund ballot initiatives in seven key states—Arizona, Colorado, Florida, Michigan, Montana, Nevada and Ohio—that take aim at the transgender community by seeking to ban "genital mutilation." The seven states targeted are either presidential battlegrounds or have competitive U.S. Senate races. None of the initiatives is on a state ballot yet.

"People that are lethargic about the election or, worse yet, they're gonna be all Trump-traumatized with the news cycle—this issue will get people to come out and vote," Wallnau said. "That ballot initiative can deliver swing states."

The last prong of Ziklag's 2024 strategy is Operation Steeplechase, which urges conservative pastors to mobilize their congregants to vote in this year's election. This project will work in coordination with several prominent conservative groups that support former president Trump's reelection, such as Turning Point USA's faith-based group, the Faith and Freedom Coalition run by conservative operative Ralph Reed and the America First Policy Institute, one of several groups closely allied with Trump.

Ziklag says in a 2023 internal video that it and its allies will "coordinate extensive pastor and church outreach through pastor summits, church-focused messaging and events and the creation of pastor resources." As preacher and activist John Amanchukwu said at a Ziklag event, "We need a church that's willing to do anything and everything to get to the point where we reclaim that which was stolen from us."

Six tax experts reviewed the election-related strategy discussions and tactics reported in this story. All of them said the activities tested or ran afoul of the law governing 501(c)(3) charities. The IRS and the Texas attorney general, which would oversee the Southlake, Texas, charity, did not respond to questions.

While not all of its political efforts appeared to be clear-cut violations, the experts said, others may be: The stated plan to mobilize voters "sympathetic to Republicans," Ziklag officials openly discussing the goal to win the election, and Wallnau's call to fund ballot initiatives that would "deliver swing states" while at the same time voicing explicit criticism of Biden all raised red flags, the experts said.

"I am troubled about a tax-exempt charitable organization that's set up and its main operation seems to be to get people to win office," said Phil Hackney, a professor of law at the University of Pittsburgh and an expert on tax-exempt organizations.

"They're planning an election effort," said Marcus Owens, a tax lawyer at Loeb and Loeb and a former director of the IRS' exempt organizations division. "That's not a 501(c)(3) activity."

Print Citations

CMS: Kroll, Andy, and Nick Surgey. "Inside Ziklag, the Secret Organization of Wealthy Christians Trying to Sway the Election and Change the Country." In *The Reference Shelf: Reproductive Rights,* edited by Micah L. Issitt, 61-68. Amenia, NY: Grey House Publishing, 2024.

MLA: Kroll, Andy, and Nick Surgey. "Inside Ziklag, the Secret Organization of Wealthy Christians Trying to Sway the Election and Change the Country." *The Reference Shelf: Reproductive Rights,* edited by Micah L. Issitt, Grey House Publishing, 2024, pp. 61-68.

APA: Kroll, A., & Surgey, N. (2024). Inside Ziklag, the secret organization of wealthy Christians trying to sway the election and change the country. In M. L. Issitt (Ed.), *The reference shelf: Reproductive rights* (pp. 61-68). Amenia, NY: Grey House Publishing. (Original work published 2024)

Supreme Court's Blow to Federal Agencies' Power Will Likely Weaken Abortion Rights— 3 Issues to Watch

By Jessica L. Waters
The Conversation, July 17, 2024

The Supreme Court wrapped up its term at the beginning of July 2024 with a range of rulings that reshape everything from the power of the presidency to how federal agencies carry out their work.

One of the court's most significant decisions was *Loper Bright Enterprises v. Raimondo*. This ruling, at its core, determines the balance of power between the judiciary branch's federal courts and the executive branch's federal agencies.

When Congress passes laws, legislators know that many will have gaps and ambiguities. It is generally the job of federal agencies—staffed with subject-matter experts—to issue regulations to fill in that detail.

Before the Supreme Court's July ruling, courts deferred to those agency decisions. Now, in a reversal of 40 years of precedent, courts, not agencies, will have the last word on interpreting federal law.

Loper did not automatically reverse all agency determinations made over the past 40 years. But, going forward, *Loper's* shift of power from federal agencies to the federal courts will have profound effects on many different policies and laws—including those that deal with abortion and reproductive rights.

Lawyers and scholars like me who study reproductive rights understand that federal agencies, such as the Department of Health and Human Services and the Food and Drug Administration, generally have the scientific and medical expertise necessary to set guidance for and implement effective, evidence-based reproductive health care policy.

For example, the FDA first approved mifepristone, one of the two drugs that can cause nonsurgical medical abortions, in 2000. The agency's medical and scientific experts reviewed decades of evidence from clinical trials and highly technical scientific studies and found that the drug was safe and effective.

Credit line: From *The Conversation*, July 17 © 2024. Reprinted with permission. All rights reserved.

Here are three abortion and reproductive rights issues in which federal agency decision-making could be tested in the months and years to come.

1. The FDA and Mifepristone

> EMTALA requires hospitals to perform emergency abortions if a pregnant patient's life or health is in danger.

This spring, the Supreme Court also issued a ruling related to the FDA's approval of mifepristone, in a case called FDA v. Alliance for Hippocratic Medicine.

This case's origins trace back to 2022, when this alliance, a coalition of medical professionals who oppose abortion, sued the FDA. It wanted to remove mifepristone from the U.S. market on the theory that the FDA never should have approved the drug—despite mifepristone's long record of safety and efficacy. A Texas federal court agreed with the Alliance for Hippocratic Medicine, effectively reversing the FDA's approval and removing the drug from the market. The FDA then appealed to the Supreme Court.

The Supreme Court held in June 2024 that these medical professionals did not have "standing"—that is, they were not the correct plaintiffs to bring the case because, as medical professionals who don't provide abortions, they weren't affected by mifepristone's availability. The Supreme Court did not actually consider whether mifepristone should be removed from the market.

However, it is almost certain that a similar challenge to the FDA's authority to regulate mifepristone will soon be back before the Supreme Court. Indeed, the lawyers for the Alliance for Hippocratic Medicine have already signaled that they will continue the medical abortion case, this time with U.S. states as plaintiffs.

And when this case reaches the Supreme Court, it is an open question whether the justices will defer to the FDA's authority to approve and regulate mifepristone—or whether they will substitute their own judgment for the FDA's. The court could, for instance, reverse the FDA's determination that mifepristone should be available by telemedicine, without an in-person appointment, or even reverse the FDA's approval of the drug.

Given that medical abortion—often with mifepristone—is the most common way someone has an abortion in the U.S., such a decision could dramatically reduce access to this safe abortion method, including for patients who have no other safe options.

2. Emergency Abortion Care

Similar issues about federal agencies' power come up when considering emergency abortions—meaning abortions precipitated by a medical emergency that places the pregnant person's health on the line.

Abortion is considered the standard treatment for some pregnancy emergencies, such as when a pregnant person's water breaks before the fetus is viable.

This spring, the Supreme Court took up a conflict between a federal law called the Emergency Medical Treatment and Active Labor Act, or EMTALA, and an Idaho state abortion ban.

EMTALA requires that emergency rooms provide care to all patients regardless of their ability to pay. After the Supreme Court overturned *roe* in June 2022, the Department of Health and Human Services issued guidance stating that EMTALA requires hospitals to perform emergency abortions if a pregnant patient's life or health is in danger. This is true even if the abortion happens in a place like Idaho that has a near-total abortion ban.

The court considered whether Idaho emergency rooms had to comply with the Department of Health and Human Services' guidance and provide emergency abortions.

In a plot twist, the court declined to give an answer and instead punted the case back to a lower court. The Idaho case will now make its way to the 9th U.S. Circuit Court of Appeals. In the meantime, Idaho emergency rooms can and must provide emergency abortion care.

However, the 5th U.S. Circuit Court of Appeals came to the opposite decision in a nearly identical case, Texas v. Becerra. That court ruled in January 2024 that, despite the federal mandate, Texas doctors cannot provide emergency abortion care to protect a patient's health.

So now, the validity of federal guidance on emergency abortions depends on the state in which a pregnant person lives and which judge hears the case—almost guaranteeing that this issue will be back before the Supreme Court.

3. Department of Education and Title IX

Loper's effect on reproductive rights could also be felt in a more tangential sense, such as in current higher education court cases.

At least 20 states around the country are challenging the Department of Education's interpretation of Title IX. Title IX is a federal law that prohibits sex discrimination in education.

The Department's Title IX regulations provide enhanced protections for LGBTQIA+ students and sexual harassment survivors and protect students from discrimination based on "pregnancy or related conditions," including whether they have had or need to get an abortion.

States such as Louisiana, Mississippi, Montana and Iowa have successfully sued in federal district court to halt implementation of the new regulations.

A pending case in a Texas federal court highlights how abortion access could be implicated in these broader challenges to the agency's Title IX regulations.

In that case, two University of Texas at Austin professors said that they will, contrary to the Department of Education's guidance, discriminate against students who get abortions by penalizing students who miss class to terminate a pregnancy and refusing to employ teaching assistants who help others get abortions.

If the Texas federal court rules in favor of the Texas professors, it will join the other courts that have dismissed agency rulemaking and erode protections for college students who have abortions.

A Collision Course with *Loper*

In her *Loper* dissent, Justice Elena Kagan wrote: "In every sphere of current or future federal regulation, expect courts from now on to play a commanding role."

Loper will fundamentally change how federal agencies do their work, particularly those that deal with highly complex medical or scientific issues.

Kagan's dissent raises the specter of judges across the country—not doctors or scientists or educators, nor even politicians, who at least must answer to the public—playing a "commanding role" in reproductive rights policy.

Print Citations

CMS: Waters, Jessica L. "Supreme Court's Blow to Federal Agencies' Power Will Likely Weaken Abortion Rights—3 Issues to Watch." In *The Reference Shelf: Reproductive Rights*, edited by Micah L. Issitt, 69-72. Amenia, NY: Grey House Publishing, 2024.

MLA: Waters, Jessica L. "Supreme Court's Blow to Federal Agencies' Power Will Likely Weaken Abortion Rights—3 Issues to Watch." *The Reference Shelf: Reproductive Rights*, edited by Micah L. Issitt, Grey House Publishing, 2024, pp. 69-72.

APA: Water, J. L. (2024). Supreme Court's blow to federal agencies' power will likely weaken abortion rights—3 issues to watch. In M. L. Issitt (Ed.), *The reference shelf: Reproductive rights* (pp. 69-72). Amenia, NY: Grey House Publishing. (Original work published 2024)

Justice Thomas: SCOTUS "Should Reconsider" Contraception, Same-Sex Marriage Rulings

By Quint Forgey and Josh Gerstein
Politico, June 24, 2022

Justice Clarence Thomas argued in a concurring opinion released on Friday that the Supreme Court "should reconsider" its past rulings codifying rights to contraception access, same-sex relationships and same-sex marriage.

The sweeping suggestion from the current court's longest-serving justice came in the concurring opinion he authored in response to the court's ruling revoking the constitutional right to abortion, also released on Friday.

In his concurring opinion, Thomas—an appointee of President George H.W. Bush—wrote that the justices "should reconsider all of this Court's substantive due process precedents, including *Griswold*, *Lawrence*, and *Obergefell*"—referring to three cases having to do with Americans' fundamental privacy, due process and equal protection rights.

Since May, when *Politico* published an initial draft majority opinion of the court's decision on Friday to strike down *Roe v. Wade*, Democratic politicians have repeatedly warned that such a ruling would lead to the reversal of other landmark privacy-related cases.

"If the rationale of the decision as released were to be sustained, a whole range of rights are in question. A whole range of rights," President Joe Biden said of the draft opinion at the time. "And the idea [that] we're letting the states make those decisions, localities make those decisions, would be a fundamental shift in what we've done."

The court's liberal wing—Justices Stephen Breyer, Sonia Sotomayor and Elena Kagan—echoed those concerns in a dissenting opinion released on Friday, writing that "no one should be confident that this majority is done with its work."

The constitutional right to abortion "does not stand alone," the three justices wrote. "To the contrary, the Court has linked it for decades to other settled freedoms involving bodily integrity, familial relationships, and procreation."

The court's past rulings in *Roe*, *Griswold v. Connecticut*, *Lawrence v. Texas*, *Obergefell v. Hodges* and other cases "are all part of the same constitutional fabric," the three justices continued, "protecting autonomous decision making over the most personal of life decisions."

Credit line: From *Politico*, June 24 © 2022. Reprinted with permission. All rights reserved.

The court's majority opinion, written by Justice Samuel Alito, repeatedly insists that the justices' decision to abandon *Roe* poses no threat to other precedents.

"Our decision concerns the constitutional right to abortion and no other right," Alito wrote.

"Nothing in this opinion should be understood to cast doubt on precedents that do not concern abortion."

> **Roe recognized the fundamental right to privacy that has served as a basis for so many more rights that we've come to take for granted.**

However, the court's liberal wing argued that assurance was unsatisfactory, given Thomas' simultaneous invitation on Friday to open up numerous other precedents for review.

"The first problem with the majority's account comes from [Thomas'] concurrence—which makes clear he is not with the program," Breyer, Sotomayor and Kagan wrote, adding: "At least one Justice is planning to use the ticket of today's decision again and again and again."

Still, no other justice joined Thomas' concurring opinion, which largely reiterated his long-stated views on the legal theories behind many of those decisions.

Furthermore, it appears doubtful that many of Thomas' conservative colleagues would be eager to revisit issues like contraception and same-sex marriage anytime soon, considering the claims in Alito's majority opinion that the court's ruling on Friday casts no doubt on those decisions.

Still, by declining to explicitly repudiate Thomas' stance, his conservative colleagues provided fodder to the court's liberal members and left-leaning critics to warn that more overrulings of precedent are on the way.

Of those in the majority on Friday, Justice Brett Kavanaugh came closest to rejecting Thomas' position, although without mentioning him by name. In a solo concurring opinion, Kavanaugh wrote: "Overruling *Roe* does not mean the overruling of those precedents, and does not threaten or cast doubt on those precedents."

Speaking from the White House shortly after the decision was released, Biden directly invoked Thomas' concurring opinion and reasserted that the ruling "risks the broader right to privacy for everyone."

"*Roe* recognized the fundamental right to privacy that has served as a basis for so many more rights that we've come to take for granted, that are ingrained in the fabric of this country," Biden said. "The right to make the best decisions for your health. The right to use birth control. A married couple in the privacy of their bedroom, for God's sake. The right to marry the person you love."

With his concurring opinion, Thomas "explicitly called to reconsider the right of marriage equality [and] the right of couples to make their choices on contraception," Biden continued. "This [is an] extreme and dangerous path the court is now taking us on."

Print Citations

CMS: Forgey, Quint, and Josh Gerstein. "Justice Thomas: SCOTUS 'Should Reconsider' Contraception, Same-Sex Marriage Rulings." In *The Reference Shelf: Reproductive Rights,* edited by Micah L. Issitt, 73-75. Amenia, NY: Grey House Publishing, 2024.

MLA: Forgey, Quint, and Josh Gerstein. "Justice Thomas: SCOTUS 'Should Reconsider' Contraception, Same-Sex Marriage Rulings." *The Reference Shelf: Reproductive Rights,* edited by Micah L. Issitt, Grey House Publishing, 2024, pp. 73-75.

APA: Forgey, Q., & Gerstein, J. (2024). Justice Thomas: SCOTUS "should reconsider" contraception, same-sex marriage rulings. In M. L. Issitt (Ed.), *The reference shelf: Reproductive rights* (pp. 73-75). Amenia, NY: Grey House Publishing. (Original work published 2022)

Following Trump's Lead, Republicans Adopt Platform That Softens Stance on Abortion

By Maggie Haberman, Shane Goldmacher, and Jonathan Swan
New York Times, July 8, 2024

Donald J. Trump told officials on Monday that he supports a new Republican Party platform, one that reflects the presumptive nominee's new position on abortion rights and slims down policy specifics across all areas of government.

The new platform, as described to the *New York Times* by people briefed on it, cements Mr. Trump's ideological takeover of the G.O.P. The platform is even more nationalistic, more protectionist and less socially conservative than the 2016 Republican platform that was duplicated in the 2020 election.

Mr. Trump, who has had the draft for several days, called into a meeting of party officials on Monday and said that he supports it. The document overwhelmingly was approved during a vote by the platform committee on Monday, passing 84 to 18, according to a person briefed on the matter.

The abortion section has been softened. There is no longer a reference to "traditional marriage" as between "one man and one woman." And there is no longer an emphasis on reducing the national debt, only a brief line about "slashing wasteful government spending."

The rest of the document reflects Mr. Trump's priorities as outlined on his campaign website: a hard-line immigration policy, including mass deportations; a protectionist trade policy with new tariffs on most imports; and sections on using federal power to remove policies in academia, the military and throughout the U.S. government put in place by what it describes as radical Democrats.

Mr. Trump and his top aides have alienated some activists by shutting them out of the development of the platform. The former president was especially focused on softening the language on abortion—the issue he views as his biggest vulnerability in the wake of the Supreme Court's decision overturning *Roe v. Wade*.

A Trump campaign spokesman did not respond to an email seeking comment.

The section on protecting human life has been significantly watered down in the 2024 draft platform. In the 2016 and 2020 platform, that section included extensive specific details about what the Republican Party would do to limit abortions, including supporting a federal ban on abortion after 20 weeks. It stated that "the unborn child has a fundamental right to life which cannot be infringed."

Credit line: From the *New York Times*, July 8 © 2024. Reprinted with permission. All rights reserved.

The 2024 draft platform, as described to the *Times*, is called "America First: A Return to Common Sense," and softens that abortion language and shifts the issue from one of conscience to a matter best handled by the states. "We believe that the 14th Amendment to the Constitution of the United States guarantees that no person can be denied life or liberty without due process and that the states are, therefore, free to pass laws protecting those rights," the draft platform reads.

> **The 2024 draft platform softens the abortion language and shifts the issue from one of conscience to a matter best handled by the states.**

The document makes no mention of a federal abortion ban, which Mr. Trump has said he opposes. Instead, the new platform stresses that Republicans oppose "late term abortion" and emphasizes that the party supports "access to birth control, and IVF (fertility treatments)."

Marjorie Dannenfelser, the president of Susan B. Anthony Pro-Life America, who had been concerned about changes to the platform before the committee's approval, sounded approving of it.

"It is important that the G.O.P. reaffirmed its commitment to protect unborn life today through the 14th Amendment," she said in a statement. "Under this amendment, it is Congress that enacts and enforces its provisions. The Republican Party remains strongly pro-life at the national level." She added: "The mission of the pro-life movement, for the next six months, must be to defeat the Biden-Harris extreme abortion agenda."

Ralph Reed, the chairman of the socially conservative Faith and Freedom Coalition, also expressed optimism about the new language.

"The Republican Party platform makes clear the unborn child has a right to life that is protected by the Constitution under the due process clause of the 14th amendment," Mr. Reed said, adding that it has long been in the Republican platform and praising Mr. Trump. "While aspirational, it applies to both the states and the federal government. The proposed ban on late-term abortion also implies federal as well as state action."

But Tony Perkins, the president of the Family Research Council and a member of the platform committee, was disappointed, and he criticized the process.

"The 2024 platform is a decent statement of campaign priorities, but not necessarily the enduring principles of a party," he said in a statement. "Unfortunately, the process was unbecoming of constitutional conservatives which did not allow the document to be amended or improve."

The new platform language also affirms Mr. Trump's position on Medicare and Social Security as the Republican Party's stance, saying that Mr. Trump "will not cut one penny" from either program. The 2016 platform, in contrast, stated, "We reject the old maxim that Social Security is the 'Third Rail' of American politics" and that "all options should be considered to preserve Social Security."

Notably, the platform also eliminated language supporting statehood for Puerto Rico, something that has been a staple of Republican platform language for decades.

The platform's new preamble also includes a broad line that "the Republican Party must stand for equal treatment for all," adding that applies to anyone "regardless of political affiliation or personal beliefs."

But then it goes on to make oblique reference to the multiple indictments Mr. Trump faces, and one set of felony convictions. "Recent Democrat-led political persecutions threaten to destroy 250 years of American principle and practice and must be stopped," it reads.

In general, the platform appears explicitly geared toward winning in 2024 rather than outlining a broader vision for the Republican Party. The first two chapters are devoted to the issues that Mr. Trump wants to make central to this race: inflation and immigration.

The platform committee is meeting in Milwaukee on Monday ahead of the full convention next week. Following the committee's vote to approve the document, the platform will head to a full vote next week.

Print Citations

CMS: Haberman, Maggie, Shane Goldmacher, and Jonathan Swan. "Following Trump's Lead, Republicans Adopt Platform That Softens Stance on Abortion." In *The Reference Shelf: Reproductive Rights,* edited by Micah L. Issitt, 76-78. Amenia, NY: Grey House Publishing, 2024.

MLA: Haberman, Maggie, et al. "Following Trump's Lead, Republicans Adopt Platform That Softens Stance on Abortion." *The Reference Shelf: Reproductive Rights,* edited by Micah L. Issitt, Grey House Publishing, 2024, pp. 76-78.

APA: Haberman, M., Goldmacher, S., & Swan, J. (2024). Following Trump's lead, Republicans adopt platform that softens stance on abortion. In M. L. Issitt (Ed.), *The reference shelf: Reproductive rights* (pp. 76-78). Amenia, NY: Grey House Publishing. (Original work published 2024)

3
Contraception

Photo by Sarahmirk, CC BY-SA 4.0, via Wikipedia.

Over-the-counter oral contraceptives are available at most pharmacies, like this CVS in Portland.

Preventing Pregnancies

Of the many issues in the broader subject of reproductive health, contraception should be one of the *least* controversial. Across the board, Democrats, Republicans, and Independents are agreed that mainstream methods of contraception, including condoms, birth control pills, and intrauterine devices (IUDs) should remain legal in all or, at least, most cases. Even with conservative circles few Americans see any reason or justification to restrict access to these important family planning technologies.[1] However, the small minority who feel that contraception is a threat are extremely dedicated and powerful and so, even with such a gulf in public opinion, the future of contraception is now in question for many Americans.

Why Ban Contraception?

Among those who want to either ban on restrict access to contraception, several justifications are common. Some argue that contraception is "unnatural," because it involves using medication to interfere with natural body processes. Others believe that contraception is a form of abortion that involves "killing" potential lives that might have resulted from sex without the use of contraception. Others believe that contraception interferes with spiritual dictates and the degree to which God or gods can determine when someone gets pregnant. Others argue that contraception divorces the act of sex from the act of reproduction and so encourages engagement in nonreproductive sex.[2]

All of these objections are rooted in the ancient history of the Abrahamic Faiths, the sister religions of Judaism, Christianity, and Islam, in order of their invention. All three of these faiths emerged within societies in which they were originally radical, fringe faiths. The ancient Jews were persecuted in their home societies because of their faith, because leaders of the ruling elite of that time saw the Jewish movement as a challenge to the primacy of their power. Religions often serve as measures of social conformity and control, and minority religions are often perceived, by members of the majority, as a threat to their power and privilege. Consider how Christians in America sometimes view Muslims, perceiving them as a threat to the future of Christian dominance within the United States. This was how members of the dominant religious/cultural traditions once viewed Jewish people where the religion first started.

This persecution was part of the reason that the Jews embraced, in the Old Testament, a highly reproductive view of sex. The more Jewish babies that were born, would mean more Jewish people in the next generation, and would therefore provide Jewish communities with more protection, solidarity, and, ultimately, political power. The same story can be applied to Christianity, which emerged first as a radical sect of Judaism. The early Christians were persecuted by the Jews and also by the Roman Empire, again because the radical Christian sect was seen as a threat to those elites in power who claimed that their power was divine in origin. The Christians also developed a highly patriarchic view of sexuality in which nonreproductive sex was prohibited. The basic idea was that Christians needed to produce more Christians and thus were encouraged to have as many children as possible. This prohibition on nonreproductive sex was then used to prohibit same sex sexuality, which was also classed as a sin in Christian lore.

Over the years that followed, as contraception technologies became more widely available, some Christians came to believe that the use of these technologies was immoral and defied God's perceived plan for Christians to continue producing more Christians. Others, forgetting about the ancient effort to increase the size of the Christian population, began to view this issue through more of a generalized moralist lens, seeing contraception as a tool that had no place in decisions *made* by God, such as when and *if* a person was to become pregnant or carry a child.

All Christian beliefs about sexuality in the early years of Christianity, and in the years since, have likewise been influenced by patriarchy. The control of feminine sexuality was one of the aims of moral guidelines related to sexuality, and sexual control of females is explicitly stated in biblical scripture. Prohibitions against contraception and female sexual autonomy continue to reflect the influence of patriarchic thought as it was seen to apply to sexual behavior. Contraception, long before medicated birth control or IUDs had been invented, was a way for women to make decisions about their own reproductive lives, as was abortion, which predates Christianity and Judaism. Prohibitions against these methods of controlling reproduction were considered immoral, in part, because of the effort to enforce male dominance over female bodies and lives. Women were, in Christian tradition, relegated to domestic and subservient roles, and the expression of feminine sexuality and sexual agency was seen as a threat to this traditionalist model of gender roles and a threat to the privileges and benefits that males received by exploiting females as sexual and domestic servants.[3]

Thus, some Christians have retained a traditionalist conservative view of sexuality and its purpose in human life, which is based on the tradition of Christian expansion that was meant to maximize population growth, and the preservation of traditional gender roles which, themselves, reinforce male dominance within Christian societies. Many opponents of nonreproductive sexuality in the modern world would be unaware of these historic influences on Christian thought and might simply see themselves are promoting proper Christian morality, unaware that these moral guidelines were shaped by a contest of power that was measured in the size of one's adherents and the level of control that dominant males were able to exert over women in their families and communities.

Nonreproductive Sex

The belief that contraception is a threat because it encourages unreproductive sex is more complex. On one hand, those who embrace this view are often influenced by Christian fundamentalist thinking, which derives from scripture the belief that the purpose of sex is solely reproduction, and that sexual pleasure is meant only for those who engage in sexuality in the approved Christian way. Not everyone defines the appropriate Christian sex in the same way, but among fundamentalist conservatives this typically means that sex must be between a man and a woman who are married in accordance with church law and do not utilize any method that would prevent the perceptively divine occurrence of conception. However, even within far-right Christian circles, perception of contraception is varied. Roman Catholics have long disproved of contraception, which makes sense given that they represent the direct link to the oldest Christian traditions and directly to the time when increasing Christian numbers was essential to building political power. It was the Catholics who made Christianity a dominant tradition, incorporating Christian thought into the Roman Empire to create the Holy Roman Empire, which then spread Christianity around the world. Non-Catholic Christians, on the other hand, often have very different ideas about contraception and some are more willing to embrace the idea that not *all* sex needs to be reproductive.

In many cultures throughout history, people have embraced the many nonreproductive reasons that people have for engaging in sex. Sex can be used purely for recreation or pleasure, or to cement and affirm bonds between bonded individuals, or for physical exercise, or even for spiritual purposes. In some traditions, sexual behavior, whether solitary or ingroups, has been considered a form of meditation, a health practice, and a way of expressing and exploring emotions, beyond the reproductive function that sex can also serve. In Christian tradition, therefore, nonreproductive sex has often been considered immoral, but this does not reflect some base state of human morality, but merely one perspective amidst a spectrum of approaches to sex and sexuality throughout history.

Americans are clearly not aligned with the traditionalist conservative Christian model on sex. Polls indicate that 99 percent of Americans have premarital sex, and even for women born in the 1940s, during which time traditionalist gender paradigms held more sway in American society, nearly 90 percent reported sex before marriage. This is the kind of data that shows clearly why abstinence-only sex education programs are routinely proven to be ineffective, but also shows that the vast majority of Americans are having sex without the intention of reproduction. The traditionalist view, quite simply, does not reflect American lives or desired ways of living.[4]

Some opponents of contraception argue that the availability of contraception encourages nonreproductive sex among individuals who "should not" be having sexual intercourse, regardless of the reason. This might include persons who are considered underage or persons who are in committed relationships and engaging in adultery. Such concerns to not shift the needle on public opinion on contraception for a variety of reasons. For one, the idea that the possibility of pregnancy is an effective deterrent to sex simply does not match with what many people understand about sexual desire from their own experiences. Second, years of data suggest that a lack of access to birth control does not discourage sex, but does result in many additional unplanned pregnancies, which, in turn, increases the demand for abortion and results in many other unfortunate consequences, including child abandonment, child abuse, and poor parental care. Increasing the number of unwanted pregnancies does nothing to support the goal of enhancing child welfare and, in fact, has the opposite effect. Unwanted pregnancies have been positively associated with psychological abuse, neglect, and violence against children, and poorer outcomes for children in general.[5]

A Minority Movement

Given the overwhelming level of public support for legal contraception and the highly subjective nature of objections to contraception use, it might seem like prohibiting contraception would be a very low priority in American politics, even for those who see this as a goal. This is not necessarily the case, however, because small dedicated groups of political activists can have a tremendous influence in US politics, when their movements become important to conservative political fortunes. In all of the major arenas of reproductive health that are being debated in American culture, public opinion favors maintaining adult access to things like abortion care and, more so, to family planning measures like sex education and contraception. There is, however, a small minority of conservatives in America who would like to exert a higher level of control over American sexuality in ways that, in general, discourage nonreproductive sexuality and encourage reproductive sexuality. This group is not only interested in prohibiting abortion to achieve this goal, but also seeks to restrict access to contraception.

To see how this minority, extremist political view worms its way into the mainstream, consider the Trump administration's new health department rules issued in 2017. These rules rolled back what was known as the "birth control mandate," which stated that employers needed to cover birth control in employer offered health insurance plans. To defend this decision, the administration claimed that certain types of contraception may not "advance government interests," and that "imposing a coverage Mandate on objecting entities whose plans cover many enrollee families who may share objections to contraception could, among some populations, affect risky sexual behavior in a negative way."

These claims are based on nothing. Scientists and experts in human behavior who have studied birth control use have found no links between the use of birth control and risker sexual behavior. A study by Dr. Jeffrey Peipert and colleagues at Washington University in St. Louis found that providing access to birth control had no influence over "risky" sexual behavior in terms of sexual behavior and reduced the likelihood of sexually transmitted disease. This study was part of a trial in the St. Louis area where women and female teens were given free birth control, of their choice, and were told about the benefits of utilizing birth control. Rates of both abortion and pregnancy in the study group fell significantly, to less than 25 percent of the national average. Of the Trump administration's effort to roll back federal birth control requirements, Dr. Peipert told *Time Magazine* in 2017, "These are myths that are to the detriment of public health. I would argue that not providing contraception is clearly increased risk-taking behavior."[6]

The Trump administration's subtle attack on the availability of birth control was a political tactic. Given the low cost of birth control, the new rules were unlikely to result in a serious backlash for Trump, but the move was a signal to potential supporters within that small group of conservatives who oppose contraception and would like to see contraceptive access reduced. Thus, Trump was able to all but guarantee support among a group of dedicated voters, without making a much more blatant move that would've reduced support among the majority, for whom contraceptive access is still seen as a benefit rather than a threat.

The threat to contraception is therefore that conservative politicians will bargain that the majority of their supporters will still vote for them, because they prioritize other issues, if they approve of policies that might weaken contraception access. It is unlikely that very many mainstream politicians with hopes of winning elections, will openly oppose the legality of contraception, but conservative politicians can benefit from making less overt moves that signify their allegiance with this brand of extremist social conservatism and willingness to embrace authoritarian controls on behavior as a way of influencing America's future cultural evolution.

Of course, the level of public support for legal contraception access also means that conservative politicians who wish to capture the support of this extremist minority will not be able to approach the issue in an honest or open manner. Just as the Trump administration claimed that contraception might increase "risky" sexual behavior and so the federal government could not require insurance companies to provide coverage, politicians often seek to use misinformation and false claims to disguise opposition to contraception as a form of public health or child welfare stance. These are overwhelmingly false positions to adopt, as all available scientific research supports the idea that contraception is overwhelmingly safe and that the availability of contraception prevents rather than encourages unwanted outcomes. The perspective that contraception poses a danger is therefore merely political propaganda used to disguise the motivations behind political positions in ways that allow politicians to signify their allegiance to a small but very engaged group of ultraconservative voters, without having to commit openly to all the ways members of this group would seek to institute additional controls or influence American sexuality.

As of 2024, conservative groups are actively attempting to utilize the *Dobbs* decision to prohibit contraception by claiming that preconception prevention of pregnancy is a form of birth control. Such a claim would require courts and American voters to decide whether all gametes (eggs and sperm) count a fetuses for the purpose of prohibiting abortion. Such an extreme view will not meet with majority support, even in far-right leaning states, but this has not stopped reproductive activists from attempting to manipulate existing court precedent to achieve this legal goal. Eight separate states have enacted or proposed laws regarding access to contraception. A law in Indiana, for instance, restricted access to IUDs, utilizing the claim that they "cause abortions," which is not biologically, medically, or in any other way an accurate depiction of how IUDs function. A bill in Oklahoma, which was defeated, attempted to link IUDs to abortion and would have resulted in the banning of these devices.[7]

While conservative activism since the 1970s has not shifted the needle in public opinion on contraception towards the right, the dependence of right-wing politicians on fringe groups within their electorate, coupled with low engagement among liberal and progressive voters, has created an opportunity for ultraconservative groups to pursue policies that are very much contrary to the beliefs and wishes of the vast majority of American voters. Mainstream Republican politicians, like Donald Trump, have voiced opposition to the idea of prohibiting contraception, but Republican victories, at any level of the state or federal government, will empower those among the majority within the conservative sphere who feel that this kind of moral legislation will benefit their long-term goals. Most voters who cast votes for Trump or other high-profile Republicans will therefore not see prohibiting contraception as part of their broader goals, but will make it more likely that activists within these groups, as unpopular as their ideas might be, can achieve at least some of their agenda.

Works Used

Abrams, Abigail. "No, Birth Control Doesn't Make You Have Riskier Sex, Researchers Say." *Time Magazine*, 12 Oct. 2017, time.com/4975951/donald-trump-birth-control-mandate-sexual-behavior/.

Barr, Beth Alison. *The Making of Biblical Womanhood: How the Subjugation of Women Became Gospel*. Brazos Press, 2021.

Forouzan, Kimya. "Midyear 2024 State Policy Trends: Many US States Attack Reproductive Health Care, as Other States Fight Back." *Guttmacher Institute*, June 2024, www.guttmacher.org/2024/06/midyear-2024-state-policy-trends-many-us-states-attack-reproductive-health-care-other.

"Moral Case Against Contraception." *BBC*, 2014, Ethics Guide, www.bbc.co.uk/ethics/contraception/against_1.shtml.

Pratasava, Veleryia. "Unwanted Pregnancies: Outcomes for Children." *Drexel University*, 18 Feb. 2022, drexel.edu/medicine/academics/womens-health-and-leadership/womens-health-education-program/whep-blog/unwanted-pregnancies-outcomes-for-children/.

"Premarital Sex Is Nearly Universal Among Americans and Has Been for Decades." *Guttmacher Institute*, 19 Dec. 2006, www.guttmacher.org/news-release/2006/premarital-sex-nearly-universal-among-americans-and-has-been-decades.

Skelley, Geoffrey, and Holly Fuong. "How Americans Feel about Contraception." *FiveThirtyEight*, 12 July 2022, fivethirtyeight.com/features/abortion-birth-control-poll/.

Notes

1. Skelley and Fuong, "How Americans Feel About Abortion and Contraception."
2. "Moral Case Against Contraception," *BBC*.
3. Barr, *The Making of Biblical Womanhood: How the Subjugation of Women Became Gospel.*
4. "Premarital Sex Is Nearly Universal Among Americans, and Has Been for Decades," *Guttmacher Institute*.
5. Pratasava "Unwanted Pregnancies: Outcomes for Children."
6. Abrams, "No, Birth Control Doesn't Make You Have Riskier Sex, Researchers Say."
7. Forouzan, "Midyear 2024 State Policy Trends: May US States Attack Reproductive Health Care, as Other States Fight Back."

Social Media Will Tell You Birth Control Causes Mental Health Issues, Weight Gain, and Infertility: Here Are the Facts

By Christopher O'Sullivan
The Conversation, April 9, 2024

Social media is full of bad advice when it comes to your health. With so much of this content created by influencers who don't actually have medical qualifications, it's no wonder that misinformation about health spreads so easily online.

In recent years, there's been a rise in misinformation about hormonal contraceptives on social media. Some women are reportedly even stopping their birth control as a result of misleading posts they've seen on TikTok and Instagram.

These three common misconceptions about birth control are cropping up online and need to be put in context:

1. Contraception Causes Depression

Countless videos on social media discuss the effect hormonal contraceptives have on mental health—with some creators claiming birth control causes mood changes and even depression.

But these videos are anything but definitive. Although there's some correlation between mental health and some forms of contraception, there are many factors at play.

Evidence shows that modern, combined hormonal contraceptives (which contain artificial versions of the reproductive hormones progestin and oestrogen) do not have any affect on mood or mental function. Some research has even highlighted cases where patients who took combined oral contraceptives had lower levels of depression than patients who received a placebo dose.

But research has shown a correlation between progesterone-only types of contraception (such as the mini-pill and the medroxyprogesterone acetate or Depo-Provera injection) and mood change. This is why some contraceptives list mood change as a "common" side effect (occurring in between one to ten or one in 100 women, depending on the brand). The evidence suggests depression is more common in adolescent girls—and diminishes after the first two years of taking these forms of birth control.

Credit line: From *The Conversation*, April 9 © 2024. Reprinted with permission. All rights reserved.

Despite these links being drawn, a 2018 large-scale review disputes this, claiming that more high quality research needs to be undertaken. The Faculty of Reproductive and Sexual Health (FSRH), one of the leading voices in sexual and reproductive healthcare, also state in its prescribing guidelines that the evidence does not directly prove a relationship between the mini pill and depression—rather, it only shows a link.

> **Many of the misconceptions around contraception have been sensationalised on social media.**

At present, there's little conclusive evidence that contraception (both hormonal and non-hormonal types) cause mental health problems. But if you have experienced mood changes or feel depressed after starting birth control (especially progesterone-only contraception) it's worth speaking to your doctor as they may be able to prescribe you another type that works better for you.

2. Contraception Causes Weight Gain

Another common social media claim is that birth control causes weight gain. This again is not the full picture.

A 2019 report published by the FSRH concluded there was no evidence that any form of oral hormonal contraceptive (including the pill, implant and intrauterine device or IUD) caused weight gain. They did, however, find evidence showing the majority of reproductive-age women tend to gradually gain weight as they get older—regardless of whether they used contraceptives or not. This can be due to the hormonal and metabolic changes that occur with age.

Other reviews have also reached similar conclusions. This study found that it's unlikely that hormonal contraceptives cause major weight gain. But the authors of this review did acknowledge that these findings don't rule out the possibility that some individual women might in fact gain weight. They are calling for more research to be done that directly compares weight changes between birth control users and people who don't use a contraceptive.

There is one form of contraception that is linked to weight gain. The Depo-Provera injection, which is administered every 12 weeks, has been proved to cause weight gain. This weight gain is more prevalent in people who were already obese before starting the injection. According to one study, women who took the Depo-Provera shot gained almost 5kg in one year.

This weight gain may be due to the progesterone in the shot, which can cause people to feel hungrier—potentially leading to overeating and weight gain.

If you're concerned about potential weight gain, the injection is not the only form of contraception available. Other forms of hormonal and non-hormonal contraceptives have not been shown to affect your weight.

3. Birth Control Lowers Your Fertility

Another common claim on social media is that birth control causes fertility issues. This is not true. Research shows hormonal contraceptives have no affect on fertility.

There's also concern online that the IUD will could cause pelvic inflammation, leading to infertility. Again, evidence shows that IUDs pose no risk to fertility. A systematic review reports no specific differences in fertility between hormonal and non-hormonal IUDs.

Social media users have also claimed the Depo-Provera injection causes infertility. But again, there's no evidence to support this. Research shows pregnancy rates are similar for women who had previously used the Depo-Provera injection compared with those who had used other types of contraceptives.

It may take a few months for your menstrual cycle to return to normal after ceasing the injection. This is because of the larger build up of active ingredient in the body, which stops your periods and takes some time to dissipate. Your menstrual cycle may also be different for between two and four cycles after stopping oral contraception.

Many of the misconceptions around contraception have been sensationalised on social media. Contraception is rarely the primary cause of any issue. As with any medication, it may interact with conditions you already have, so it's important to seek advice about contraception from your doctor or nurse—not TikTok.

Print Citations

CMS: O'Sullivan, Christopher. "Social Media Will Tell You Birth Control Causes Mental Health Issues, Weight Gain, and Infertility: Here Are the Facts." In *The Reference Shelf: Reproductive Rights,* edited by Micah L. Issitt, 88-90. Amenia, NY: Grey House Publishing, 2024.

MLA: O'Sullivan, Christopher. "Social Media Will Tell You Birth Control Causes Mental Health Issues, Weight Gain, and Infertility: Here Are the Facts." *The Reference Shelf: Reproductive Rights,* edited by Micah L. Issitt, Grey House Publishing, 2024, pp. 88-90.

APA: O'Sullivan, C. (2024). Social media will tell you birth control causes mental health issues, weight gain, and infertility: Here are the facts. In M. L. Issitt (Ed.), *The reference shelf: Reproductive rights* (pp. 88-90). Amenia, NY: Grey House Publishing. (Original work published 2024)

Opinion: Birth Control Access May Get Easier—Here's Why It's Not Enough

By Lucy Tu and Jocelyn Viterna
Undark, February 9, 2023

Just weeks after the Supreme Court overturned *Roe v. Wade*, Paris-based company HRA Pharma applied for Food and Drug Administration approval of the country's first over-the-counter birth control pill. The application was a timely response to Justice Clarence Thomas's concurring opinion in *Dobbs v. Jackson Women's Health Organization*, where he suggested the Court "should reconsider" its 1965 ruling that codified rights to contraceptive access. If HRA Pharma's petition is approved, people in the United States could purchase birth control pills from pharmacy shelves, next to condoms and menstrual products, without a prescription.

The possibility of an OTC birth control pill could remove key barriers to contraceptives, especially in the post-*Dobbs* era. And since one in three reproductive-aged women report difficulty obtaining a birth control prescription or refills, such an option may also help repair the U.S.'s fragmented state of reproductive rights.

But birth control has not always been synonymous with bodily autonomy. Contraceptives may allow people to manage their fertility, but they have also been pushed as a panacea for social problems like poverty, crime, and, more recently, climate change. Accordingly, tensions between the right to choose birth control and contraceptive coercion, or pressuring someone to use or not use a particular method of contraception, have influenced social policy since the birth control movement began in 1914.

Over-the-counter birth control is no exception. Removing the pill's prescription requirement would be a historic advancement in reproductive health care. But the FDA's decision, which is expected to be announced in mid-2023, isn't enough to resolve disparities in access to contraception for communities of color and low-income women, who face long-standing barriers to contraceptive care, including out-of-pocket costs, pharmacy deserts, and medical mistrust.

The availability of an OTC pill means little if patients can't afford or access the pill, or are simply suspicious of it. For the OTC pill to realize its potential for improved reproductive health and liberation, we must acknowledge contraception's tangled history with reproductive coercion. It's the only way to ensure equitable access, choice, and education.

Credit line: From *Undark*, February 9 © 2023. Reprinted with permission. All rights reserved.

Advocates from "Free the Pill," the coalition that helped lay the groundwork for regulatory approval, emphasize that contraception is critical for family planning and reproductive health care in the U.S. The American Medical Association and the American College of Obstetricians and Gynecologists, or ACOG, have also voiced support for the over-the-counter option.

But historical lessons warn against hopes that mere approval of the OTC pill will have an equalizing effect for all people. While more than three-quarters of reproductive-aged women support the OTC pill, low-income women and women of color report greater concern over the contraceptive's safety, showing a lingering distrust of birth control.

Indeed, researchers from the Bixby Center for Global Reproductive Health found that Black and Latina women were more likely to believe that the government encourages contraceptive use to limit minority populations. They were also more likely to use non-hormonal methods of contraception—or no method at all.

Such medical mistrust is well-founded considering the legacy of reproductive coercion and its ramifications for racial minorities in the U.S. For example, in the 1920s, American reproductive policies included eugenics-inspired programs aimed at decreasing the population of low-income, disabled, or non-White individuals. Indeed, sociologist Melissa Wilde argues that it was the eugenics movement—and its message of limiting the large family sizes of so-called "undesirable" Catholic immigrants from Ireland and Italy—that first pushed the Catholic church to ban artificial forms of birth control in 1930.

In the 1970s, U.S. doctors sterilized an estimated 25 to 42 percent of Native American women of childbearing age, often without their knowledge or consent. In the 1990s, lawmakers in many states proposed bills that would have forced poor women, primarily women of color, to use the long-acting contraceptive Norplant to qualify for welfare benefits—a proposal that continues to have cachet among politicians into the 21st century. Former Arizona state Sen. Russell Pearce was quoted in 2014 saying, "You put me in charge of Medicaid, the first thing I'd do is get [female recipients] Norplant, birth-control implants, or tubal ligations."

Although the U.S. has made major advances in improving contraceptive access, including the Affordable Care Act's 2011 mandate that insurance plans provide contraceptive coverage, it has not escaped its legacy of contraception and population control. Reproductive coercion exists on a spectrum, according to Leigh Senderowicz, an assistant professor at the University of Wisconsin-Madison who studies contraceptive autonomy. Although the term is typically used in reference to intimate partnerships, Senderowicz argues that reproductive coercion also includes the more quotidian and systemic restrictions that especially impact marginalized communities, including a lack of access to affordable, effective, and trustworthy contraceptive options.

Like the "Plan B" emergency contraceptive, the OTC pill would be sold by grocery stores and big box retailers, but pharmacies would serve as the primary distributor. Yet even access to pharmacies is not ensured for marginalized communities. In Los Angeles, for example, one-third of Black and Latino neighborhoods meet the criteria for a pharmacy desert. Pharmacy closures are also more common in these neighborhoods across the U.S., making residents and their reproductive health collateral damage in an already fractured network of contraceptive access. As Ebony Jade Hilton, an anesthesiologist based in Charlottesville, Virginia, noted on Twitter, "Options mean nothing [without] access."

> **Birth control has not always been synonymous with bodily autonomy. The availability of an OTC pill means little if patients can't afford or access the pill.**

"Free the Pill" advocates have acknowledged these barriers and the long-term solutions they require. The more immediate concerns are the unresolved legal obstacles to OTC contraceptives, even if the FDA approves the new option.

Currently, 13 states have policies known as "conscience clauses" that allow pharmacists to refuse to provide medication when it conflicts with their religious or moral beliefs. These clauses have been invoked in notable cases of pharmacists denying patients emergency contraception or prescriptions for medication abortion. The U.S. Department of Health and Human Services recently clarified that, at least for prescription birth control, these refusals violate the ACA's anti-discrimination provisions. But it's unclear where OTC birth control would fall under these guidelines. Given that 10 of the conscience clause states have severe abortion restrictions or total bans, disparities in contraceptive access now carry bigger stakes.

Similar problems may prevent the OTC option from being affordable. The ACA allows insurance companies to require a prescription before covering OTC birth control expenses, which loops many patients back to the beginning of their contraceptive conundrum. For uninsured and low-income patients, a menu featuring only these two options—paying high out-of-pocket costs for the OTC option or obtaining prescriptions from a provider who may be geographically inaccessible—leaves the OTC pill firmly out of reach.

As the FDA considers OTC approval, health care providers and policymakers must recognize that women are responsible enough to decide whether this new option is right for them. Clinicians opposed to OTC contraceptives often report concerns with patients' ability to correctly use the pill. But research demonstrates that women can effectively self-screen to make sure they are a good candidate for hormonal birth control and follow medication instructions. Misguided perceptions of patient incompetence compound on historical themes of favoring clinician expertise over women's contraceptive preferences.

Additionally, dismantling the culture of fear surrounding birth control will require a lot more than recognizing historical inequities. People who can access OTC birth control should still have the option of supportive contraceptive counseling. ACOG has encouraged physicians to conduct such counseling with a reproductive justice framework—one that acknowledges historical and ongoing reproductive coercion and prioritizes the patient's values and lived experiences. The American

Pharmacists Association should encourage similar practices for pharmacists, who will play a key role in reproductive health care if the OTC pill is approved.

OTC birth control opens an important option for reproductive health care in the post-*Dobbs* era. But until we grapple with our past and present systems of reproductive coercion and their continuing effects on marginalized communities, the OTC pill will be unable to deliver on its promise of choice.

Print Citations

CMS: Tu, Lucy, and Jocelyn Viterna. "Opinion: Birth Control Access May Get Easier—Here's Why It's Not Enough." In *The Reference Shelf: Reproductive Rights*, edited by Micah L. Issitt, 91-94. Amenia, NY: Grey House Publishing, 2024.

MLA: Tu, Lucy, and Jocelyn Viterna. "Opinion: Birth Control Access May Get Easier—Here's Why It's Not Enough." *The Reference Shelf: Reproductive Rights*, edited by Micah L. Issitt, Grey House Publishing, 2024, pp. 91-94.

APA: Tu, L., & Viterna, J. (2024). Opinion: Birth control access may get easier—Here's why it's not enough. In M. L. Issitt (Ed.), *The reference shelf: Reproductive rights* (pp. 91-94). Amenia, NY: Grey House Publishing. (Original work published 2023)

Contraception in the United States: A Closer Look at Experiences, Preferences, and Coverage

By Brittni Frederiksen, Usha Rajni, Michelle Long, Karen Diep, and Alina Salganicoff

KFF, November 3, 2022

Contraceptive care is an important component of overall health care for many people. Federal and state policies shape access to and the availability of contraceptive care, but factors such as provider characteristics, as well as individual preferences and experiences also impact contraceptive choices and use. This report provides a close examination of reproductive age (18–49) females' (including those who identify as women and other genders) experiences with contraception, insurance coverage, contraceptive preferences, and interactions with the health care system based on an analysis of the 2022 *KFF* Women's Health Survey, a nationally representative survey of females ages 18 to 64 in the U.S.

Use of Contraceptives

The majority of females 18 to 64 (90%) have used contraception at some point in their reproductive years and many have used more than one contraceptive method throughout their lifetime (76%). People's needs and preferences for different types of methods can change and speaks to the importance of having a broad range of contraceptive options available. Not surprisingly, most people use contraception to prevent pregnancy (85%), but four in ten also say that they use contraception for another reason such as managing a medical condition or preventing a sexually transmitted infection (STI).

Not all people who want to prevent pregnancy use contraceptives. One in six (17%) sexually active females who say they are not trying to get pregnant are not using contraception. There are many reasons why people may not use contraceptives, ranging from concerns about side effects, lack of desire to use a method, to those who aren't trying but would not mind if they got pregnant or have religious reasons.

Credit line: From *KFF*, November 3 © 2022. Reprinted with permission. All rights reserved.

Contraceptive Coverage

Although the ACA has required contraceptive coverage for over a decade, many still do not know about the policy and some privately insured females are still paying for their contraceptives. Four in ten (41%) females of reproductive age do not know that most insurance plans are required to pay the full cost of birth control for women.

While most females (70%) with private insurance say their insurance covered the full cost of their most recent birth control method, a quarter say they paid at least part of the cost out-of-pocket. Of those who paid out of pocket, 16% say it was because they wanted a certain brand of contraception that was not covered by their plan (even though their plan should cover it if their provider recommends it for them). Others say it is because their prescribing provider (10%) or pharmacy (5%) was out of network. Half did not know why they had to pay.

Cost can be a barrier to contraceptive use for some. One in five uninsured females of reproductive age say they had to stop using a contraceptive method because they couldn't afford it. A smaller share of those on Medicaid (6%) or with private coverage (3%) cited cost as a barrier to continued use. For low-income women, 17% said cost was the leading reason they weren't using their preferred method.

Contraceptive Preferences and Side Effects

Overall, one quarter of females who are using contraception are not using their preferred method. The leading reason for this is concern about side effects, a theme that comes up in many aspects of contraceptive care. Almost one-third of contraceptive users (31%) say they are experiencing side effects from their current method, and just over half (52%) say the side effects are more severe than they expected.

Just 30% of females say they received all the information they needed before choosing their birth control method. This is even lower among Asian/Pacific Islander females, just 12% of whom say they had all the information they needed before choosing a method, compared to more than a quarter of Hispanic (26%) and Black (28%) females and one-third of White females (34%). Person-centered contraceptive counseling is a key element to assuring people can select the contraceptive method that suits them. However, only 40% of those receiving contraceptive care rate their most recent contraceptive counseling as "excellent."

Accessing Contraception

The majority of reproductive age females get their birth control care at a doctor's office (77%) and prefer to get their care there, even as more services have become available online with growing numbers of online contraception platforms. Many also rely on clinics and health centers for their care, particularly those who are low-income, uninsured, Black or Hispanic. Far fewer (7%) have received a prescription or obtained a health care service from an online company in the prior 12 months. Convenience is the main reason those who would prefer to get their birth control care from an online company cite for their preference.

The majority of females 18 to 64 (90%) have used contraception at some point in their reproductive years.

Emergency contraceptive pills (EC) are an effective form of back up birth control, but a sizable minority of people who might benefit from them don't know where to get them or that they're available over the counter. Emergency contraceptive pills, which can be taken to prevent pregnancy after a contraceptive failure or unprotected sex, have been available over the counter for more than 15 years. One in four reproductive age females (27%) either don't know EC pills are available over the counter or have never heard of them. Among those who have heard of EC pills and could become pregnant, three in ten (31%) don't know where they could get it.

Not only was there a lack of awareness about where to get emergency contraceptive pills, but even before the Supreme Court overturned *Roe v. Wade*, few knew where they could get an abortion if they needed one. Prior to the ruling in *Dobbs*, just one-quarter (26%) of females ages 18–49 said they knew what clinic or health care provider they could go to for an abortion if they wanted or needed one. Smaller shares of females living in rural areas, where services are more limited, knew where they could go to get an abortion compared to females living in more urban areas (16% vs. 28%).

Access to abortion and contraception continues to remain at the center of policy debates across the nation. Not only has abortion access been banned in many states, but access to effective methods to *prevent* pregnancy, like emergency contraceptive pills and long-acting reversible contraception (such as IUDs), may also become restricted. Doctors and health care providers are trusted sources of information for many people, which means they could play an important role in filling information gaps and addressing misinformation. While the ACA preventive services coverage requirement has markedly improved the affordability of contraceptives, the policy is being challenged yet again in the courts by those who object to preventive services such as contraception on religious or moral grounds. The outcomes of these debates, along with state, federal and private sector actions will continue to shape the availability and use of contraceptive care for millions in the years to come.

Print Citations

CMS: Frederiksen, Brittni, Usha Rajni, Michelle Long, Karen Diep, and Alina Salganicoff. "Contraception in the United States: A Closer Look at Experiences, Preferences, and Coverage." In *The Reference Shelf: Reproductive Rights,* edited by Micah L. Issitt, 95-98. Amenia, NY: Grey House Publishing, 2024.

MLA: Frederiksen, Brittni, et al. "Contraception in the United States: A Closer Look at Experiences, Preferences, and Coverage." *The Reference Shelf: Reproductive Rights,* edited by Micah L. Issitt, Grey House Publishing, 2024, pp. 95-98.

APA: Frederiksen, B., Rajni, U., Long, M., Diep, K., & Salganicoff, A. (2024). Contraception in the United States: A closer look at experiences, preferences, and coverage. In M. L. Issitt (Ed.), *The reference shelf: Reproductive rights* (pp. 95-98). Amenia, NY: Grey House Publishing. (Original work published 2022)

Emergency Contraception: Here's What You Probably Don't Know, but Should

By Cathryn Brown
The Conversation, August 31, 2023

Things don't always go to plan when it comes to sex. Sometimes condoms break (or are even forgotten altogether) and daily contraceptive pills can be missed. Whatever the reason, if you need to prevent an unplanned pregnancy you might decide to use emergency contraception.

There are three main options for emergency contraception: levonorgestrel tablets (known as Levonelle in the UK and Plan B in the US), ulipristal tablets (Ella-One in the UK and Ella in the US) and having a copper intra-uterine device (IUD—sometimes called the coil) fitted.

In the UK and US, you can get levonorgestrel and ulipristal from pharmacies. In UK pharmacies, there's typically no charge if it's offered as part of an NHS service. In other parts of the world, levonorgestrel is often easier to access than ulipristal. For emergency IUD fittings, you need to go to a contraceptive and sexual health clinic, or your GP or gynaecologist.

How Does It Work?

Although we often call emergency contraceptives "the morning-after pill," the hormonal pill options can be taken up to five days after unprotected sex. The IUD can sometimes be used even later.

Levonorgestrel and ulipristal both work by delaying ovulation. This means that if there are sperm inside the fallopian tubes, there won't be an egg for them to meet and fertilise.

Ulipristal is more effective when ovulation is expected within a day, as it can still delay the release of an egg even after the ovulation process has started (when levels of a hormone called luteinising hormone start to rise). Levonorgestrel can't delay ovulation once this starts.

In a typical menstrual cycle, you're most at risk of pregnancy on days nine to 14. But even if you're more than halfway through your typical monthly cycle, these tablets can still work. This is because you can't actually calculate when precisely ovulation has occurred until the next time your period arrives—so it's better to get help than spend time stressing at home.

Credit line: From *The Conversation*, August 31 © 2023. Reprinted with permission. All rights reserved.

The IUD works by making the environment within the uterus unfriendly to sperm, and so prevents the sperm fertilising an egg that may have been released. It can be inserted up to five days after the earliest date you could have ovulated. For example, if you usually have 28 day cycles, you could use this up to day 19 (18 days after the day your last period started).

> There's zero shame in using an emergency contraceptive if you need it.

It's important to note that all of these methods are contraceptives, and don't cause abortions. If you're already pregnant, these won't stop a pregnancy.

Emergency contraceptives also cannot protect against sexually transmitted infections (STIs) —so if you think you've been exposed to one, it's important to visit a sexual health service or your doctor.

How Effective Is It?

The IUD is over 99% effective at preventing pregnancy, even when used as an emergency contraceptive.

The coil can also be left in as a regular method of contraception afterwards.

While it's the most effective form of emergency contraception, it can be uncomfortable or even painful to have an IUD fitted. It's also somewhat less convenient than popping to a local pharmacy for a pill or using GP or online doctor services.

Ulipristal can be taken up to five days after unprotected sex. It's at least 95% effective at stopping pregnancies when taken within this time frame.

Levonorgestrel is 95% effective at preventing pregnancy if taken within 24 hours of unprotected sex. But this drops to 58% effectiveness if taken between two and three days after unprotected sex.

Depending on the point in your cycle when you had unprotected sex, ulipristal is often a better option. But both tablets are up to 95% effective at stopping pregnancies when taken soon after unprotected sex.

Levonorgestrel and ulipristal are preferably only taken once in each monthly cycle, as they are possibly less effective if used more than once. It's also important to continue with other forms of contraception, such as condoms or the contraceptive pill, until your next period arrives—ulipristal can reduce the effectiveness of some contraceptive pills, so speak to your healthcare provider about taking it.

In my practice as a community pharmacist, I always prefer to recommend ulipristal because of its longer period of effectiveness. It is more expensive though, and so sometimes it isn't always available as part of a free service. Both levonorgestrel and ulipristal are available without prescription in the UK.

Certain medical conditions (especially those affecting your gastrointestinal system, such as Crohn's) and medications (such as antiepileptic drugs) can affect how well the pills work. In this circumstance, it's worth speaking with a doctor about your options as an IUD may work better for you.

What Should You Expect?

Nausea and vomiting are the most common side effects from taking the morning-after pill. It may also cause your next period to begin earlier or later than normal. Some people have also reported headaches or dizziness.

The IUD can make periods heavier or more painful. This often subsides after three to six months if you have chosen to keep it in.

Ectopic pregnancy (when a fertilised egg implants in a fallopian tube) may be possible if emergency contraception fails. If you have lower stomach pain (even if your period arrives), it's important to seek immediate help as this can be very serious.

If your period is more than seven days late or is shorter or lighter than normal, you should take a pregnancy test to check the emergency contraception has worked.

There's zero shame in using an emergency contraceptive if you need it. Just remember it's less effective than regular forms of contraceptives, so only use it as a backup plan. It's also worth noting that emergency contraceptives have no effect on long-term fertility and can be used even if you plan to have children later on.

Print Citations

CMS: Brown, Cathryn. "Emergency Contraception: Here's What You Probably Don't Know, but Should." In *The Reference Shelf: Reproductive Rights,* edited by Micah L. Issitt, 99-101. Amenia, NY: Grey House Publishing, 2024.

MLA: Brown, Cathryn. "Emergency Contraception: Here's What You Probably Don't Know, but Should." *The Reference Shelf: Reproductive Rights,* edited by Micah L. Issitt, Grey House Publishing, 2024, pp. 99-101.

APA: Brown, C. (2024). Emergency contraception: Here's what you probably don't know, but should. In M. L. Issitt (Ed.), *The reference shelf: Reproductive rights* (pp. 99-101). Amenia, NY: Grey House Publishing. (Original work published 2023)

The GOP Doesn't Want to Talk About Abortion: Harris Wants to Make Them

By Megan Messerly and Alice Miranda Ollstein
Politico, July 24, 2024

Democrats for the last month have been too busy fighting over whether President Joe Biden should lead the ticket to keep voters' attention on abortion. Vice President Kamala Harris is trying to bring the focus back.

On Monday, Harris told campaign staff in Wilmington, Delaware, that she would prevent Republicans from enacting a national ban because "the government should not be telling a woman what to do with her body." On Tuesday, she concluded a rally in a Milwaukee suburb by promising to sign legislation that would "restore reproductive freedoms." And on Wednesday, the Harris campaign said it plans to counter former President Donald Trump's rally in Charlotte with an abortion-focused event in North Carolina featuring Hadley Duvall, a Kentucky woman who was raped by her stepfather when she was 12.

Democrats have made abortion rights a cornerstone of the 2024 campaign, but Biden's disastrous debate and a month's worth of questions over whether his campaign could continue sidelined the issue that the party has used to boost their electoral prospects since *Roe v. Wade* was overturned two years ago.

As Harris begins to delineate herself as a presumptive presidential nominee rather than Biden's running mate, she is leaning into abortion to mobilize voters as she builds out the rest of her policy platform.

"We who believe in reproductive freedom will stop Donald Trump's extreme abortion bans, because we trust women to make decisions about their own body and not have their government tell them what to do," Harris said at the Tuesday rally. "And when Congress passes a law to restore reproductive freedoms, as president of the United States I will sign it into law."

Trump has said abortion rights should be left to the states, attempting to neutralize Democrats' attacks. Abortion was barely mentioned at the Republican National Convention in Milwaukee last week, and the GOP recently removed calls for a national ban from its party platform. Harris, even before becoming the presumptive nominee, argued that Trump is responsible for every state abortion ban and owns the suffering of patients unable to access the procedure. And she has long been more comfortable than Biden talking about the issue, from using the word "abortion" when campaigning to becoming the first vice president to visit an abortion clinic in March.

Credit line: From *Politico*, July 24 © 2024. Reprinted with permission. All rights reserved.

"Having her at the top of the ticket, with her proven record, with her authenticity on this issue, with her passion and with her prosecutorial skills, going after the guy—the criminal—who's responsible for this crisis, it's already so energizing," said Mini Timmaraju, the president of Reproductive Freedom for All, which endorsed Harris on Sunday. "It's going to make sure this issue is front and center for the election, as it should be, because it's the top persuasion issue of this election."

> **Harris told campaign staff that she would prevent Republicans from enacting a national ban.**

Reproductive Freedom For All launched its first TV and digital ad in support of Harris this week, which features a clip of the candidate talking about voters' power to push back against abortion bans. The six-figure ad buy, shared exclusively with *Politico*, is part of the group's planned $2 million campaign targeting voters under 35 and people of color.

Both abortion-rights and anti-abortion groups say they are eager to have Harris bring the topic back into the spotlight and force GOP candidates to respond.

While abortion-rights groups expect Harris to pursue more progressive policies on abortion than Biden, she so far only pledged to sign legislation protecting "reproductive freedoms," without providing further detail. Her campaign did not respond to a request for comment seeking clarification.

Anti-abortion groups that have long been frustrated at Republicans' post-*Roe* position on abortion are equally enthused by Harris' elevation to the top of the Democratic ticket. They believe they can use her record of aggressive action on reproductive rights—as an attorney general, senator and vice president—to paint her as extreme in a way that they couldn't with Biden.

"We find Kamala to be a larger threat to the life cause than Joe Biden," said John Mize, president of Americans United for Life. "In a perverse way, it gives the pro-life movement a bit more juice, or a bit more energy, to combat the radical agenda."

Kelsey Pritchard, director of state public affairs for Susan B. Anthony Pro-Life America, said the organization plans to highlight Harris' role as "Biden's abortion czar"—including her nationwide reproductive rights tour—as part of its $92 million campaign across battleground states and those with abortion-rights measures on their ballots.

Some anti-abortion activists frustrated by many Republicans' avoidance of the issue after the fall of *Roe v. Wade*, and particularly with the issue's near-total absence at the recent Republican National Convention in Milwaukee, said they expected Harris' candidacy to pressure Republican candidates to more directly articulate where they stand.

"There's going to be hundreds of millions of dollars spent on abortion advertising. So does the GOP intend to say nothing?" said Kristi Hamrick, the chief policy strategist for Students for Life of America. "The Republicans are going to need to answer. They're going to need to be fearless. They're going to need to be ready."

But abortion-rights proponents in states where protections for the procedure are or could be on the ballot believe they will see the opposite effect. Voters who were unimpressed by Biden, they hope, will be energized and excited by Harris' candidacy and buoy ballot measures in states like Nebraska.

"She's a better messenger than Biden on abortion. When you hear Biden talk about abortion you get the impression that he is not actually a supporter of abortion rights," said Nebraska state Sen. Megan Hunt, an independent. "We need a candidate who can speak soberly and seriously and just say like, 'What the f*** are we doing, what the hell are we doing in this country that this has become so normalized?'"

Some strategists, however, are unconvinced that Harris' candidacy will change the underlying dynamics of the race, arguing that Biden had already made abortion rights a pillar of his reelection campaign and most voters who care about the issue have made up their minds.

"Abortion politics is already baked into the 2024 presidential sweepstakes, and that does not change because Kamala Harris may lead the ticket," said Stan Barnes, a political consultant and former GOP state representative from Arizona. "Those who care most ardently about that topic and want to vote their conscience already know what they're doing. It's not going to move the needle."

Print Citations

CMS: Messerly, Megan, and Alice Miranda Ollstein. "The GOP Doesn't Want to Talk About Abortion: Harris Wants to Make Them." In *The Reference Shelf: Reproductive Rights,* edited by Micah L. Issitt, 102-104. Amenia, NY: Grey House Publishing, 2024.

MLA: Messerly, Megan, and Alice Miranda Ollstein. "The GOP Doesn't Want to Talk About Abortion: Harris Wants to Make Them." *The Reference Shelf: Reproductive Rights,* edited by Micah L. Issitt, Grey House Publishing, 2024, pp. 102-104.

APA: Messerly, M., & Ollstein, A. M. (2024). The GOP doesn't want to talk about abortion: Harris wants to make them. In M. L. Issitt (Ed.), *The Reference Shelf: Reproductive rights* (pp. 102-104). Amenia, NY: Grey House Publishing. (Original work published 2024)

4
Assisted Reproduction

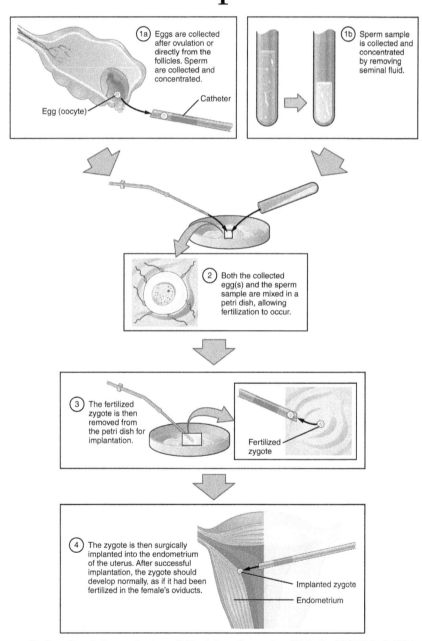

A diagram of IVF treatment.

Fertility Treatments in the United States

Writing about infertility for the United States Conference of Catholic Bishops, John M. Haas writes:

> Husbands and wives "make love," they do not "make babies." They give expression to their love for one another, and a child may or may not be engendered by that act of love. The marital act is not a manufacturing process, and children are not products. Like the Son of God himself, we are the kind of beings who are "begotten, not made" and, therefore, of equal status and dignity with our parents.
>
> In IVF, children are engendered through a technical process, subjected to "quality control," and eliminated if found "defective."[1]

This reflects the broad thinking on in vitro fertilization, or IVF, a treatment method designed to help those who are struggling to conceive and carry children, to succeed in this process. IVF involves the purposeful creation and harvesting of eggs and the creation of embryos and, for this reason, some see the process as unnatural or even as a usurpation of a role that magic and divine intervention is supposed to play in human lives. Others believe that the necessary destruction of embryos, in a very early stage of development, nonetheless means that IVF is akin to abortion and so object to the process as a form of killing.

Recent changes in the American political system have given increased power to a minority of ultraconservative Americans who seek to restore traditionalist Christian culture through a variety of means. One of these methods, is to place more stringent controls on female reproduction and to eliminate access to reproductive technologies that do not fit with their vision of traditionalist conservative sexuality and reproduction. Because this minority now holds outsized power, thanks to the Republican Party's lack of broader social capital and dependence on the support of far-right fringe groups, IVF, contraception, and many others "unnatural" forms of family planning are now under threat.

Childlessness in America

Much of human culture centers around having and raising children, about the experience of childbirth, parenthood, and the trials and tribulations of growth and maturity, both from the perspective of the children and from the perspective of parents trying to guide children through those stages of their lives. The stories and myths that undergird many human cultures present having children as the endpoint of the story, treating this aspect of life as the ultimate goal for every human and the ultimate triumph for every romance and love story. This is true of many different ancient myths and is still reflected in our modern myths, like how sitcom love stories so often end with the "will-they-wont-they" couple having children. The act is seen as drawing completion to a romance, representing their shared commitment to one another and ending the first act of their lives as they embark together on the next: parenthood.

Reproduction is a central drive for every kind of animal and though we cannot know how nonhuman animals feel about this aspect of their lives, for human men and women who find themselves unable to have children, the experience can be devastating, both emotionally and culturally. Both women and men who don't have children may be subject to cultural and social isolation and may feel excluded from many aspects of life in their communities, and among their circle of friends. Prejudiced and cruel people utilize childlessness to belittle others, to make them feel lesser and less important. Consider white potential vice president of the United States chose to say to criticize presidential hopeful Kamala Harris,

> We're effectively run in this country, via the Democrats, via our corporate oligarchs, by a bunch of childless cat ladies who are miserable at their own lives and the choices that they've made, and so they want to make the rest of the country miserable, too. And it's just a basic fact. You look at Kamala Harris, Pete Buttigieg, AOC—the entire future of the Democrats is controlled by people without children.[2]

Kamala Harris has two stepchildren, and Pete Buttigieg has adopted children, which means that Vance apparently does not consider either adoption or stepparenting to count as "real" parenting. Alexandria Ocasio-Cortez became engaged to web developer Riley Roberts in 2022, so it remains to be seen whether or not the representative will attempt to have children in the future. The assertion that childless people are less fit to lead, have less interest in their world, or should have a diminished role in shaping their society is demonstrably ignorant, prejudiced, and self-centered and has no logical or empirical defense. Vance presents himself as a promoter of family, but actually uses this issue to advance himself, equating the biological state of fatherhood with social superiority. Vance even takes this idea further, suggesting that persons who have children should perhaps be afforded "more votes" in elections than those who do not have children. In 2021 Vance stated, "When you go to the polls in this country as a parent, you should have more power. You should have more of an ability to speak your voice in a democratic republic than people who don't have kids."

This does not reflect Vance's love of children, of course, but reflects his embrace of a patriarchic, cis-gender, heterosexual ideal in which children are born to married couples, and the woman does not work outside the home. This is reflected in Vance's support for eliminating a requirement for employers to partially fund maternity leave for working mothers and when doing so, specifically said that he did not support this for working "mothers," not "parents."

Prejudiced and self-serving ideologues like Vance demonstrate the way that childless persons are discriminated against in the United States and excluded from central aspects of American life, even to the point of being classed as lesser citizens by extremists like J. D. Vance and allies. Like many other issues in the reproductive rights debate, this comes down to the embrace of a traditionalist model of Christian family, which is itself, rooted in the patriarchic traditions of Christianity and in the reproductive contests for power that existed at the dawn of Christianity.

All of this also demonstrates the tremendous pressure that Americans experience to "become parents" and how this act, unachievable for some, can even define whether or not the person will be seen as a full member of their society or an outcast. Given this pressure, medical science has invested heavily in technologies to help those who want to have children but face biological difficulties, to achieve this goal. Among the most extreme types of technology in this vein is the science of IVF.

IVF Primer

Infertility refers to a disorder in which a person has been trying to conceive for twelve months or more with no success. The IVF process is one of the ways that scientists have found to try and combat biological issues that get in the way of successful conception. The process basically has five steps:

> First, a females egg production is accelerated and enhanced through stimulation or "superovulation," which typically involves injecting follicle stimulating hormone (FSH). This causes the woman's body to produce more eggs each cycle, which means more chances of successful fertilization. Ultrasounds are used to check the female's ovaries during this process.
>
> Second, a hormone injection is given that helps the eggs to mature more quickly, and then the eggs are removed in a minor surgical procedure known as "follicular aspiration," in which the eggs are "sucked" into a syringe.
>
> Third, sperm is collected from a partner or donor and these sperm are then washed and spun to retrieve only the healthiest sperm.
>
> Fourth, the specialists combine the best sperm from the sample with the most developed eggs. This can be done simply by letting the sperm and egg interact, or sperm can be injected directly into the egg in a process known as "intracytoplasmic sperm injection."
>
> Fifth, embryos are transferred into the uterus of the female, along with medications that help to prepare the lining of the uterus to property associate with the developing embryo.[3]

IVF is controversial for several reasons. During the process embryos are typically discarded. In some cases, embryos are discarded because they show chromosomal anomalies that would lead to development problems, or because they are not viable and show signs of deterioration. In other cases, embryos are discarded simply because they are not needed.[4]

It must be noted that embryos at the stage at which they are used for IVF are merely a collection of cells with the *potential* to develop into a being, they are not, by themselves, living beings. Each cell in the body of an organism is living, but not independent. A neuron in the brain is a living thing, but it is not a being, it does not function without being incorporated into a brain, in conjunction with other cells. Likewise, the embryos used in IVF are not beings, because an embryo does not create a child. An embryo is a collection of cells that can be used to make a child, but it is not the cells that become the child, but the body that makes those cells into a child. The body provides the hormones, nutrients, and other materials needed by those cells to make something. Without the body, the cells are merely tissue. In other words, the process of conception is a process in which a person uses their body along with cells from an external source, to build a being. This process requires the person to give cells from her body to the developing embryo, and this is what allows it to grow. The embryo does not do this on its own, or simply by virtue of its being a special set of cells called an "embryo," it does this as a function of the body.

It is further important to note that the formation of an embryo does not guarantee development into a fetus, even when the right conditions are provided. Many embryos fail at various stages of development and few embryos can be used, by the body, to create a surviving fetus. Rather than being a chance at a child, therefore, embryos at the stage at which they are harvested for use in IVF might be seen as a chance to create a fetus, which then is a chance at creating a child.

Therefore, the tissues involved in IVF cannot be factually classified, on the medical or biological level, as "fetuses" or as "children." Despite the complete lack of medical or biological data to justify the position, the Alabama Supreme Court ruled, in 2024, that frozen embryos can be considered "children" under state law. The decision immediately sparked intense medical and scientific criticism, citing the extreme ideological bias that was needed to motivate such a position, but also meant that many IVF clinics in the state ceased operations. If embryos are considered children, IVF cannot be effectively conducted, because the IVF process in which physicians are forced to use every potentially viable embryo is unsustainable. Writing in the *Washington Post*, Monica Hesse stated, "Embryos are vessels of hope, pain and love. But they are not children."[5]

Empiricism versus Metaphysics

The belief that, as members of the Alabama court ruled, that "embryos are children waiting to be born," is not medically or biologically sound, any more than it would be appropriate to say that a sperm cell or a female oocyte is a person, but therein lies the difficulty in approaching this issue in American society. The Alabama Supreme Court is not operating on empirical data and is not adopting defensible positions that can be debated in a contest of data and information, but is operating from a metaphysical belief that all parts of the reproductive process are divine and constitute personhood. The demarcation, between life and nonlife, or between person and nonperson, is therefore not rooted in our understanding of life as a biological process, but in the belief that supernatural forces dictate aspects of our lives, including the process of reproduction and development.

Those who have embraced this view of the world, as one shaped by supernatural forces beyond their full comprehension, but which they must honor in whatever way they see as appropriate, the process of reproduction is a divine one. Critics of assisted reproduction techniques like IVF have argued that it is immoral to eliminate genetic abnormalities, or to discard potentially dysfunctional embryos and argue that these are aspects of birth and life that are the exclusive purview of a god or, at least, should be shaped by supernatural influence. From this perspective, it is easy to see why so many Americans would not share this view.

First, some Americans are not religious and do not see reproduction as a miraculous or supernatural process in any way shape or form. Second, some Americans who are religious are not Christian, and so do not embrace the particular approach to the spiritual conception of reproduction that has become common among certain facets of Christianity. Third, many Americans who *are* Christian still do not conceive of the reproductive process in such a way that human intervention is considered immoral or inappropriate. Fourth, even some Americans who have been raised in Christian traditions that oppose things like abortion or IVF still choose to utilize these technologies, prioritizing other aspects of their lives or well-being over this adherence to Christian fundamentalism.

Members of the Roman Catholic faith have long been the stalwarts in the promotion of the traditionalist view of gender roles and reproduction. Over the years, the Catholic church has officially been *against* IVF treatments for two main reasons. First, the church argues that "procreation is intrinsic to the physical union of the couple," and thus that the intervention of medicine interferes what "should be" a natural process. Second, because IVF involves discarding unused embryos, the church objects. However, Catholic officials have not, as members of the extremist Alabama Supreme Court have recently done, classify these embryos as children. Instead the Catholic church looks upon these embryos as having, "the promise of life that develops into a child."[6] Despite these long objections and outright prohibitions, a Pew Research Survey in 2023 found that 55 percent, over half, either used IVF or knew someone who had. A far back as 2013, only 12 percent of Catholics said that using IVF was "morally wrong," and this percentage has continued to fall in the years since.[7]

So, how do the American people, as a whole, view IVF and other forms of assisted reproduction? A May 2024 survey from Pew Research Center found that 70 percent of Americans feel that access to IVF is a good thing. A further 22 percent were not sure, which is unsurprising given how little many people know about and understand the IVF process. The percentage of people who felt that IVF was a "bad thing" was around 8 percent. Catholics and white evangelicals were more likely to say that access to IVF was a bad thing, with 9 percent of white evangelicals and 8 percent of Catholics voicing this view. Even among these groups, however, the view was at best fringe, if not outright extremist. Among white evangelical protestants, a full 63 percent said that IVF was a "good thing" and among Catholics, 65 percent approved.[8] Studies show further that a dominant majority of Americans (67 percent) even believe that health insurance plans should be *required* to provide IVF coverage, with only 7 percent opposed.[9]

Repeated surveys and studies show that Americans would prioritize allowing their fellow Americans to utilize technology to achieve parenthood, rather than prioritizing the well-being of cells with the potential to be used to create beings. While not as high as support for contraception, which some ultraconservatives also see as interfering with divine dictates, the public support for IVF indicates that any law prohibiting the process, such as those that might emerge after the Alabama Supreme Court's extremist ruling, would not be embraced by the public. This, however, might not matter. The future of assisted reproduction, like many aspects of the reproductive debate, is not a top priority for many voters. Voters who support Donald Trump, for whatever reason, will empower extremist views on reproduction held by a small minority, but given increased power because Trump and like-minded politicians are dependent on these ultraconservative groups and, without them, would be unable to win elections. This makes the 7 to 8 percent of Americans who think that IVF is morally wrong, in many ways more influential than the nearly 70 percent who feel that access to IVF is an important aid to individuals, couples, and families seeking to experience the process of parenthood.

Works Used

"Abortion Viewed in Moral Terms: Fewer See Stem Cell Research and IVF as Moral Issues." *Pew Research Center*, 15 Aug. 2013, www.pewresearch.org/religion/2013/08/15/abortion-viewed-in-moral-terms/#:~:text=is%20morally%20acceptabl[...]tion,-https://www.pewresearch.org/short-reads/2024/05/13/americans-overwhelmingly-say-access-to-ivf-is-a-good-thing/For%20comparison%20purposes.

Borelli, Gabriel. "Americans Overwhelmingly Say Access to IVF Is a Good Thing." *Pew Research Center*, 13 May 2024, www.pewresearch.org/short-reads/2024/05/13/americans-overwhelmingly-say-access-to-ivf-is-a-good-thing/.

Caldwell, Noah, Katia Riddle, and Ailsa Chang. "The Family Politics Behind J. D. Vance's 'Childless Cat Ladies' Comment." *NPR*, 25 July 2024, www.npr.org/2024/07/25/nx-s1-5051873/the-family-politics-behind-j-d-vances-childless-cat-ladies-comment.

DeRose, Jason. "Despite Church Prohibitions, Catholics Still Choose IVF to Have Children." *NPR*, 22 Mar. 2024, www.npr.org/2024/03/22/1239879602/despite-church-prohibitions-catholics-still-choose-ivf-to-have-children.

Haas, John M. "Begotten Not Made: A Catholic View of Reproductive Technology." *United States Conference of Catholic Bishops*, www.usccb.org/issues-and-action/human-life-and-dignity/reproductive-technology/begotten-not-made-a-catholic-view-of-reproductive-technology.

Hesse, Monica. "Embryos Are Vessels of Hope, Pain and Love: But They Are Not Children." *Washington Post*, 21 Feb. 2024, www.washingtonpost.com/style/power/2024/02/21/embryos-alabama-supreme-court-ruling/.

Robertson, Rachael. "Why Discarding Embryos Is Inherent to the IVF Process." *Medpage Today*, 28 Feb. 2024, www.medpagetoday.com/obgyn/infertility/108932.

"A Step-By-Step Look at the IVF Process." *Penn Medicine*, 20 Apr. 2020, www.pennmedicine.org/updates/blogs/fertility-blog/2020/april/how-does-the-ivf-process-work.

"Survey Shows Strong Support for Increased Access to Fertility Treatments." *American Society for Reproductive Medicine (ASRM)*, 23 Apr. 2024, www.asrm.org/news-and-events/asrm-news/press-releasesbulletins/survey-shows-strong-support-fertility/.

Notes

1. Haas, "Begotten Not Made: A Catholic View of Reproductive Technology."
2. Caldwell, Riddle, and Chang, "The Family Politics Behind J. D. Vance's 'Childless Cat Ladies' Comment."
3. "A Step-By-Step Look at the IVF Process," *Penn Medicine*.
4. Robertson, "Why Discarding Embryos Is Inherent to the IVF Process."
5. Hesse, "Embryos Are Vessels of Hope, Pain and Love: But They Are Not Children."
6. DeRose, "Despite Church Prohibitions, Catholics Still Choose IVF to Have Children."
7. "Abortion Viewed in Moral Terms: Fewer See Stem Cell Research and IVF as Moral Issues," *Pew Research Center*.
8. Borelli, "Americans Overwhelmingly Say Access to IVF Is a Good Thing."
9. "Survey Shows Strong Support for Increased Access to Fertility Treatments," *American Society for Reproductive Medicine (ASRM)*.

Why the Southern Baptists' Vote Opposing IVF Could Change National Politics

By Megan Messerly
Politico, June 12, 2024

INDIANAPOLIS—The Southern Baptist Convention, the nation's largest and most politically powerful Protestant denomination, voted Wednesday to oppose in vitro fertilization.

The move may signal the beginning of a broad turn on the right against IVF, an issue that many evangelicals, anti-abortion advocates and other social conservatives see as the "pro-life" movement's next frontier—one they hope will eventually lead to restrictions, or outright bans, on IVF at the state and federal levels.

The vote comes as Democrats in Washington, hoping to drive a wedge among Republicans, prepare to hold a vote on legislation to protect IVF, while former President Donald Trump struggles with how to message to evangelicals on abortion and other reproductive health issues that they would like to see him take stronger positions on in the post-*Roe* era.

IVF has come under increasing scrutiny since the Supreme Court's *Dobbs* decision two years ago. Many on the right have begun to question whether the practice, which often discards fertilized eggs, is at odds with their beliefs on when life begins, even as it is relied upon by millions of Americans to grow their families and is supported by the overwhelming majority of evangelicals.

"It's going to be a long process. It took us 50 years to take down *Roe*," said Brent Leatherwood, president of the Ethics and Religious Liberty Commission, the public policy arm of the SBC. "It may take us a similarly long time frame to get people to a place where they are thinking more deeply about something like this. It's okay. It takes time. We have to be patient."

The resolution, which was passed by nearly 11,000 so-called messengers to the Southern Baptist Convention's annual meeting, declares that IVF "most often participates in the destruction of embryonic human life" and calls on Southern Baptists to adopt and "only utilize reproductive technologies" that affirm "the unconditional value and right to life of every human being."

Though the resolution is nonbinding, nearly 13 million Southern Baptists across 45,000 churches may now face pressure from the pulpit or in individual conversations with pastors to eschew IVF.

While Catholics have long opposed IVF, many Protestant denominations have largely ignored it even as they have preached on the sanctity of life as it relates to

---

Credit line: From *Politico*, June 12 © 2024. Reprinted with permission. All rights reserved.

abortion. That is starting to change in the wake of the Alabama Supreme Court's decision in February that ruled that frozen embryos created during the IVF process should have full personhood rights.

The Southern Baptists' Wednesday vote could encourage other evangelical denominations and churches to follow suit in declaring—or at least teaching about—their ethical concerns with IVF.

"This is a very powerful faith group," said Christa Brown, an advocate for reform within the denomination as it relates to sexual assault and women's issues. "They have huge influence not only because of their own numbers but because they're a bellwether for all of white evangelicalism."

The IVF conversation has put Republicans in an uncomfortable position as they stare down polling showing overwhelming popular support for IVF. A CBS News/YouGov poll earlier this year found that 86 percent of respondents thought IVF should be legal, and a survey released in December by a firm run by Kellyanne Conway, former President Donald Trump's former senior counselor and campaign manager, found that IVF had 78 percent support among self-identified "pro-life advocates" and 83 percent among evangelical Christians.

The Alabama high court's decision forced many evangelicals to for the first time think deeply about the ethical implications of the procedure, which as commonly practiced in the U.S. results in the destruction of excess embryos. Doctors create extra embryos to ensure the best chance of a successful pregnancy. The leftover embryos are frozen, destroyed or donated to medical research.

Many evangelicals are now coming around to the fact that their conviction that life begins at conception must be applied to IVF, too. If abortion is murder, the destruction of viable embryos created during the IVF process is as well.

"I know friends—fellow believers—that have struggled with fertility issues," said Katie Royce, a member of Birchman Baptist Church in Fort Worth, Texas. "It does pain my heart to see them not just invest so much money into IVF because they want to have a natural-born baby of their own, but it breaks my heart because I think, well, have you done all the research behind it? Or did you just cock the gun and pull the trigger?"

Some Republicans in Washington have responded to the IVF discourse by signing onto legislation creating broad federal protections for IVF or introducing their own bills to expand access to the procedure. Last month, Sen. Ted Crux (R-Texas), a Southern Baptist, and Katie Britt (R-Ala.) introduced legislation to strip Medicaid funding from any state that bans IVF, a proposal the Ethics and Religious Liberty Commission resoundingly condemned in a recent letter.

Albert Mohler, a prominent evangelical theologian, president of the Southern Baptist Theological Seminary and one of the two people who submitted the IVF resolution for consideration, said Republican elected officials need to do better.

"I'm very frustrated. A lot of them are responding out of political expediency, not out of moral principle. You can't say on one hand life begins at fertilization and then on the other hand say but now we're not so concerned about that in this other arena," Mohler said. "I find the initiatives and legislation to be deeply troubling and I think they reveal a lack of seriousness on the part of many social conservatives."

Mohler and Andrew Walker, an ethics professor at Southern Baptist Theological Seminary, have long advocated on the IVF issue. But they said the Alabama Supreme Court decision created an opportunity for a wider conversation about the practice within the denomination.

> **Many evangelicals are now coming around to the fact that their conviction that life begins at conception must be applied to IVF, too.**

"Do I think this means that Southern Baptist couples will never ever pursue IVF again? No, I don't think that's the case," Walker said. "I think that this is a very helpful point in time brought about by national circumstances that is allowing us to make an initial but very important statement on IVF."

Still, the issue can be hard for Republicans who want to tout their "pro-life" credentials but not alienate the vast majority of their constituents who accept IVF as a common way to bring life into the world. Even House Speaker Mike Johnson, a Southern Baptist and former ERLC trustee, has struggled with how to talk about the issue. He has publicly underscored his support for IVF while declining to weigh in on whether the destruction of unused embryos is murder.

"We've seen many politicians come out in support of IVF, and the messaging often clearly is, we want to support families in expanding and growing their families. We want to say 'yes and amen' to that, but not by any means possible," said Jason Thacker, a senior fellow and director of the research institute at the ERLC. "We have to consider the ethical implications and realities of these technologies and making sure that we're valuing human life even in the embryonic stage."

As evangelicals become more educated on the issue, they are largely falling into two camps: those who believe that IVF can be practiced ethically if no embryos are destroyed, and those who like Mohler and Walker believe IVF is inherently unethical because it separates conception from the act of sex between husband and wife. Walker, acknowledging the former view, noted the resolution was "drafted to pass."

A last-minute amendment sought to make clear that IVF is permissible in some circumstances, but failed.

The vote followed emotional testimony from an Ohio man, Zach Sahadak, who said his son was conceived through IVF and his wife is pregnant with another IVF child. They have 10 more embryos in cold storage.

"I am for the sanctity of life and the sanctity of embryos," Sahadak said. "I am against the idea that this technology is so wicked that it cannot be employed."

Throughout the week, Southern Baptists were grappling with whether they agreed.

Erick Sessions, a pastor at Graceland Church in New Albany, Indiana, and his wife struggled to conceive for seven years but decided against IVF because of ethical concerns and opted instead to foster children. Nearly 15 years later, they have four adopted and five naturally conceived children.

"Anytime you get outside of the normal means within which procreation occurs, the more foreign you get or the more alien you get from that, the more you have to consider its moral implications," Sessions said. "When you divorce it now from the actual physical act of sex, and you put it into a laboratory, it just becomes further and further away from the normal means within the natural world of procreation."

But he said he is unsure whether his congregation is ready to hear about IVF from the pulpit. One of the pastors at his church, he said, has had a child through IVF.

Karen Patrick, whose husband is senior pastor at First Baptist Church of Sylacauga, Alabama, said she had conversations with friends immediately after the state Supreme Court decision forced many families to pause the IVF process as the Legislature scrambled to pass a bill that would allow procedures to resume in the state. Patrick said there was "a lot of confusion" about IVF in the women's study group she leads at church.

"I had conversations just immediately after that with some friends who were struggling with how this decision impacted people that they knew personally, whose process of IVF had been put on hold and not knowing what was going to happen with that, and just trying to help people think through that while being sympathetic to those who were very much wanting to have children," Patrick said. "Until recently, I didn't really think through that deeply either."

Her husband, Rick, said Monday that he planned to support the IVF resolution. Though he said he normally preaches on abortion, not IVF, he said he's gotten more questions on the latter from congregants in advance of this week's meeting.

"I'm sensitive to the couple that wants to have a child. Certainly you want to help them. It's just disheartening. The bottom line is, life begins at conception and I firmly believe it does. The way we would do any kind of IVF, we need to not produce the additional fertilized eggs that are going to assuredly be destroyed," he said. "That is just unconscionable that we would kill those lives. We don't want murder, to murder those human beings."

For Kelsey Melvin, who attends International Baptist Church in Arlington, Texas, it's personal. She and her husband are deciding whether to move forward with IVF; if they do, they plan to have as many children as viable embryos are created.

Melvin, after hearing Mohler speak to the Danbury Institute, a Christian advocacy organization, on Monday, said she appreciated his tone and his tenor.

"I just disagree with him on this particular issue," she said. "We're pro-life, and I feel like that is another way that we can be pro-life. I believe it is a way that God has given us to have children."

Print Citations

CMS: Messerly, Megan. "Why the Southern Baptists' Vote Opposing IVF Could Change National Politics." In *The Reference Shelf: Reproductive Rights,* edited by Micah L. Issitt, 114-118. Amenia, NY: Grey House Publishing, 2024.

MLA: Messerly, Megan. "Why the Southern Baptists' Vote Opposing IVF Could Change National Politics." *The Reference Shelf: Reproductive Rights,* edited by Micah L. Issitt, Grey House Publishing, 2024, pp. 114-118.

APA: Messerly, M. (2024). Why the Southern Baptists' vote opposing IVF could change national politics. In M. L. Issitt (Ed.), *The reference shelf: Reproductive rights* (pp. 114-118). Amenia, NY: Grey House Publishing. (Original work published 2024)

Alabama Ruling Frozen Embryos Are Equivalent to Living Children Has Worrying Implications for IVF

By Alex Polyakov
The Conversation, February 26, 2024

In December 2020 in Alabama, a hospital patient gained unauthorised access to an adjoining IVF storage facility, which was not adequately secured. The patient is said to have removed several frozen embryos, which they then dropped on the floor, owing to a freeze-burn to their hand. The embryos were destroyed.

In Alabama, the Wrongful Death of a Minor Act allows parents of a deceased child to recover punitive damages for their child's death, and three couples affected by the incident subsequently brought lawsuits against the clinic under this legislation.

When this case was heard recently in the Supreme Court of Alabama, the majority of justices opined this statute applies to frozen embryos because: *an unborn child is a genetically unique human being whose life begins at fertilization and ends at death.*

This essentially means frozen embryos are protected under Alabama law to the same extent as any living child. While this was a civil matter, it's not inconceivable that, based on this interpretation, anyone who destroys a frozen embryo in Alabama—accidentally or on purpose—could face criminal penalties, such as manslaughter or even murder charges.

Likely for fear it's too risky, clinics in the state are now limiting their IVF services, leaving patients having to seek treatment elsewhere.

Ascribing personhood to frozen embryos is not a novel idea, but such a conviction is held only by the very fringes of the religious and conservative spectrum. There are clear political dimensions to this ruling, which appears to be an extension of a radical agenda on the altar of which the Supreme Court of the United States recently sacrificed the right to abortion.

This ruling from the Supreme Court of Alabama reflects a profound ignorance about how the process of IVF works.

Creating Multiple Embryos Is Essential for Overall IVF Success

The process of in vitro fertilisation, or IVF, begins with a "stimulated" cycle, where hormones are injected into a woman to stimulate an ovary to produce multiple eggs.

Credit line: From *The Conversation*, February 26 © 2024. Reprinted with permission. All rights reserved.

These eggs are then collected and combined with sperm, forming embryos that are placed in an incubator to grow.

Five days later, the embryos are assessed. Some develop into "good quality" embryos suitable for transfer into a woman's uterus. The hope is that following the transfer, the embryo will implant

> **Anyone who destroys a frozen embryo in Alabama—accidentally or on purpose—could face criminal penalties.**

and result in a viable pregnancy, ultimately leading to the birth of a healthy child. Any good-quality embryos not used in a stimulated cycle are usually frozen for future attempts.

Unfortunately, IVF is somewhat inefficient, with attrition a prominent feature at every stage. Not all collected eggs are suitable for fertilisation, not all fertilise, not all embryos fertilise normally, and not all normally-fertilised embryos are of good quality. Poor-quality eggs, abnormally-fertilised embryos and poor-quality embryos are routinely discarded.

The practical implications of this process and the heartbreaking reality for individuals and couples undergoing IVF is that it takes, on average, three to five eggs to produce one good-quality embryo. However, this number is age-dependent and significantly higher for older women.

The chance of achieving pregnancy from one embryo transfer is also significantly influenced by the woman's age, being as high as 50% in younger women but decreasing exponentially as a woman gets older. At the age of 46, it can be as low as 1–2%.

So it's vital to be able to safely produce as many good-quality embryos as possible from one stimulated IVF cycle in case multiple sequential embryo transfers are needed to achieve a healthy pregnancy.

Should the initial embryo transfer fail to produce a viable pregnancy, and frozen embryos are available, those can be thawed and transferred into a woman's uterus in a "thaw" cycle. These cycles usually don't require the use of injectable hormones or an egg collection and, in most instances, require only monitoring (including ultrasounds and blood tests), and timed embryo transfer.

The risks associated with IVF, such as bleeding and infections, are mostly confined to the stimulated cycles, while thaw cycles pose minimal risk. Notably, the most labour-intensive, and, therefore, costly portion is the stimulated cycle, while a thaw cycle can be around three to four times cheaper.

Should embryo freezing become unavailable, all people undergoing IVF would have to rely solely on stimulated cycles to achieve pregnancy, significantly increasing the risks and radically escalating the costs.

The Judge's Error in Interpreting Australian Practice

Tom Parker, the Chief Justice of the Supreme Court of Alabama, made the following statement in his judgement: *in Australia and New Zealand, prevailing ethical standards dictate that physicians usually create only one embryo at a time.*

He implied that in Australia, the only IVF cycles ethically permitted are stimulated cycles, where just one embryo is created and transferred, with no embryos being frozen.

However, this assertion is demonstrably false. There are no guidelines or regulations in Australia that discourage the creation of multiple embryos, as this practice enhances overall pregnancy rates, while making IVF safer and more cost-effective.

What is discouraged is the *transfer* of multiple embryos at one time, as this increases the likelihood of multiple births, which carry heightened medical risks for both mothers and babies.

It seems the Chief Justice has fundamentally misunderstood the Australian regulatory framework. Ironically, the excellent IVF outcomes and very low rates of multiple births in Australia are largely attributable to the widespread use of frozen embryo transfer cycles—a practice now under threat in Alabama.

Print Citations

CMS: Polyakov, Alex. "Alabama Ruling Frozen Embryos Are Equivalent to Living Children Has Worrying Implications for IVF." In *The Reference Shelf: Reproductive Rights*, edited by Micah L. Issitt, 119-121. Amenia, NY: Grey House Publishing, 2024.

MLA: Polyakov, Alex. "Alabama Ruling Frozen Embryos Are Equivalent to Living Children Has Worrying Implications for IVF." *The Reference Shelf: Reproductive Rights*, edited by Micah L. Issitt, Grey House Publishing, 2024, pp. 119-121.

APA: Polyakov, A. (2024). Alabama ruling frozen embryos are equivalent to living children has worrying implications for IVF. In M. L. Issitt (Ed.), *The reference shelf: Reproductive rights* (pp. 119-121). Amenia, NY: Grey House Publishing. (Original work published 2024)

Republicans Can't Be Trusted to Protect IVF

By Sarah Jones
New York Magazine, February 29, 2024

When the Alabama Supreme Court ruled that frozen embryos are children, it threatened hopeful parents across the state. Several clinics have now paused IVF treatments while they consider the legal implications of the ruling. "We were at the doctor's office when the doctors and the clinics said they would close down. The very next day, I got progesterone shots delivered. It's just been gut punch after gut punch for us," one Alabama woman told The 19th. Most Americans support the legality of IVF, and as outrage grows, Republicans struggle in a trap of their own making. This isn't what they wanted, they insist: They support IVF. In Congress, Nancy Mace of South Carolina said in a statement she would "stop any and all efforts to ban IVF," and Byron Donalds of Florida expressed support for the procedure on *Meet the Press*. "We really want the Alabama legislature to make sure that that procedure is protected for families who do struggle with having children, that helps them actually create great families, which is what our country desperately needs," he said.

But did he tell the truth?

Donalds, like Mace, co-sponsored the Life at Conception Act in 2021. The bill defined a human being as a "member of the species homo sapiens at all stages of life, including the moment of fertilization or cloning, or other moment at which an individual member of the human species comes into being," the *Washington Post* reported. Not only would it have banned almost all abortions, it did not protect access to IVF. Neither Mace nor Donalds have co-sponsored the reintroduced bill, the *Post* added, but they also have yet to square their current positions on IVF with their previous support for the legislation. Senate Republicans are hardly more moderate. On Wednesday, Senator Cindy Hyde-Smith of Mississippi blocked a bill that would have created federal protections for IVF and other fertility treatments.

Senator Tammy Duckworth, a Democrat from Illinois, had reintroduced the bill to protect IVF—and to call the GOP's bluff. Duckworth, who had two daughters with the help of IVF, used a legislative procedure "that allows any one senator to object and stop it in its tracks," the *New York Times* reported, and Hyde-Smith took the bait. (She also blocked the bill in 2022, when Duckworth first introduced it after *Dobbs*.) The bill was full of "poison pills," the senator from Mississippi said, because it went beyond ensuring access to IVF and allegedly lacked restrictions on surrogacy

---

Credit line: From *New York Magazine*, February 29 © 2024. Reprinted with permission. All rights reserved.

and human cloning. Tony Perkins, who heads the far-right Family Research Council, called the bill "deceptive" and claimed, falsely, that the bill would "legalize" cloning, gene-edited designer babies, and the creation of human-animal hybrids, or "chimeras." Hyde-Smith later appeared on his broadcast program, Washington Watch, where she accused Democrats of trying to "exploit emotions."

> **Tammy Duckworth's bill protects women from prosecution for pursuing IVF and doctors for performing it.**

Duckworth's bill does not legalize "chimeras." The senator has said it does "three things and three things only": It protects women from prosecution for pursuing IVF and doctors for performing it, and it further allows insurance companies to cover the procedure. In response, Republicans can only dissemble. House Speaker Mike Johnson said on Thursday that he supports IVF and that it must be done "ethically," whatever that means. Johnson, too, cosponsored the Life at Conception Act and believes in fetal personhood—an overtly religious notion that the fetus is a person from the time of its conception. He is hardly alone. For many on the right, fetal personhood has long been the basis of their opposition to abortion. In 1973, the year the Supreme Court decided *Roe v. Wade,* a Maryland congressman proposed the first Human Life Amendment, which said the U.S. should not deprive any human being, "from the moment of conception," of life without due process. Lawmakers would introduce 330 versions of the bill over the next 40 years, ProPublica reported.

Jeannie Suk Gersen observed in a 2019 piece for the *New Yorker* that "the abortion fight we are gearing up for departs from the realm of uneasy compromise and re-engages the clash of absolutes." Now we live with the consequences, and so must the GOP. If an embryo is a person, the conventional IVF process is murderous. Republicans haven't squared their professed support for IVF with their opposition to abortion because they can't. For the same reason, they can't be relied on to protect IVF. They're bound by their own logic, as Duckworth found out. "If this is urgent and you care deeply about this as you say you do—like you've been saying in the last 72-plus hours since the Alabama Supreme Court ruling—then don't object," she said on Wednesday. "Let this bill pass." They didn't, because they couldn't. Republicans can't escape the personhood problem. Though Republican lawmakers in Alabama have introduced some early proposals meant to protect IVF, Democrats say they're still dodging the question of personhood, which threatens the entire endeavor.

Compromise is neither possible nor advisable. Let us remember the two absolutes at work. One holds that a woman has the right to her own body. The other grants rights to embryos, which transforms women into non-human vessels. The first view is compatible with modern notions of equality and citizenship, and the other is not. Only one view should prevail—and if it does, it will do so without any help from the right.

Print Citations

CMS: Jones, Sarah. "Republicans Can't Be Trusted to Protect IVF." In *The Reference Shelf: Reproductive Rights,* edited by Micah L. Issitt, 122-124. Amenia, NY: Grey House Publishing, 2024.

MLA: Jones, Sarah. "Republicans Can't Be Trusted to Protect IVF." *The Reference Shelf: Reproductive Rights,* edited by Micah L. Issitt, Grey House Publishing, 2024, pp. 122-124.

APA: Jones, S. (2024). Republicans can't be trusted to protect IVF. In M. L. Issitt (Ed.), *The reference shelf: Reproductive rights* (pp. 122-124). Amenia, NY: Grey House Publishing. (Original work published 2024)

Why IVF Looks Different in the US Than in the Rest of the World

By Rachel M. Cohen
Vox, March 26, 2024

Earlier this month the *[The] Atlantic* ran an opinion piece describing the American fertility industry as "strangely undeveloped" from a regulatory perspective. The two authors—a conservative political analyst and an anti-abortion bioethicist—claimed the landscape for assisted reproductive technology has left "parents, children, clinics and practitioners" without basic protections and safety guardrails.

Their ominous arguments are part of a much older debate over whether the US fertility industry is sufficiently regulated, a conversation that has reignited now that in vitro fertilization is back in the national headlines.

In the wake of Alabama's Supreme Court concluding that frozen embryos created through IVF count as "children" under state law, anti-abortion groups have jumped to say this moment offers a new chance to protect human life. When Alabama's legislature moved to protect IVF providers from liability, the advocacy group Students for Life said it would amount to an industry "get-out-of-regulation free card."

Critics sometimes charge the $5.34 billion fertility sector with being a "Wild West" that places profit on a pedestal above ethics and safety. Defenders say there's plenty of regulation; to the extent that other countries have more rules, it's because they have more centralized government-run health care systems and far less rabid anti-abortion politics.

"This specialized medical field is often criticized as being a 'Wild West' in which anything goes," Kerry Lynn Macintosh, a professor at Santa Clara University School of Law, told me. "In my opinion, that criticism is inaccurate and unfair."

Untangling the various arguments thrown around in the discussion can get complicated. There are potential regulations for patient safety, such as inspecting cryogenic storage tanks and accrediting fertility clinics. There are potential regulations that some religious conservatives want to see in the name of protecting embryo "dignity" or heterosexual marriage—like rules around embryo disposal or who may be eligible to use the assisted reproductive technology at all. And there are other potential regulations that pertain to complex and divisive societal issues—like sperm donor anonymity and screening embryos for sex and other genetic characteristics.

These regulatory questions are not new, but they're resurfacing now within the new post-Roe era, where the technology continues to advance at a rapid clip and

Credit line: From *Vox*, March 26 © 2024. Reprinted with permission. All rights reserved.

the risks of government overreach into reproductive health care are more acute than ever.

How IVF Is Regulated in the United States

There are more than 450 fertility clinics across the country, and like most aspects of US health care, the IVF industry is regulated by a patchwork of federal and state rules as well as professional self-governance, all with varying levels of penalties and enforcement mechanisms.

Unlike many other aspects of US health care, though, insurance coverage for assisted reproductive technologies is rare, with companies generally ducking services like IVF due to its high cost. Some experts and insurers also reject the idea that infertility is a disease, despite bodies like the World Health Organization labeling it as such.

The primary consumer protection law governing IVF is the Fertility Clinic Success Rate and Certification Act of 1992, which requires clinics to report their live birth success rates to the federal government. Around 90 percent of clinics participate, though there is no real legal consequence for those that don't. The Centers for Disease Control and Prevention also audits a sample of clinics each year to validate the self-reported data.

Doctors who provide IVF must be licensed to practice medicine, and if they violate medical norms, they can lose their privileges. In one notorious example, the doctor who transferred multiple embryos into a woman who would give birth to the first surviving octuplets had his license revoked by the state of California.

Another major mechanism for regulation is the courts: American tort law allows patients to sue clinics, doctors, and manufacturers for damages if they feel they've been injured by medical malpractice. Between January 2009 and April 2019, patients brought more than 130 lawsuits over destroyed embryos. One lawsuit in 2021 won a nearly $15 million judgment.

"Believe me, fertility clinics and their suppliers heard that message loud and clear," Macintosh, the Santa Clara law professor, said.

Some states require fertility clinics to be accredited and inspected, while others do not. Louisiana is the only state to outright prohibit the destruction of embryos, requiring patients to either pay forever to store their unused embryos, or donate them to a married couple. Most states allow patients to decide what to do with any excess genetic material.

Much of the standard-setting in IVF comes from the American Society for Reproductive Medicine, the professional association representing practitioners in the field. The ASRM provides influential guidance to members on appropriate conduct, and can censure, suspend, or expel members deemed unethical. It has a sister organization—the Society for Assisted Reproductive Technology—which collects data on IVF cycles to report to the government and requires labs to get accredited if they wish to become members. (Most clinics are members.)

Sean Tipton, the chief advocacy and policy officer for the American Society for Reproductive Medicine, disagrees that IVF in the US lacks oversight and accountability, and emphasized that IVF is the only medical procedure for which doctors must report their success rates to the US government.

"The idea that this field is unregulated is completely wrong, and people who make that argument are either grossly misinformed or intentionally misleading," he told Vox.

> **Critics charge the $5.34 billion fertility sector with being a "Wild West" that places profit above ethics and safety.**

Tipton is proud of his group's self-regulatory record, and pointed out that 20 years ago, when it became clear that too many IVF pregnancies were leading to twins and triplets, his group promoted data that showed one can reduce the number of embryos transferred without hurting the live birth success rate. Practitioners took note and there's since been an enormous reduction in multiple births.

Tipton also said the tort system is simply a fundamental differentiator for regulation of health care in the US compared to other countries. "In American medicine, we don't try to have a 9,000-page set of regulations because the field changes way too fast for that," he argued. "Instead we have patients who, if they feel they have been victimized by someone in accidental or malicious ways, they have the right to sue and get relief."

Is There Room for More or Better Regulation?

Despite the aforementioned guardrails, many critics maintain the US can do better. They fault a fertility industry they see as too freewheeling, chaotic, and profit-driven. They want to see more safety testing on FDA-approved storage tanks, and lament all the voluntary rules which they say will do too little to prevent the most unscrupulous actors from causing harm.

The industry is "cavalier about rules, casual about paperwork, irritated by government interference," David Plotz, a journalist who wrote a book about a mysterious sperm bank with highly elite and accomplished donors, once said.

Naomi Cahn, a University of Virginia law professor who focuses on reproductive technology, told *Vox* she thinks more state and federal oversight is needed for cryopreservation tanks even once they're approved by the FDA for use.

"It may be difficult to determine just what that oversight should be: How often do tanks need to be inspected? What types of safety procedures must be implemented? It is impossible to protect against all errors, but it is so important to be able to have confidence that one's reproductive material is being stored safely," she said.

Critics also note certain practices are allowed in the US that are frequently banned in other countries, like screening for sex or eye color, or allowing sperm donor anonymity. One survey found nearly 73 percent of US fertility clinics offer patients the ability to select their embryo's sex.

"IVF clinics have had pretty free rein, and some would look at their pathway as being a bit free and easy in terms of new developments," Francis Collins, the former director of the National Institutes of Health, told the *Washington Post* in 2018.

Past Efforts to Reach Consensus National Positions on IVF Have Flopped

Many critics of American IVF like to point to the UK as a model for superior governmental oversight. There, an independent agency—the Human Fertilisation and Embryology Authority—oversees all clinic licensing, regulates storage of embryos, and sets national rules all clinics must abide by to use assisted reproductive technology. It was formed via a 1990 statute and originated in a national report published in 1984.

But there's a far less organized and aggressive anti-abortion movement in Britain, which allowed UK leaders to reach compromise positions on embryo research and creation that could not be replicated at the same time in America.

As the technology was first being developed in the 1970s and '80s, the US government made a significant effort to come together on some national policies around IVF.

In the late '70s, a 13-person national committee composed of seven doctors, two attorneys, one businessman, a philanthropy representative, a philosopher, and a religious ethicist took up the task of crafting recommendations for IVF research. This "Ethics Advisory Board" solicited testimony and held public hearings across the country. In its final report in 1979, it concluded research on IVF was ethically acceptable and recommended the federal government lift its research funding ban on human embryos up to the age of 14 days.

Anti-abortion groups mobilized hard against this. Activists sent nearly 13,000 letters to Congress opposed to the Ethics Advisory Board's conclusions and placed an ad in the *New York Times* calling IVF a "morally abhorrent technology."

The 1980s saw similar pushback to federal deliberation. "We found it impossible in this country to find common ground when there were congressional committees tasked with trying to come up with policies that could gain a consensus," Margaret Marsh, a Rutgers historian who has studied IVF's rise, told me. "Anti-abortion activists opposed the technology and some conservative politicians believed family law was the province of the state, not the national government."

By 1996, under pressure from anti-abortion groups, Congress passed the Dickey-Wicker Amendment—a rider that bans any federal funds going toward human embryo research. It's been tacked onto appropriations bills annually since, leaving the American public sector effectively out of researching most fertility technologies and significantly limiting its oversight role.

Tipton says what's happening right now in Alabama and the "rabid anti-choice movement" are speaking loud and clear about present-day possibilities for federal rule-making. "In 2024, if anyone thinks they're going to have a rational discussion about national [IVF] regulation they are gravely mistaken," he said.

Macintosh, who focuses on biotechnology law, echoed Tipton's skepticism. "In the United States, anything to do with human reproduction is contentious, and I would not trust a federal agency to make decisions based on science alone," she said.

And some Republicans still just ideologically resist federal rules altogether. "I don't see any need to regulate [IVF] at the federal level," Republican Sen. Roger

Marshall told *Politico* recently. "I think the *Dobbs* decision puts this issue back at the state level."

The US's Lighter-Touch Regulatory Landscape Is Directly Tied to Anti-Abortion Politics

The debate over whether IVF is adequately regulated has resurfaced over the last month.

After Alabama's court ruling, Democratic Sen. Tammy Duckworth brought a bill to establish a national right to IVF up for a vote. Her Access to Family Building Act would override state limits on assisted reproductive technology and give individuals the right to decide how to use or dispose of their genetic reproductive materials, thus shielding patients and doctors from liability.

It was blocked, however, by Republican Sen. Cindy Hyde-Smith, who claimed it had "poison pills" that would allegedly legalize human cloning and commercial surrogacy, subject anti-abortion groups to "crippling lawsuits," and lift the federal ban "on the creation of three-parent embryos." (The bill does not mention these things.)

Conservatives and other groups affiliated with the anti-abortion movement echoed the opposition, insisting Duckworth's bill would unleash untold consequences under a broad legal interpretation. Tony Perkins, the head of the Family Research Council, blasted the bill as part of Democrats' "radical, Frankensteinian agenda." Jordan Boyd, a staff writer for the Federalist, called it an attempt "to stifle oversight and regulation of Big Fertility."

Duckworth and IVF advocates rejected these arguments.

"The idea that my Access to Family Building Act would interfere with federal or state safety regulations surrounding IVF is a false claim aimed at distracting people from what my legislation would actually do," Duckworth told *Vox*. "It is Republicans' crusade to redefine the concept of a human being to include embryos that poses an existential threat to IVF—and any future questions surrounding safety regulations."

Other countries do have tougher federal rules and penalties governing their fertility sectors. For example, operating a non-accredited clinic in Australia can lead to up to a decade in prison. Countries like Norway, Finland, and New Zealand ban anonymous sperm donations. Other countries like Canada ban embryo sex selection except in rare medical circumstances.

But in the US, with its much stronger culture of privacy and its more intense anti-abortion politics, similar policies have been largely off the table. Progressive activists have long raised concerns about how fertility regulations could hurt the most vulnerable Americans, just as abortion bans disproportionately affect low-income women and people of color.

"What we have not done in this country, at least until the demise of *Roe v. Wade*, is have the government in the business of making decisions about people's reproductive lives," Marsh said.

Defenders of the US regulatory landscape also note that many of the more heavily regulated countries have often left patients in those places without access to care. Thousands of couples travel to the US for fertility treatment (sometimes dubbed "reproductive tourism") or rely on shipments of anonymous American sperm because their own countries have major shortages.

Prominent anti-abortion groups have been going on offense since Alabama's Supreme Court ruling, accusing Republicans of "sanctioning murder" for supporting IVF, and doubling down on "personhood" bills that threaten treatment access. Some activists have called for more regulation of embryos, like tracking where they go, how they're stored, and what happens to them.

Such tracking would amount to a significant increase in government oversight. Cahn, the University of Virginia law professor, said it could also fundamentally encroach on privacy protections.

"While the government does keep track of the number of [assisted reproductive technology] cycles for legal purposes, it does not keep track of *who* is undergoing those cycles," she told me. "And while births are reported, we don't—and shouldn't—keep track of each menstrual cycle that produces eggs nor each time someone tries to get pregnant."

Cahn co-authored a paper in 2022 proposing a new independent federal agency to oversee reproductive technologies, and others have suggested reforms like requiring all fertility clinics to obtain certification from the Society for Assisted Reproductive Technology, rather than leave such accreditation optional.

Many of these ideas sound reasonable, and some aspects of the rapidly growing reproductive technology sector really do warrant at the very least more public discussion. But such discussion is unlikely to come in practicable form any time soon, as some activists increasingly make their long-term hope of ending IVF known. And the politics of regulation look exceedingly difficult, too, when 126 House Republicans are currently co-sponsoring federal legislation to give constitutional rights to embryos.

Print Citations

CMS: Cohen, Rachel M. "Why IVF Looks Different in the US Than in the Rest of the World." In *The Reference Shelf: Reproductive Rights*, edited by Micah L. Issitt, 125-130. Amenia, NY: Grey House Publishing, 2024.

MLA: Cohen, Rachel M. "Why IVF Looks Different in the US Than in the Rest of the World." *The Reference Shelf: Reproductive Rights*, edited by Micah L. Issitt, Grey House Publishing, 2024, pp. 125-130.

APA: Cohen, R. M. (2024). Why IVF looks different in the US than in the rest of the world. In M. L. Issitt (Ed.), *The reference shelf: Reproductive rights* (pp. 125-130). Amenia, NY: Grey House Publishing. (Original work published 2024)

The Connection Between Fertility Treatments and the Overturning of *Roe v. Wade*

By Fiorella Valdesolo
Vogue, January 27, 2023

Last month, Tammy Duckworth, the Democratic senator from Illinois, along with Senator Patty Murray of Washington, introduced legislation called the Right to Build Families Act, which aims to codify the protection of assisted reproductive technologies for patients (so they have a say over their own genetic material) and for doctors who provide fertility services. What Duckworth and Murray have a keen understanding of is that while access to abortion care may be the primary health care service impacted by the overturning of *Roe v. Wade* earlier this year, it's certainly not the only one that the Supreme Court decision put at risk. Patients, doctors, and legal experts alike are concerned that abortion bans could actually have more far-reaching effects, namely on fertility treatments. The senators' bill aims to anticipate those effects. As Duckworth said: "This is part of the abortion debate that most Americans were unaware of until *Roe vs. Wade* fell." In honor of the 50th anniversary of the *Roe v. Wade* ruling this week, here's a look at how its overturning impacts fertility.

What Is IVF, and How Does It Work?

In vitro fertilization, or IVF, is a process that dates back to 1978, whereby patients receive injections of medication designed to stimulate the ovaries so they can produce mature eggs. Those eggs are then removed from the ovaries and, in a lab, combined with viable sperm so they can develop into embryos. The embryos are, in many cases, tested for genetic issues and then usually frozen to be transferred to the patient's uterus at a later date. "There are many situations where IVF may be needed," says Angeline Beltsos, MD, double board certified in obstetrics and gynecology and reproductive endocrinology and the clinical CEO at Kindbody. "IVF is used to help patients where natural conception is not occurring, to preserve fertility or to help couples decrease the chance of miscarriage or disease in their child."

Credit line: From *Vogue*, January 27 © 2023. Reprinted with permission. All rights reserved.

Why Is There a Concern That the *Roe* Decision Will Impact IVF?

"Fertility treatments, contraception, and abortion are all on the spectrum of full-scale reproductive health care," says Lucky Sekhon, MD, a reproductive endocrinologist, infertility specialist, and ob-gyn at RMA of New York, a fertility center. "The common thread between what fertility doctors, ob-gyns, and abortion-care providers do is that we allow people to have agency over their bodies." Her colleague, Tia Jackson-Bey, MD, MPH, at RMA of New York, says reproductive medicine encompasses all aspects of family planning. "I often discuss abortion care and IVF as two points on the same continuum," she adds. "The decision to have a family when and how you want necessitates the full spectrum of reproductive rights, including access to safe abortion and fertility treatments like IVF." And there are several reasons for concern about the impact of the *Roe* decision on said fertility treatments. First, the long-standing association between IVF and embryo research and the anti-abortion movement. "This is why we are restricted in the US from embryo research with federal (NIH) funds," explains Marcelle Cedars, MD, an ob-gyn and reproductive endocrinologist in San Francisco, pointing to the Reagan years and the Dickey-Wicker amendment. Then, says Cedars, there is the possibility of fertility patients having pregnancy complications that require termination. And the belief by anti-choice groups that human life begins at the moment of fertilization means that IVF, which fertilizes many eggs at once, is something they may take issue with.

What Are Personhood Amendments, and Why Do They Pose a Specific Threat?

Personhood amendments were once a fringe idea, but the overturning of *Roe* emboldened many anti-abortion groups to bring it to the mainstream. "One way abortion and IVF are linked is through personhood laws, which are vague measures that classify fetuses, embryos, and/or fertilized eggs as people starting at the point of conception," says Karla Torres, senior human rights counsel at the Center for Reproductive Rights, adding that these ambiguous amendments significantly undermine an IVF patient's ability to make decisions about their care and a doctor's ability to provide it for them. Cedars wonders if this will limit the number of eggs that can be inseminated. What about embryos that don't survive in culture (easily 50%) or don't survive freezing and thawing? Will there be legal ramifications? Will efforts to reduce the number of embryos transferred by selection processes, improving maternal and childhood health, be thwarted? All these limitations would lead to lower odds of conceiving. While personhood amendments have been introduced more than 300 times in Congress, there are few states (like Georgia, Arizona, and Alabama) where those laws are in effect, and there is still confusion about how to apply them. "Some states even have overlapping laws, like Alabama, which has both a trigger ban and a fetal personhood law that further adds to the lack of clarity surrounding IVF care," says Torres. "There is also concern that IVF may become even more expensive as providers figure out how to continue providing care in states that enact abortion bans or personhood laws." This further cuts them off for the uninsured and those for whom fertility care was already cost prohibitive. And Sekhon underscores that using personhood as the basis of criminal proceedings is not new: It's been used to incarcerate pregnant women who test positive for drug screens or are accused of engaging in behaviors deemed potentially harmful to the fetus. "In Alabama, there have been hundreds of prosecutions of pregnant and postpartum women for chemical endangerment of a fetus," she adds.

> The decision to have a family when and how you want necessitates the full spectrum of reproductive rights.

Are Certain IVF Practices More of a Target?

Selective reduction may be one, says Sekhon. The procedure performed at the end of the first trimester will terminate one of multiple pregnancies in the uterus. And there are a number of reasons a pregnant person would choose to undergo it: Multifetal pregnancies put them at higher risk of complications like diabetes and high blood pressure (or preeclampsia), which can result in stroke or death, and embryos can be affected by genetic imbalances or serious diseases that are detected in genetic testing. "Despite often being medically indicated for the health of the pregnancy and the person who is pregnant, selective reduction comes into question as it involves performing an abortion, terminating a pregnancy, on one or more fetuses," Sekhon explains. Preimplantation genetic testing (or PGT) is another common practice that could be targeted. Genetic imbalances and mutations could lead to significant medical issues or syndromes and increase the risk of future cancers and conditions, and the process of testing for them is especially important for pregnant patients over 35, when the odds of these issues begin to rise. There are also, says Sekhon, numerous studies proving that PGT doesn't harm the embryo, which, if the family doesn't want to discard it, can also be donated to reproductive research. "The use of PGT, which has revolutionized IVF and led to safer and more effective outcomes, may decrease as these practices create ethical or legal dilemmas of how to handle disease-affected or chromosomally abnormal embryos," says Jackson-Bey. "This is a significant disadvantage to the field and the families who need these technologies to safely grow their families." Jackson-Bey adds that the current recommendation for transfer of a single chromosomally normal (euploid) embryo could be threatened if providers or families can't afford to store additional embryos or are criminalized for discarding them.

Does Restrictive Access to Some Medication Pose a Challenge for Fertility Treatments Too?

Limited access to a drug like misoprostol—which is used for a number of indications, including medical abortion—can be problematic. "It can be used to induce uterine contractions and speed up the process of a miscarriage for a patient with a nonviable pregnancy," says Sekhon. This is key as most miscarriages do not occur spontaneously, and incomplete ones can lead to infections and hemorrhages. Misoprostol can also be used to soften the cervix in preparation for reparative uterine surgeries (to remove fibroids, polyps, or scar tissue) and to contract the uterine muscles to prevent blood hemorrhaging after a miscarriage or delivering a baby. "Pharmacies in states with abortion restrictions often balk at dispensing misoprostol to treat patients who need it for reasons other than abortions," says Sekhon. "This can lead to delays in treating incomplete miscarriages and increases risk of infection, bleeding that can be life-threatening or require blood transfusions."

Are Doctors or Fertility Companies Doing Anything—or Should They Be Doing Anything—to Protect In Vitro Embryos?

Beltsos reports that Kindbody patients, particularly in states where there have been legislative changes after *Roe*, are concerned about what will happen to their frozen embryos. Embryos created through IVF are stored in laboratories to keep them safe for future use. "As the question of personhood begins to surface, patients and clinics are considering what they should do, and in certain states there is consideration to move embryos to potentially safer locations where jurisdictions of how they can be managed may be less restrictive," says Beltsos. Some Kindbody patients have asked to have their embryos transferred to locations in other states. The company, like many others, is constantly monitoring the situation and working with organizations like the American Society for Reproductive Medicine, which Cedars is the president of, and the American College of Obstetricians and Gynecologists.

What Is the Legal Status of IVF Right Now?

Right now, IVF remains legal in all 50 states, though state abortion bans could impact access to certain practices like freezing or discarding unused embryos. "While IVF remains legal in the US, the threats to providing and accessing it should not be understated," says Torres. "Fertility doctors and their patients, whether they live in a state that safeguards access to abortion or not, have been experiencing anxiety because of the uncertainty and chaos caused by the patchwork of legal abortion access currently happening across the country and what that may mean for IVF access and care." Sekhon points out that certain states (like South Carolina and Alabama) provide specific exemptions for IVF in their bans, but in a state like Louisiana, embryos are legally considered a person, so patients are not permitted to discard unused ones. Anti-abortion legislators have been bolstered by the *Roe* decision: Legislation potentially banning IVF is reportedly being discussed in Ohio, Virginia, and Texas; personhood legislation that may impact IVF is expected to be introduced in Florida; and Virginia has filed a bill for next year stating that life begins at fertilization. Sekhon encourages everyone to support and follow organizations like ASMR and Resolve, "patient and physician education and advocacy organizations that are paying close attention to the changing landscape of reproductive rights and access to care in the US." Cedars suspects that the likelihood of IVF being explicitly criminalized is low, but she adds: "Who really thought *Roe v. Wade* would be overturned?"

Print Citations

CMS: Valdesolo, Fiorella. "The Connection Between Fertility Treatments and the Overturning of *Roe v. Wade*." In *The Reference Shelf: Reproductive Rights,* edited by Micah L. Issitt, 131-135. Amenia, NY: Grey House Publishing, 2024.

MLA: Valdesolo, Fiorella. "The Connection Between Fertility Treatments and the Overturning of *Roe v. Wade*." *The Reference Shelf: Reproductive Rights,* edited by Micah L. Issitt, Grey House Publishing, 2024, pp. 131-135.

APA: Valdesolo, F. (2024). The connection between fertility treatments and the overturning of *Roe v. Wade*. In M. L. Issitt (Ed.), *The reference shelf: Reproductive rights* (pp. 131-135). Amenia, NY: Grey House Publishing. (Original work published 2023)

How IVF Is Complicating Republicans Abortion Messaging

By Lexie Shapitl
NPR, March 16, 2024

In-vitro fertilization has become the latest front in the political battle over reproductive rights, and it's left some Republicans grappling with how to square their support for IVF with their past stances on reproductive rights.

In the weeks since the Alabama Supreme Court ruled that embryos are children under the law, threatening access to IVF in the state, Congressional Republicans have lined up to voice their support for the procedure.

Republicans have tried to send a clear and unified message. The Senate GOP campaign arm advised those running for office to "clearly state [their] support for IVF" and "publicly oppose any efforts to restrict access" to the treatment in a memo to candidates obtained by *NPR*. In her Republican response to President Biden's State of the Union, Alabama Sen. Katie Britt said "we strongly support continued nationwide access to in-vitro fertilization."

But many GOP lawmakers have spent years arguing that life begins at conception—the same basic premise that upheld the Alabama decision, which threw fertility clinics and patients in the state into limbo.

Since the Alabama ruling, Republicans have struggled to articulate what distinguishes their views from the court's.

Kansas Sen. Roger Marshall, a practicing obstetrician, said he welcomes "every day 200 babies that are born because of in-vitro fertilization in this country."

"There's nothing more pro-family than supporting the birth of babies."

He's also one of the senators who co-sponsored the Life at Conception Act, a bill that would have granted constitutional protection to embryos at "the moment of fertilization." If enacted, that legislation could have threatened access to IVF, during which embryos are often discarded or stored for years.

Asked if he saw any tension between those two stances, Marshall said: "I've wrestled with this for over 25 years as a practicing obstetrician. And when I talked to the spiritual experts, they can't agree on this particular issue. But I am absolutely certain that in vitro fertilization is a great thing, that God has given us this technology and we should use it."

Many Republicans have rallied around the message that IVF is "pro-life."

"As a pro-life guy, I think that IVF is pro-life," said Sen. Josh Hawley, R-Mo. "It helps people start their family or add to their family if they want to."

Credit line: From *NPR*, March 16 © 2024. Reprinted with permission. All rights reserved.

Hawley also co-sponsored the Life at Conception Act. When he was asked about the destruction of embryos through the process, he reiterated: "Having a baby is a pro-life thing. So I'm in favor of it."

Past Support for "Life at Conception Act" Causes Strife

The Life at Conception Act bill had more than 160 republican cosponsors in the House before the Supreme Court struck down the right to an abortion.

Republican congressman Don Bacon was one of those early co-sponsors. But he didn't sign onto the bill in 2023, over concerns that the language would be used to challenge IVF.

"I just think in principle, on a normal pregnancy, we want to respect that that is a—it's human. It's alive," Bacon said. "I want to help mom and dads become mom and dads. That's my goal."

Congresswoman Michelle Steel faced criticism for signing onto the Life at Conception Act after publicly discussing her experience using IVF. She has been an active supporter for IVF treatment access.

She recently became the first lawmaker to take her name off the bill since Alabama's court ruling, citing "confusion" about her stance

"Nothing is more pro-life than helping families with children, and I do not support federal restrictions on IVF," she said on the House floor on March 7.

Florida Sen. Marco Rubio acknowledged the tension facing conservatives.

"The ethical dilemma that this poses is, in order to create life, you have to destroy life because you'll create embryos that are not going to be used," Rubio said. "And it's a very difficult bioethical issue, and it's one that the practitioners themselves confront."

"That's what makes it complex," Rubio added. "And it's a balancing act that as a society we're going to have to make."

Emma Waters, a religion, life and bioethics associate at the conservative think tank The Heritage Foundation, said the group has been having discussions with members of Congress about what a "pro-life vision for IVF" would look like.

To Waters, that means not destroying embryos in the process of IVF for any reason. She suggested the U.S. could adopt policies limiting the number of embryos created during treatment or requiring that all embryos get implanted.

"I think a lot of Republican lawmakers in particular feel like they're forced into this strict binary where either they have to say, 'I'm fully in support of IVF, do whatever that entails, no limitations, no regulation, and just like I'm in support, go for it,'" Waters said. "Or they're going to have or they're going to be painted as being totally in opposition to IVF and not caring about women, not caring about children."

Fertility groups say regulations on embryo storage, like the ones Waters proposes, would threaten IVF access, decrease effectiveness and increase risks.

Barbara Collura—the CEO and president of RESOLVE: The National Infertility Foundation—said in a statement that "any changes to the clinical guidelines for IVF that try to regulate the creation of embryos will cause an incredible burden to the patient."

> **Fertility groups say regulations on embryo storage would threaten IVF access.**

"Doing so would add cost, interfere with the patient and provider relationship, and have disastrous pregnancy outcomes," Collura continued.

How Congress Might and Might Not Respond

The Alabama legislature has resolved the issue there—for now. Lawmakers passed a bill in March to shield IVF providers from legal liability. But the law doesn't address the larger, underlying questions posed by the court decision.

Democrats in Congress have introduced legislation to protect IVF nationally. Rep. Susan Wild, D-PA., and Sens. Tammy Duckworth, D-Ill., and Patty Murray, D-Wash., have introduced the Access to Family Building Act, which would codify the right to "assisted reproductive technology" without overly burdensome regulation. President Biden called on Congress to pass those protections during his State of the Union address.

Republican Rep. Nancy Mace, R-S.C., has also introduced a resolution expressing support of assisted reproductive technology, but it would not be legally binding or enact any policy change.

The Heritage Foundation and Susan B. Anthony Pro-Life America came out against both of those efforts. SBA said in a statement that the Access to Family Building act is a "sweeping anything goes" bill that would violate religious freedoms. Waters said the bill would "open the floodgates to a host of really concerning practices," such as cloning and genetic editing.

So far, New York Rep. Marc Molinaro is the only Republican to sign onto the legislation. Molinaro has taken a softer stance on abortion than many of his Republican colleagues; while he says he is "personally pro-life," he does not support a national ban, and supports exceptions for rape and incest.

In a statement first shared with *Axios*, Molinaro said, "I'm a parent who has personal experience with IVF and support all women and families who choose IVF to bring life into this world. Protecting it is just common sense."

Rep. Anna Paulina Luna, R-Fla., announced Thursday that she is introducing a "Right to Try IVF" bill. Text of the bill was not yet available.

But any legislation is unlikely to advance in the House: Republican Speaker Mike Johnson has said he supports IVF access, but that it is "a states issue" that Congress will not take up.

That doesn't mean, though, that it won't be an issue on the campaign trail. Michigan Congresswoman Elissa Slotkin is running for Senate. And she says Republican messages of support are meaningless unless they sign on and support legislative action.

"I'm running against someone who came out loud and proud, 'I support IVF,' except he co-led four bills that would do the exact same thing as the Alabama ruling," Slotkin said. "It's not what these guys say. It's what they do."

Print Citations

CMS: Shapitl, Lexie. "How IVF Is Complicating Republicans' Abortion Messaging." In *The Reference Shelf: Reproductive Rights,* edited by Micah L. Issitt, 136-139. Amenia, NY: Grey House Publishing, 2024.

MLA: Shapitl, Lexie. "How IVF Is Complicating Republicans' Abortion Messaging." *The Reference Shelf: Reproductive Rights,* edited by Micah L. Issitt, Grey House Publishing, 2024, pp. 136-139.

APA: Shapitl, L. (2024). How IVF is complicating Republicans' abortion messaging. In M. L. Issitt (Ed.), *The reference shelf: Reproductive rights* (pp. 136-139). Amenia, NY: Grey House Publishing. (Original work published 2024)

5
Maternal Health

Photo by Jno.skinner, CC BY-SA 4.0, via Wikipedia.

A crisis pregnancy center (foreground) in Nebraska deliberately located across from an abortion clinic.

Women's Reproductive Health

The debate over reproductive rights often focuses on "potential children." This is the approach favored by right-wing activists and ideologues, because they see the ultimate goal of their movement as the mission to "protect children," but this focus reduces the focus on the lives of American women, for whom reproductive rights can have many different consequences.

Reproductive Rights and Women's Rights

There is an important historical reason that abortion and contraception are associated with the women's rights and women's liberation movements around the world. The ability to control one's reproduction is a matter of bodily autonomy, freedom, and societal personhood. Since prehistory, the control of female reproduction was used to reinforce societal gender roles, which were in turn used to maintain females in a state of dependency and subservience. This pattern of oppression is visible throughout history in many different manifestations and has, at times, been quite overt, with male leaders of societies utilizing religion, mythology, and other claims to justify male dominance and to mandate female subservience. Cultural norms and taboos have been shaped by this and, though the language has changed, the pattern remains in place.[1]

The long struggle for autonomy, for American women, included the right to contraception and abortion, as women struggled to achieve control of their reproductive potential, without sacrificing the other aspects of sexuality that define human life. In her prize-winning study of reproductive rights *Abortion and Woman's Choice*, professor of political science Rosalind Pollack Petchesky argues, "The ability of women to participate equally in the economic and social life of the Nation has been facilitated by their ability to control their reproductive lives."[2] This quote could go on to be used by the Supreme Court in rejecting a challenge against Planned Parenthood of Southern Pennsylvania.

In 2022, a study of women's achievements and rights in US states found that women's achievements in arenas like the economy, health, family planning, and representation, were closely aligned with the degree to which the state supported reproductive freedoms. Maryland achieved top place in the list, while also being one of the states in which abortion rights are protected. At the lowest end of the list was Alabama, Kentucky, Louisiana, and Utah, states that severely curtailed reproductive freedoms, even before the Supreme Court ruling in the *Dobbs* case gave legislators in these states the power to ban abortion care outright.[3]

This is not merely a matter of American rights and freedoms, but holds true around the world. Nations in which reproductive rights are sharply curtailed also have lower levels of achievement and representation for women. Around the world, more than 200 million people do not have access to modern contraception, abortion and related care is denied to many millions of women, and these inequities in reproductive control have devastating effects on the lives of women. Banchiamlack Dessalegn, a director at MSI Reproductive Choices in Ethiopia write for *Al Jazeera*,

> In Addis Ababa, where I grew up, I saw first hand what a lack of access to reproductive health information and services can do. Someone I knew died by suicide after becoming pregnant because she did not know who to turn to. Another girl disappeared from class one day, never to return; we then heard rumors that she had ingested bleach in an attempt to end her pregnancy...the situation today is not too different. Across Africa and Latin American about three-quarters of abortions are unsafe; globally almost half of abortions are performed through dangerous methods.[4]

Dessalegn goes on to argue, "Gender equality isn't possible without abortion and contraception."

Protecting Some Kinds of Life

Critics of abortion and contraception typically argue that embryos and/or fetuses are living beings who need to be protected. Often this is intermingled with religious views based on claims about the sanctity of children's lives and/or of the miraculous nature of reproduction, conception, and childbirth. Given this claim, one might expect that individuals who favor limitations on reproductive controls like contraception and abortion, would also support measures that provide alternatives for individuals struggling reproductive challenges or would, at the very least, demonstrate commitment to the lives of children in other ways.

This does not turn out to be the case. A *New York Times* study from 2022 found that states with abortion bans in place were also the least supportive of mothers and children. Such states had the worst results in studies of maternal health, and well-being and outcomes for both women and children, and also tended to have the most limited social service systems.[5]

A study by the Center for American Progress fond that abortion ban states have the highest rates of child poverty in the nation. Mississippi, the worst-ranked state in the nation, had a childhood poverty rates of 27.9 percent, meaning that more than one out of every four Mississippi children lived in poverty.[6] More than half of the states in the bottom ten states for child poverty are ones in which reproductive rights have been sharply curtailed. When the Supreme Court was hearing arguments on the fate of abortion access, a union of 154 economists wrote that legal abortion has led to women attaining higher levels of education and professional occupations and, through this and other effects, has led to lower rates of child poverty around the world.[7]

The desire to protect potential children is therefore not associated with a deeper commitment to improving maternal care or child welfare long term but appears to be focused primarily on enacting prohibitions against actions that individuals within those states deem immoral. Once conception has occurred, therefore, a woman may be required, under penalty of law, to carry that child to term. In some cases, and in some states, exceptions are not given even for situations in which the pregnancy is the result of rape, incest, or in cases where the pregnancy threatens the life of the mother.

While this may seem contradictory, if reflects the fact that the Republican Party is not a united stream of thought, but a collection of interest groups whose interests often conflict in practice and in principle. Abortion bans and restrictions have relatively low-economic impact for another group of potential voters very important to Republican Party fortunes, the wealthy elite class and corporations. For these individuals, the proper manifestation of conservative values is often more focused on enabling those who have wealth to maintain that wealth and this is represented in Republican economic policies, which often provide significant tax relief to corporations and wealthy Americans. To provide one of many examples, the 2023 tax bills proposed by the GOP included $608 billion in tax cuts for the richest one-fifth of Americans, while the poorest one-fifth would receive $1.4 billion in tax relief, spread out among a far larger proportion of the population. The richest 1 percent of Americans would, under this plan, receive $28.4 billion in tax relief.[8] This portion of the voting electorate also tends to oppose social welfare systems which they claim, typically without evidence, do not work and which represent, to them, an unnecessary tax burden. This same facet of the conservative voting population also typically opposes efforts to increase funding for child care, education, and other services provided to children.

The interests of fiscal conservatives and social conservatives, like those in the antiabortion movement, overlap in the nebulously defined realm of "family values." Conservative social values are often defended as an attempt to support and preserve "traditional families" or "traditional values." This is often defined as heterosexual, married, childbearing couples. For some conservatives, this focus is only on *white* Christians, because white supremacists, when aligned with one of the major political parties, are typically aligned with the Republican Party. There has, in fact, been a resurgence in white supremacism driven by the fact that mainstream Republican politicians have voiced support for white nationalist conspiracy theories.[9]

Fiscal conservatives can also achieve some of their goals, by claiming that their aim is to preserve traditional family values. A lack of funding for maternal care might be justified with the claim that an appropriate family should contain a breadwinning male, which would then mean that women should not need state assistance. It might even be argued, despite a lack of evidence to support the claim, that social assistance programs "discourage marriage" and traditional lifestyles. Likewise, refusals to fund public education has been justified by the claim that public education systems dilute traditional values and norms, such as might be better received through Christian education or parents. The fiscal and social sides of the conservative population thus align through the belief that their efforts preserve an imagined ideal of American family life and morality, which also happens to correspond with the belief that corporations and wealthy individuals should not be held responsible for contributing to the collective resources used to support children, mothers, and families.

For social conservatives, the goal of protecting potential life is also often tied to perceptions of personal responsibility. When a woman suffers from rape, abuse, or otherwise experiences an unplanned pregnancy, some see this as the woman's responsibility and feel less moral duty to support that woman, because the woman's choices resulted in the situation. Likewise, child welfare is considered a matter of parental responsibility and so when a child suffers as the result of parental neglect, this might be seen as a failure of the parent but is not connected to the broader issue of protecting potential life through restrictions on reproductive care, without providing a large safety net for the people whose lives are shaped by those restrictions. In some cases, these beliefs might even be given spiritual justification by observing that potential lives are free from sin and thus more perfect than existing lives. A woman's health and welfare may thus be considered less important than the goal of ensuring that a potential life can be spared, as this potential life might be more perfect than the life of the woman who created it.

Outcomes for Women, Adolescents, and Nontraditional Families

The formation of opinions on reproductive rights is complex. Some approach the issue from an entirely religious point of view, staking their political positions on an associated system of belief that they have developed through their perception of their faith and how that faith has been manipulated by political actors seeking to claim their support. Others come to their beliefs through secular channels, or through their education or experience in the health-care system, as parents, as men and women living in America. Opinion on abortion, the most controversial of all issues in the reproductive rights debate, shows that America is not merely divided among pro and con voices, but that Americans tend to approach this and other reproductive health issues with more nuance and subtlety.

In 2024, the debate over reproductive rights is dominated by far-right activists whose approach to this issue is proscriptive and based largely on the view that prohibitions on consensual behavior will reduce the desire of individuals to engage in those behaviors. But when these ideas are put into practice, the effect on the welfare of people is significant. Critics of recent restrictive health-care laws have indicated that maternal mortality is likely to rise, have raised issues in which women with serious medical issues have been unable to receive lifesaving care, and have reported on lowered expectations and life satisfaction for adolescents and women. While advocates often speak of wanting to *encourage* reproduction, the opposite appears to be occurring, with more and more women choosing to avoid reproduction or sex, out of fear that they will not be in control when such an event occurs.

What is important to note, also, is that the drive for protecting potential life or prohibiting technologies that individuals utilize to shape the reproductive process in their interests, is aligned with many other views that are prejudicial. Many of those most committed to issues like the antiabortion movement also support proposals to limit lesbian, gay, bisexual, transgender, and queer (LGBTQ) parental rights or rights to adopt children. The focus on preserving ideal family is not one that is all inclusive, but refers only to those seen by those same activists as constituting appropriate family members. This may not include those who pregnancies can only be achieved through alternative methods, like adoption, or in vitro fertilization (IVF), or who want to parent with a same-sex partner. The focus on family values only applies to those who are seen, by external judges, as appropriate members of the kind of family that they see as legitimate. The movement is less, therefore, about the sanctity of all life as it is about deciding what kind of life deserves to exist and to thrive.

Works Used

Badger, Emily, Margot Sanger-Katz, and Claire Cain Miller. "States with Abortion Bans Are Among Least Supportive for Mothers and Children." *New York Times*, 28 July 2022.

Clark, Simon. "How White Supremacy Returned to Mainstream Politics." *CAP*, 1 July 2020, www.americanprogress.org/article/white-supremacy-returned-mainstream-politics/.

Dessalegn, Banchiamlack. "Gender Equality Isn't Possible Without Abortion and Contraception." *Al Jazeera*, 18 Mar. 2023, www.aljazeera.com/opinions/2023/3/18/gender-equality-isnt-possible-without-abortion-and-contraception.

Hubbard, Kaia. "The Link Between Abortion Rights and Gender Equality." *U.S. News & World Report*, 25 Aug. 2022, www.usnews.com/news/best-states/articles/how-abortion-rights-are-linked-to-gender-equality.

Ma, Adrian, and Wailin Wong. "Abortion Access Tends to Lower Child Poverty Rates, Economists Say." *NPR*, 26 May 2022.

Mies, Maria. *Patriarchy and Accumulation on a World Scale: Women in the International Division of Labor*. Zed Books, 1998.

Petchesky, Rosalind Pollack. *Abortion and Women's Choice: The State, Sexuality, and Reproductive Freedom*. Verso, 1989.

Treisman, Rachel. "States with the Toughest Abortion Laws Have the Weakest Maternal Supports, Data Shows." *NPR*, 18 Aug. 2022, www.npr.org/2022/08/18/1111344810/abortion-ban-states-social-safety-net-health-outcomes.

Wamhoff, Steve. "Trio of GOP Tax Bills Would Expand Corporate Tax Breaks While Doing Little for Americans Who Most Need Help." *ITEP*, 11 June 2023, itep.org/gop-tax-bills-expand-corporate-tax-breaks/.

Notes

1. Mies, *Patriarchy and Accumulation on a World Scale*.
2. Petchesky, *Abortion and Women's Choice: The State, Sexuality, and Reproductive Freedom*.

3. Hubbard, "The Link Between Abortion Rights and Gender Equality."
4. Dessalegn, "Gender Equality Isn't Possible Without Abortion and Contraception."
5. "Badger, Sanger-Katz, and Cain Miller, "States with Abortion Bans Are Among Least Supportive for Mothers and Children."
6. Treisman, "States with the Toughest Abortion Laws Have the Weakest Maternal Supports, Data Shows."
7. Ma and Wong, "Abortion Access Tends to Lower Child Poverty Rates, Economists Say."
8. Wamhoff, "Trio of GOP Tax Bills Would Expand Corporate Tax Breaks While Doing Little for Americans Who Most Need Help."
9. Clark, "How White Supremacy Returned to Mainstream Politics."

Abortion Bans Are Changing What It Means to Be Young in America

By Julie Maslowsky
The Conversation, June 17, 2024

Adolescence and young adulthood is a time of identity formation, when young people figure out who they are and who they want to be. One of the ways they do this is by considering the world around them, paying attention to social issues and starting to understand their society and their place in it. Laws and policies signal to young people what society thinks of their value, their role in society and their opportunities for the future.

But the experience of growing up in the post-*Roe v. Wade* era looks very different from that before the 50-year precedent was overturned in 2022.

Following the *Dobbs v. Jackson Supreme Court* decision, more than half of U.S. adolescents, ages 13-19, now live in a state with severely restricted or no legal abortion access. As a result, today's young people are coming of age in what one expert in health law and bioethics has termed an "era of rights retractions."

I am a developmental psychologist and population health scientist who studies adolescent development and sexual and reproductive health, and it is clear to me from a variety of indicators that, following *Dobbs,* the experience of adolescence and young adulthood in America has fundamentally changed.

Abortion bans are not only affecting those who need an abortion – they are shaping an entire generation.

How Young People View the *Dobbs* Decision

In 2022, my colleagues and I conducted a national survey of young people between the ages of 14 to 24, beginning shortly after the leak of the Supreme Court's opinion in the case.

We asked them about their knowledge of the *Dobbs* decision, how they felt about it and how they believed it was impacting the lives of young people in their state. Our research showed that the majority of young people are aware of and alarmed by the *Dobbs* decision and its implications.

Our own research and other emerging data make it clear that abortion restrictions not only affect young people who become pregnant or seek an abortion. These restrictions are affecting how young people think about voting, where they should choose to live, study and work, and how to control their fertility. Abortion restrictions may also have serious impacts on young people's mental health.

Credit line: From *The Conversation,* June 17 © 2024. Reprinted with permission. All rights reserved.

Implications for Voting

Some 8 million young people are becoming newly eligible to vote in 2024. Research shows that young people are the most likely to support abortion rights.

Abortion is a top issue that is currently motivating young voters. Change Research found in its recent national poll that 3 in 4 young voters believe abortion should be legal in all or most cases.

More than half of young voters say they will not vote for a candidate whose position on abortion is different from theirs. In the 2022 midterm elections, young people reported that abortion was the top issue influencing their vote.

How these young people vote may shape the 2024 election at both the national and state level in important ways. Their votes could serve as a referendum on reproductive rights directly in states where the issue is on the ballot and indirectly by shaping who young people want to represent them.

Where to Attend College, Live and Work Post-*Roe*

High school seniors are considering abortion access when deciding where to go to college. Over 70% reported considering reproductive health care access in their college decision.

Abortion access also matters to those entering the workforce. In a recent national survey, two-thirds of young workers reported that they did not wish to live in a state with abortion bans.

Another survey found that 60% of young women are more motivated to move to another state now that their state has passed a ban on abortion, or would be if their state did pass a ban.

Managing Fertility

Following *Dobbs*, young people's access to contraceptive services is changing too.

In Texas in March 2024, an appeals court ruled that the state could outlaw providing contraception to minors without parental consent at Title X clinics, which receive federal funding to provide confidential contraception regardless of age, income or immigration status. This ruling removed the only confidential access to contraception available to teens in that state.

Recent research that my colleagues conducted with college students in several U.S. Southeast states shows that they are worried that more legal restrictions on contraception are coming. In our study, one young person reported: "I fear that these changes are only a precursor to more strict laws regarding contraception and health care. I fear for the rights and bodies of those like me and those who are less fortunate."

Some young people have already taken permanent action to avoid pregnancy. Nationally, there have been significant increases in the number of young people who are choosing to undergo permanent sterilization, either vasectomy or tubal ligation. The effects are largest for tubal ligation. The rate of tubal ligation was rising prior to *Dobbs*, but immediately following *Dobbs*, one large national study found that the rate jumped by about 20% and has continued to rise at nearly twice its pre-*Dobbs* pace.

These increases signal that some young people simply do not want to take the chance of becoming pregnant or impregnating someone when comprehensive reproductive health care is not available or is under threat.

> **Abortion restrictions may also have serious impacts on young people's mental health.**

Effects on Mental Health

Emerging data shows that mental health outcomes are worse in states with abortion bans.

For instance, a recent large, national study examined changes in mental health symptoms in the months before and after the *Dobbs* decision, comparing people living in states with trigger abortion bans versus those living in states without trigger bans. A trigger ban was a law designed to be "triggered," or take effect, as soon as the legal precedent set by *Roe v. Wade* no longer applied. The study found that women (but not men) ages 18 to 45 living in states with trigger bans showed greater increases in symptoms of anxiety and depression after the *Dobbs* abortion decision was announced, compared with women living in states without such bans.

Unfortunately, the study did not include young people under age 18, nor did it look separately at young adults, who have most of their childbearing years ahead of them, to determine how they were being affected. Excluding young people from research and lumping them in with middle-aged adults is a common occurrence in studies focusing on abortion access and its consequences, a problematic practice highlighted by a recent expert consensus report.

Scholars predict that mental health consequences of reproductive health care restrictions will be more severe for historically marginalized populations. I expect this will include young people.

Our initial research indicates that many young people are experiencing significant stress and worry as a result of changing access to abortion. When describing her feelings about the decision, one young woman said, "I feel so many things. Anger, sadness, outrage. It makes me scared for my own future and for other women."

Print Citations

CMS: Maslowsky, Julie. "Abortion Bans Are Changing What It Means to Be Young in America." In *The Reference Shelf: Reproductive Rights,* edited by Micah L. Issitt, 149-152. Amenia, NY: Grey House Publishing, 2024.

MLA: Maslowsky, Julie. "Abortion Bans Are Changing What It Means to Be Young in America." *The Reference Shelf: Reproductive Rights,* edited by Micah L. Issitt, Grey House Publishing, 2024, pp. 149-152.

APA: Maslowsky, J. (2024). Abortion bans are changing what it means to be young in America. In M. L. Issitt (Ed.), *The reference shelf: Reproductive rights* (pp. 149-152). Amenia, NY: Grey House Publishing. (Original work published 2024)

What to Know About the Roiling Debate over U.S. Maternal Mortality Rates

By Robin Fields
ProPublica, April 5, 2024

An unusual public dispute has erupted among leading maternal health experts over whether the striking rise of U.S. maternal mortality rates over the past two decades was the real deal—or a statistical mirage.

The challenge to what has been a long-held view among public health officials came from researchers behind a new study published in the American Journal of Obstetrics & Gynecology.

The study concluded that maternal death rates put out by the Centers for Disease Control and Prevention have been substantially inflated by misclassified data. Using an alternate way of counting deaths related to pregnancy and childbirth, the study found, U.S. maternal mortality rates would be far lower than have been reported. And they'd be stable, not rising.

The pushback followed soon after.

The CDC said it disagreed with the study's findings and criticized the researchers' methodology as a recipe for undercounting maternal deaths. The American College of Obstetricians and Gynecologists criticized the study for painting an "incomplete picture."

"To reduce the U.S. maternal mortality crisis to an 'overestimation' is irresponsible and minimizes the many lives lost and the families that have been deeply affected," Dr. Christopher Zahn, the group's interim CEO, said in a written statement.

ProPublica has been writing since 2017 about what maternal health experts condemned as unacceptably high numbers of deaths and near-deaths related to pregnancy and childbirth. Our series, "Lost Mothers," examined how most maternal deaths are preventable and how obdurate racial disparities cause Black mothers to die at far higher rates. The disproportionate toll on Black women is one point on which the CDC and the new study agree.

We also wrote about how flaws in data collection had made it challenging to understand how U.S. maternal mortality rates were changing, as well as how American outcomes compared with those of other wealthy countries.

The landscape has changed in critical ways since then. More than 20 states have banned or restricted access to abortion since the U.S. Supreme Court overturned *Roe v. Wade* in 2022; studies have shown that maternal mortality rates are higher in these states.

Credit line: From *ProPublica*, April 5 © 2024. Reprinted with permission. All rights reserved.

Thus it seems all the more urgent to revisit some key questions about this marker of reproductive health.

Why Is It So Hard to Pin Down How Many American Women Die as a Consequence of Pregnancy and Childbirth?

Health officials rely on information from death certificates to track maternal deaths. These crucial documents are filled in by doctors, turned in to state and local vital statistics offices, then funneled to epidemiologists at the CDC.

The cause-of-death information in these records has always been prone to error and often is incomplete. In the case of maternal deaths, death certificates often aren't filled out by OB-GYNs or anyone trained to recognize a connection to pregnancy or childbirth.

The simplest cases involve deaths that result directly from pregnancy, labor or postpartum complications. But pregnancy also can interact with a mother-to-be's preexisting health conditions or cause new ones, figuring into fatalities in ways that death certificates sometimes don't reflect.

For many years, research showed substantial numbers of maternal deaths were being missed—possibly as many as half. To fix this, starting in 2003, states began phasing in a revised death certificate that added a checkbox question asking whether the person who died, if female, was pregnant at the time or within a year of death.

After states added the pregnancy checkbox, they often saw their rates of maternal deaths double, experts told *ProPublica*. This eliminated the undercount, but it also brought so-called false positives: deaths counted as related to pregnancy or childbirth that really weren't. This was particularly a problem among women over 40.

The CDC highlighted these issues in several reports. In one, it found that 147 decedents over 85 had been identified as pregnant when they died or within the previous year, according to 2013 checkbox data. In another, it analyzed a sample of 2014 and 2016 maternal deaths identified via the checkbox, comparing their death certificates to hospital records; more than half the deaths were potentially false positives, the agency concluded.

In 2018, the agency made changes to improve data quality, among them that the pregnancy checkbox wouldn't be used for women who died at ages 45 and older. Last year, the CDC took another step designed to wring out errors, requiring states to start verifying checkbox information on a subset of records.

The new study's authors—a dozen researchers based mostly in Canada—say the tweaks haven't gone far enough. They propose an alternative way of counting in which deaths are classified as maternal only if at least one cause of death listed on the death certificate specifically mentions pregnancy.

Classifying deaths as maternal without this kind of evidence, based solely on the pregnancy checkbox, undermines "the very purpose of surveillance," lead author Dr. K.S. Joseph, a physician and epidemiologist at the University of British Columbia, said in an interview.

"If we are to use this cause-of-death information to institute clinical and public health programs aimed at preventing maternal death, we need proper cause of death information," he said.

He wasn't surprised that the study kicked off a firestorm: "The dominant narrative is that the U.S. has a maternal mortality crisis," he wrote in a follow-up email. "So it's not unexpected that a study such as ours is met with skepticism, at least initially."

> From 2018 to 2021, Black women have maternal mortality rates double that of women overall and 2.5 to 3 times higher than white women.

He said the researchers were confident that their findings were accurate and that the narrative would change.

The CDC, however, challenged the study's approach, arguing it would miss many maternal deaths.

One example: a mother-to-be who dies from hypertension. The checkbox should catch this, ensuring the death would be counted as maternal. Using the study's method, the death might be missed if whoever fills out the death certificate gives the cause as hypertension without adding the connection to pregnancy.

"Capturing these otherwise unrecorded maternal deaths is critical to understanding the scope of maternal mortality in the United States and taking effective public health action to prevent these deaths," the CDC said in an emailed statement.

Joseph agreed his study's method likely does underestimate maternal death rates. "But it is the best available method to answer the question of whether rates have increased over the last 20 years," he said.

So Are U.S. Maternal Mortality Rates Rising or Not?

The CDC's National Center for Health Statistics didn't publish an official U.S. maternal mortality rate for more than a decade—from 2007 to 2018—as states transitioned to using death certificates including the pregnancy checkbox.

The CDC's rate for 2018—17.4 deaths per 100,000 live births—was considerably higher than the 12.7 rate for 2007, an increase the agency attributed largely to changes in data collection. But it's less clear how much of that was driven by errors versus accurately counting maternal deaths that previously had been missed.

The agency's rates edged up again in 2019 and 2020, then leaped to almost 33 deaths per 100,000 live births in 2021. Some of this reflected the pandemic: A quarter of maternal deaths in 2020 and 2021 were associated with COVID-19, a report by the Government Accountability Office found.

The new study compares two four-year periods: 1999 to 2002 (before the checkbox) and 2018 to 2021 (after).

Using the CDC's way of counting, the maternal mortality rate more than doubled over that time frame, from about 9.7 deaths per 100,000 live births in the first period to 23.6 deaths per 100,000 live births in the second one, the study finds.

Using the researchers' formula, by contrast, maternal deaths stayed essentially flat from the first period to the second, going from 10.2 deaths per 100,000 live births to 10.4 deaths per live births.

Some of the authors' findings echo those of other researchers. For example, they found that deaths from direct obstetrical causes, such as preeclampsia and postpartum hemorrhage, decreased over time.

There have been other studies that reached similar conclusions, including one showing the rate of pregnant women who died delivering children in the hospital dropped by more than half from 2008 through 2021.

Still, the CDC's mortality data experts say they have the fundamental trend line right, particularly since the checkbox-related changes in 2018.

"We feel fairly confident that there has been an increase [in maternal mortality], particularly during the pandemic," Robert Anderson, chief of mortality statistics for the CDC, told CNN.

"We went from underestimating to overestimating, so we had to make that correction. But I feel fairly confident that the increases since 2018 are real."

What About the Data on Racial Disparities—Does This Hold Up?

Whatever method you use to calculate maternal death rates, Black women still have a substantially higher risk of dying as a result of pregnancy or childbirth.

Data from the CDC shows that for each year from 2018 to 2021, Black women have maternal mortality rates double that of women overall and 2.5 to 3 times higher than white women.

The new study, using its alternative method for counting pregnancy- and childbirth-related deaths, finds similar racial disparities over that period.

How Do U.S. Maternal Mortality Rates Compare with Those of Other Wealthy Countries?

Much of the concern about U.S. maternal death rates has been driven by its outlier status among industrialized countries and that its rates have continued to worsen as rates in many wealthy nations improved.

The 2021 rate reported by the CDC was several times those of countries like Australia and Switzerland and topped those of many middle-income countries.

By the new study's yardstick, U.S. maternal mortality rates look considerably better—similar to those of Canada and the United Kingdom though still higher than those of many other wealthy countries.

To allow rates to be compared internationally, countries around the world, including the U.S., use the World Health Organization's definition of maternal mortality.

But they often have very different systems for tracking deaths and checking the accuracy, consistency and comprehensiveness of vital statistics data. The U.K. is considered the gold standard when it comes to maternal deaths, conducting in-depth investigations into every single one.

While the new study says the CDC has been overestimating U.S. maternal mortality rates, some health experts have argued there are pregnancy-related deaths that aren't captured by the agency's data but should be.

The maternal mortality rate excludes deaths by suicide or caused by "accidental or incidental" causes, including drug overdoses. It also doesn't include maternal deaths that occur more than 42 days after giving birth. In the U.S., about 30% of pregnancy-related deaths are happening from 43 days to 365 days after delivery, a CDC report said.

"These are all issues that clinicians and public health people need to debate and to address," Joseph said. "But we haven't done it as yet."

Print Citations

CMS: Fields, Robin. "What to Know About the Roiling Debate Over U.S. Maternal Mortality Rates." In *The Reference Shelf: Reproductive Rights,* edited by Micah L. Issitt, 153-157. Amenia, NY: Grey House Publishing, 2024.

MLA: Fields, Robin. "What to Know About the Roiling Debate Over U.S. Maternal Mortality Rates." *The Reference Shelf: Reproductive Rights,* edited by Micah L. Issitt, Grey House Publishing, 2024, pp. 153-157.

APA: Fields, R (2024). What to know about the roiling debate over U.S. maternal mortality rates. In M. L. Issitt (Ed.), *The reference shelf: Reproductive rights* (pp. 153-157). Amenia, NY: Grey House Publishing. (Original work published 2024)

A Rare Disease That Underscores the Importance of Abortion Access

By Doug Johnson
Undark, September 26, 2022

It took a long time and numerous instances of nearly fainting for Renee Schmidt to figure out what was going on. Her symptoms became really noticeable as she headed to college at age 18, she recalled. About once a month, when she turned her head, she would feel herself start losing consciousness or experiencing momentary memory loss. On a few occasions, she fully passed out. Over time, the episodes occurred more frequently, sometimes 20 to 40 times per day. Schmidt had to drop out. "I couldn't do school anymore. I was pretty much in bed all day for six months at least," she said, "which was not ideal."

Three years after her symptoms emerged, Schmidt was diagnosed with Ehlers-Danlos Syndrome. EDS is a cluster of often rare, poorly understood, inherited diseases that impact connective tissues. The disorders are caused by defects in collagen, the most abundant protein in the human body, providing structural support to ligaments, tendons, and many organs. EDS symptoms can include chronic fatigue, pain, dislocations, and even surprising conditions like aortic aneurysms. In Schmidt's case, EDS was responsible for her spine's laxity, which allowed her vertebrae to compress her brainstem when she turned her head.

This past June, the Supreme Court of the United States reversed the nearly 50-year-old abortion rights case known as *Roe v. Wade*, allowing individual states to once again ban or limit access to abortion. It was a move that critics argue will likely compromise the health of people who may become pregnant—particularly those with conditions like EDS. Like many other illnesses, EDS can complicate pregnancy, and a lack of access to abortion can put people with the disorder at risk of particularly difficult pregnancies, medical experts and patients told *Undark*. For EDS, pregnancy complications can include death in rare cases.

This matter is further exacerbated by a lack of awareness of the disease among medical staff, including those involved in maternity and birth. To address this, researchers in the field have teamed up with the nonprofit Ehlers-Danlos Society to explore these complications, and establish care guidelines.

Around the world, an estimated one in every 5,000 people, or 0.02 percent of the population, has a form the disease. (By contrast, active epilepsy, which can also complicate pregnancy, affects an estimated 0.6 percent of the population. And gestational diabetes affects an estimated 4 percent of pregnant women.) Some think

Credit line: From *Undark*, September 26 © 2022. Reprinted with permission. All rights reserved.

EDS cases might be undercounted. The condition is so unknown and misunderstood among medical staff that patients can go 10 and 20 years without a diagnosis. "Within every single type of EDS—even the ultra-rare—it is being missed or underdiagnosed," said Lara Bloom, president and CEO of the Ehlers-Danlos Society.

Regardless of numbers, the team behind the Ehlers-Danlos Society project hopes that the work will make pregnancies and births safer for patients, including those in states that have banned abortion. The condition can make pregnancy more painful, uncomfortable, and potentially risky, said Sally Pezaro, an adjunct associate professor at the University of Notre Dame Australia and an assistant professor at Coventry University. Pezaro researches and practices midwifery, and is leading the EDS Society project. Because of the possible complications associated with pregnancy, she said, patients may wish to terminate—though women in states with abortion bans may not get to make this call. Still, she said she hopes that her work will make pregnancy and delivery smoother and less dangerous:

"It will hopefully increase your physician's knowledge about things to reduce the risk, or manage the risk appropriately."

Understanding EDS's impact on pregnancy and birth is complicated by the fact that there are 14 known types of the disease and an array of symptoms. Patients with the most common variety, hypermobile EDS, or hEDS, often have joint hypermobility and experience dizziness and gastrointestinal problems, among other things. Patients with the second most common type, classic EDS, often have loose skin and experience poor wound healing. One of the rarer and more dangerous types is vascular EDS, or VEDS, which comes with an increased risk for rupturing of the intestines, uterus, and various blood vessels.

According to Pezaro, EDS can complicate pregnancies in a few ways, though pregnancies with hEDS are not usually life-threatening. During pregnancy, changes in hormone levels cause joints to relax. With already weakened connective tissue, all patients with EDS can face a number of issues. For instance, they can have contractions that last for weeks, and then deliver rapidly and unexpectedly. As such, Pezaro said, they may not be near medical help when their baby comes.

Lacerations to the vaginal wall during labor and Caesarean sections may heal more slowly than is typical. EDS also increases the risk of vaginal or rectal prolapse and hemorrhage. A survey of more than 1,700 people found that those with the disorder reported higher rates of miscarriages, stillbirths, and terminations, compared to those without it. The results were published earlier this year.

Vascular EDS is associated with uterine ruptures, aortic dissections (tears in the largest artery in the body located in the heart), and even death. According to one paper from this year, the maternal mortality rates for people with VEDS can vary from 4 to 25 percent, compared to the U.S. average of 0.024 percent (23.8 deaths per 100,000 live births), according to the Centers for Disease Control and Prevention.

According to Laura McGillis, a nurse practitioner at the GoodHope Ehlers-Danlos Syndrome program in Toronto who is part of Pezaro's team, drafting the guidelines involves determining and using the best available research. But, she said,

"We don't have all the answers because there's not a lot of literature that's posted on this."

Nevertheless, since the effort began early this year, the researchers have already identified key information to be included in the guidelines, including details about the need for a multidisciplinary care team. Health care providers will also be advised to prepare for fast births, and, when necessary, to use non-dissolvable stitches because people with EDS may fail to heal before dissolvable stitches disintegrate, leaving the patient open to infection. The researchers hope to finalize the guidelines by the end of this year and then get them published.

> **EDS can complicate pregnancy, and a lack of access to abortion can put people with the disorder at risk of particularly difficult pregnancies.**

Knowledge among medical staff is quite rare, said Bloom, and EDS patients often find it hard to locate an informed practitioner. "I think, in medical school, most people are taught about EDS with a small paragraph," she said. "So that certainly needs to change."

In an email to *Undark*, Kate Connors, director of communications and public affairs for the American College of Obstetricians and Gynecologists, said the organization did not have data on how many of its members were aware of EDS and its complications. Similarly, Natalia Kimrey, associate director of marketing and communications for the American College of Nurse-Midwives wrote in an email that her group "would not have data on the relative level of awareness about EDS among midwives in the United States."

The EDS Society created an international consortium of medical professionals and experts whose names and affiliations can be found on the society's website. The website also includes a page where knowledgeable health care professionals can add their names to a directory.

People with EDS may face particular challenges in states that have banned abortion. Schmidt—who protested the end of *Roe* outside the Supreme Court—eventually got surgery for her condition in November of 2020, a month after her EDS diagnosis. (Her joints were hypermobile enough to fulfill the criteria for hEDS, though she hasn't done genetic testing to rule out other EDS types.) The surgery included the installation of a device linking her skull to a vertebra in her neck in order to keep everything in place. However, Schmidt noted, had she gotten pregnant before the procedure and had she lived in a state that banned abortion, pregnancy, labor, and delivery could have killed her.

Also, people with EDS may require medications that could harm fetuses, such as some blood pressure drugs and occasionally opioids. It may not be possible to wean off these medicines prior to an unexpected pregnancy or find alternatives that are both effective and fetus-safe, Schmidt said.

Other EDS patients share these concerns, said Mandolyn Orrell, director of the Ehlers-Danlos Syndrome Support Group of Asheville, North Carolina. The group's Facebook page has 2,727 followers. Because North Carolina recently banned abortion after 20 weeks and six days, people with EDS may be forced to carry a baby to term, and face the risks that poses. "Truly, they could lose their lives," she said of people with EDS living in states that ban abortion. "That's what it boils down to."

Currently, there are no laws prohibiting people from traveling to other states for abortions. But some states have created so-called bounty hunter laws, allowing any citizen to sue someone who helps another person get an abortion, including a partner who drives them across a state border, said Carrie Baker, a professor in Smith College's Program for the Study of Women and Gender.

Further, travel can be time-consuming, uncomfortable, and expensive for people with pre-existing conditions, according to Svetlana Blitshteyn, a neurologist at the University at Buffalo Jacobs School of Medicine and Biomedical Sciences who regularly works with people with EDS. Traveling is also expensive, which could be an issue considering many people with EDS may find it difficult to work due to discomfort or pain. Blitshteyn also noted that any abortion doctors that people with EDS go to in other states aren't likely to know about their condition or medical history.

Some people with EDS may elect to not have children—a choice that abortion bans may take away. McGillis noted that the chronic pain, joint instability, gastrointestinal issues, and migraines that can come along with EDS may be too much for a person to handle while also raising a family. As a genetic disease, EDS can be passed down to one's children: hEDS, for instance, has a 50 percent chance of being inherited. Some people may not want their children to inherit the disease. Passing down these disorders "forcibly, to a child—it's just not ok," Orrell said.

These concerns resonate beyond the EDS community. Since *Roe* was overturned, providers of reproductive healthcare have said that the contentious nature of the abortion debate has resulted in suboptimal care, and some have pointed to data indicating that abortion bans are likely to lead to higher rates of maternal mortality.

The loss of *Roe* "has spurred widespread fear and confusion amongst the public, and creates unnecessary challenges for patients who need abortion care," said Sarah Diemert, director of medical standards integration and evaluation at Planned Parenthood Federation of America, in an email to *Undark*.

Diemert added: "For many pregnant people, there are medical reasons why they may want or need to consider abortion in order to avoid serious, potentially life-threatening complications. Given the state of abortion access across the country, pregnant people may be forced to carry pregnancies to term against their will at risk of their health and life. This is unacceptable."

Many states that have banned abortion do make exceptions for things like life-threatening scenarios or irreversible physical impairment. Baker said that these vary from state to state, but also that these exceptions are often intentionally vague to dissuade doctors from performing abortions. Doctors may be cautious in making the call that someone has a life-threatening disorder that would allow them to get an abortion, for fear of losing their medical license or being charged with a crime.

Considering EDS is poorly understood, many doctors may decide that the condition is not a good enough reason for a doctor to perform an abortion, Baker said. The guidelines would note that VEDS in particular is life-threatening and, in that way, they could be useful for people with the disease who try to get an abortion in states that have banned it, according to Pezaro.

The extent to which Pezaro's work could help people with EDS who get pregnant remains to be seen. Merlin Butler is a clinical geneticist and professor emeritus at the University of Kansas Medical Center, and uses genetic testing to identify various diseases, including EDS. He noted that he's seen an increase in EDS in the past few years. In his opinion, some of the guidelines established could be common across all types of the disease. However, there are mutations in around 20 genes that are responsible for EDS, not including hEDS, for which no gene has been found responsible. As such, the guidelines should ideally be more specific to each variety of EDS, he said. Meanwhile, Blitshteyn noted that the researchers can learn a bit about the complications from the existing literature, but also that the field requires more research, and larger studies.

But Pezaro is hopeful that the guidelines will help doctors, midwives, nurses, and everyone else involved in maternity. McGillis agrees, noting the information provides "more power for patients," she said. "It's more power for practitioners to understand how to move forward safely with a pregnancy, or as safely as possible with a pregnancy."

Print Citations

CMS: Johnson, Doug. "A Rare Disease That Underscores the Importance of Abortion Access." In *The Reference Shelf: Reproductive Rights,* edited by Micah L. Issitt, 158-162. Amenia, NY: Grey House Publishing, 2024.

MLA: Johnson, Doug. "A Rare Disease That Underscores the Importance of Abortion Access." *The Reference Shelf: Reproductive Rights,* edited by Micah L. Issitt, Grey House Publishing, 2024, pp. 158-162.

APA: Johnson, D. (2024). A rare disease that underscores the importance of abortion access. M. L. Issitt (Ed.), *The reference shelf: Reproductive rights* (pp. 158-162). Amenia, NY: Grey House Publishing. (Original work published 2022)

The End of *Roe* Is Having a Chilling Effect on Pregnancy

By Lauren Leader
Politico, September 13, 2023

The end of *Roe v. Wade* in June 2022 has had a profound effect on maternal health care and abortion access across the country. Fourteen states have now completely banned abortion and two dozen more have bans at 22 weeks or less. As a result, an already grim maternal health care landscape has worsened.

New data reveals an unexpected consequence of these developments: Young women, even those in states where abortion remains legal, say they are foregoing having children because they are afraid to get pregnant because of changes that followed the *Dobbs* decision that ended *Roe*.

Polling conducted in August by my organization, All In Together, in partnership with polling firm Echelon Insights found that 34 percent of women aged 18–39 said they or someone they know personally has "decided not to get pregnant due to concerns about managing pregnancy-related medical emergencies." Put another way, poor or unavailable maternal health care post-*Dobbs* is leading people to alter some of their most important life choices.

For young people, the maternal health care crisis is deeply personal. More than a third of young people and 22 percent of young women told us they have personally dealt with or know someone who has "faced constraints when trying to manage a pregnancy-related emergency." And 23 percent of 18- to 39-year-old women say they have themselves or know someone else who has been unable to obtain an abortion in their state—a number almost three times higher than respondents in other age groups.

Perhaps most surprisingly however, these results are similar regardless of whether the respondents are living in states with abortion bans or states without restrictions on abortion access. The consistency between red and blue states suggests that the statistics on maternal mortality and the stories and struggles of women navigating the new normal on abortion access have penetrated the psyche of young people everywhere. The *Dobbs* decision, it seems, has fundamentally altered how people feel about having families and the calculus for getting pregnant.

Alexis McGill Johnson, CEO of Planned Parenthood, told me that the stories of women dying or facing near-death experiences because of abortion restrictions has struck fear in the hearts of young people, many of whom were already ambivalent about having children because of the costs and pressures that generation faces.

Credit line: From *Politico*, September 13 © 2023. Reprinted with permission. All rights reserved.

"Abortion bans make pregnancy less safe," she said, "and women are acutely aware of the consequence of restricting access to reproductive health care in their own lives."

In the wake of *Dobbs*, stories of women enduring horrific medical trauma in states where abortion is illegal have been widely reported. For instance, Carmen Broesder, an Idaho mom, documented her 19-day long harrowing miscarriage on TikTok—including her three trips to the emergency room. While only six weeks pregnant, she was denied access to a D&C (dilation and curettage) surgery because of Idaho's abortion ban.

> The hallmark of a flourishing society is one where people can fulfill their hopes and dreams.

It goes almost without saying that this is not good news for the already declining birth rates in the U.S. According to research from Pew, birth rates in the U.S. had been falling since the early 2000s and plummeted during the COVID pandemic. Fertility rates briefly rebounded after the pandemic but now, post-*Dobbs*, they have dropped again.

Should this trend continue, the reluctance of young women to have children now will have vast and long-term consequences for the American economy and fabric of the nation. Falling birth rates can affect everything from tax revenue to labor force participation, schools, housing, elder care and more.

But beyond the macroeconomic ramifications, there is also a human and emotional toll for people who may want children but are too afraid to have them. The hallmark of a flourishing society is one where people can fulfill their hopes and dreams, and for many, those dreams include raising a family. But for a generation of Americans, that dream now appears frustrated. Gen Y and Z Americans report higher rates of mental health challenges and stress than other generations. The *Dobbs* decision has clearly contributed to that anxiety.

All of this signals troubling, unexpected and ominous continuing consequences of the Supreme Court's deeply unpopular *Dobbs* ruling and the ripple effects that abortion bans, which polls show a majority of Americans oppose, have created. It's a trend worth watching and weighing—for lawmakers, for women, for families and for all Americans.

Print Citations

CMS: Leader, Lauren. "The End of *Roe* Is Having a Chilling Effect on Pregnancy." In *The Reference Shelf: Reproductive Rights*, edited by Micah L. Issitt, 163-165. Amenia, NY: Grey House Publishing, 2024.

MLA: Leader, Lauren. "The End of *Roe* Is Having a Chilling Effect on Pregnancy." *The Reference Shelf: Reproductive Rights*, edited by Micah L. Issitt, Grey House Publishing, 2024, pp. 163-165.

APA: Leader, L. (2024). The end of *Roe* is having a chilling effect on pregnancy. In M. L. Issitt (Ed.), *The reference shelf: Reproductive rights* (pp. 163-165). Amenia, NY: Grey House Publishing. (Original work published 2023)

What Overturning *Roe v. Wade* Means Psychologically for Teens Who Could Get Pregnant

By Kimberly Zapata
Parents, July 21, 2022

On Friday, June 24, the Supreme Court made a landmark decision. With a vote of 6–3, the nation's highest court overturned *Roe v. Wade*, ending nearly 50 years of federally protected abortion rights. And while this decision will have far-reaching effects—in many states, for example, pregnant people will not have access to fair, safe, or reasonable reproductive health—there are mental health implications, too. Frank C. Worrell, Ph.D., president of the American Psychological Association (APA), worries we are on the brink of a "psychological crisis."

"We are setting up a situation where we are deliberately pushing people into a psychological crisis," Dr. Worrell told Fortune, emphasizing that the decision will disproportionately hurt low-income individuals and people of color. "If you live in a state with a law that [has gotten rid of or] will get rid of abortion, your level of anxiety will go up."

"This ruling ignores not only precedent but science, and will exacerbate the mental health crisis America is already experiencing," Dr. Worrell added in a statement. "We are alarmed that the justices would nullify *Roe* despite decades of scientific research demonstrating that people who are denied abortions are more likely to experience higher levels of anxiety, lower life satisfaction, and lower self-esteem compared with those who are able to obtain abortions."

Why Teens Are Especially Impacted by the Court's Decision

Of course, pregnant people across the country will feel the effects of this decision. *Roe v. Wade* impacts individuals of all ages. But teens, particularly marginalized youths, are at-risk. Why? Because teens, tweens, and young adults already face many barriers. It is hard for youths to access and afford reproductive health. If they have to travel for said health care, they will face additional hurdles. Many teens don't have access to transportation, for example. This will make it extremely difficult to find and access care. They are also "vulnerable" to mental health issues—and mental health concerns.

"We know that self-harm and suicidal behavior in teens is associated with stress, uncertainty, and social pressures," says Sarah Gupta, M.D., a board-certified

Credit line: From *Parents*, July 21 © 2022. Reprinted with permission. All rights reserved.

physician with expertise in psychiatry and neurology. Rates of non-suicidal self-injury are increased at this age. Approximately 17% of teens have admitted to self-injuring at least once in their life. Suicide is also too prevalent. It is the second leading cause of death among children aged 15 to 19, and this number increases for LGBTQIA+ and Black teens. According to The Trevor Project, LGBTQIA+ youth are more than four times as likely to attempt suicide than their peers, and according to the AACAP, Black youth are twice as likely to die by suicide as their white counterparts.

> **The restricting and/or outright banning of abortion could also increase emotional, physical, relational, and financial stress for anyone who is pregnant or can get pregnant.**

The disparities are alarming. They are also striking and, when compared to other risk factors—like health care access—a major cause of concern.

"It's definitely possible that the overturning of *Roe v. Wade* will lead to an increase in suicidal behaviors in pregnant adolescents," Dr. Gupta adds. "The extra stress and uncertainty may also worsen anxiety and depression."

Reduced Access to Health Care Increases Mental Health Risks

Dr. Gupta's concerns are not unique, nor are they unfounded. The American Academy of Child and Adolescent Psychiatry (AACAP) voiced similar concerns hours after *Roe v. Wade* was overturned.

"Lack of abortion availability for pregnant teens with psychiatric disorders may severely impact the course of their health, including mental health and increase risk for suicide," a AACAP statement reads. "The Supreme Court's ruling, in combination with state laws criminalizing support or assistance to these youth seeking abortions can criminalize psychiatric care, impeding our ability as child and adolescent psychiatrists, to act in the best interests of our patient's overall health care needs."

The numbers don't lie, either. According to a long-term study, which followed more than 1,000 pregnant people, when individuals are denied abortions, they face increased economic hardship and—in turn—additional mental health challenges.

"It's important for folks to know that abortion does not cause mental health problems," Debra Mollen, Ph.D., a professor of counseling psychology at Texas Woman's University, who studies abortion and reproductive rights, told the APA. "What's harmful are the stigma surrounding abortion, the lack of knowledge about it, and the lack of access." The restricting and/or outright banning of abortion could also increase emotional, physical, relational, and financial stress for anyone who is pregnant or can get pregnant.

"This kind of globalized stress increases the severity of existing mental health conditions and creates vulnerabilities for new conditions to emerge," Grace Dickman, a licensed clinical social worker with her own private practice, told Verywell Mind.

Health Organizations Issue Statements of Concern

Of course, it's worth noting that other organizations have spoken out against the overturning of *Roe v. Wade*. The American Academy of Pediatrics (AAP) stresses the importance of bodily autonomy and reproductive control (i.e. adolescents should be allowed to make their own health care decisions, particularly in regard to undesired and/or unplanned pregnancy). Timely access to said care is also extremely important.

"[June 24th's] Supreme Court decision to overturn *Roe v. Wade* means that the once Constitutionally protected right to access an abortion is no longer guaranteed nationwide," Moira Szilagyi, president of the AAP, said in a statement. "This decision carries grave consequences for our adolescent patients, who already face many more barriers than adults in accessing comprehensive reproductive health care services and abortion care.... [it also means that] evidence-based care will be difficult or impossible to access, threatening the health and safety of our patients and jeopardizing the patient-physician relationship."

The JED Foundation echoed a similar sentiment, particularly in regard to how this decision affects teen and tween mental health. "Youth mental health is already in a state of crisis," according to the U.S. Surgeon General. "One in three young adults between ages 18 and 25 has experienced a mental, emotional, or behavioral health issue in the past year," a statement reads. "[And] overturning *Roe v. Wade* has added to the significant stressors that were already impacting their day-to-day lives, as well as their overall physical, emotional, and mental health."

"The Supreme Court's decision will be especially detrimental to marginalized groups," the foundation adds. "Black people will be disproportionately targeted, [as] they are more likely to live in states subject to abortion bans, and they are five times more likely to pursue abortions than white people (due to reasons such as difficulty accessing contraception, likelihood of being uninsured, and higher rates of both pregnancy complications and maternal death, among other reasons), according to the *Washington Post*. "It also disproportionately impacts LGBTQ individual."

The American Foundation for Suicide Prevention has yet to release a statement. They also declined to comment for this report.

What We Can Do to Help Teens

So what can people and parents do? How can teens cope with an unplanned and unwanted pregnancy? According to Dr. Gupta, it is essential that pregnant adolescents get support—from friends, family, and their community.

"There are excellent resources available to help pregnant teens understand their options, including parenting, kinship care, adoption, and abortion," she says. "For reproductive health information, resources, and tools, GoodRx's Reproductive Health Center and the Planned Parenthood teen website are great places to start. The latter can help teens connect with in-person services, if needed. Confidential help is also available 24/7 by calling the National Suicide Prevention Lifeline at 988 or by texting 'HOME' to Crisis Text Line at 741741, and LGBTQIA+ teens can access additional resources through The Trevor Project."

Scarleteen is another excellent resource, says Matthew Goldenberg, Psy.D., a psychologist at the Seattle Children's Hospital Gender Clinic. "Many websites offer information for teens on mental health, sexual health, and identity such as Scarleteen," he says.

The Society for Adolescent Health and Medicine also has sexual and reproductive health resources.

Print Citations

CMS: Zapata, Kimberly. "What Overturning *Roe v. Wade* Means Psychologically for Teens Who Could Get Pregnant." In *The Reference Shelf: Reproductive Rights,* edited by Micah L. Issitt, 166-169. Amenia, NY: Grey House Publishing, 2024.

MLA: Zapata, Kimberly. "What Overturning *Roe v. Wade* Means Psychologically for Teens Who Could Get Pregnant." *The Reference Shelf: Reproductive Rights,* edited by Micah L. Issitt, Grey House Publishing, 2024, pp. 166-169.

APA: Zapata, K. (2024). What overturning *Roe v. Wade* means psychologically for teens who could get pregnant. In M. L. Issitt (Ed.), *The reference shelf: Reproductive rights* (pp. 166-169). Amenia, NY: Grey House Publishing. (Original work published 2022)

More U.S. Women Are Avoiding Unwanted or Mistimed Pregnancies

By Claire Cain Miller
New York Times, May 3, 2023

Births and pregnancies in the United States have been on a long-term decline. A new data analysis provides one reason: It's becoming less common for women to get pregnant when they don't want to be.

The analysis, released Thursday in the journal *Demography* by researchers at the Guttmacher Institute, estimates the number of pregnancies in the United States—there is no single official count—and examines women's feelings about the timing of their pregnancies. In the past, most demography surveys have asked if pregnancies were intended or not, but that approach missed nuances like whether a woman was ambivalent about being pregnant—or wanted to be pregnant, but earlier or later.

The new analysis, covering 2009 to 2015, found that a growing majority of women said their pregnancies came at the right time. It uncovered a decline in the share of pregnancies that women didn't want or that happened too soon, a shift driven by young women.

It also found that a significant and increasing share of women—particularly those 35 and older—said they were getting pregnant later than they wanted.

"This just bolsters that idea that people have more control over their reproduction, especially in earlier ages," said Alison Gemmill, a demographer and epidemiologist at Johns Hopkins who studies reproductive health and was not involved in the new study.

It also reflects, she said, "a change in people's ideals about when to have kids and norms around the ideal time—when we're settled, when I have my career established. . . ."

The new data is one of the clearest indicators that the drop in fertility during the Great Recession was not just a temporary delay, as often happens in recessions. Instead, it seems to have coincided with a broader shift in what women wanted, and increased access to contraception.

The analysis combined reports and surveys from the National Center for Health Statistics; abortion data from Guttmacher; and estimates of total pregnancies and miscarriages.

The data is from before two seismic events that affected fertility: the pandemic, followed by the *Dobbs* decision that ended the nationwide right to abortion. It's unclear what long-term changes those will bring. There is early evidence that at the

---

Credit line: From the *New York Times,* May 3 © 2023. Reprinted with permission. All rights reserved.

beginning of the pandemic, many people delayed getting pregnant. There could also be an increase in the share of unwanted or mistimed births in states with new abortion bans.

The United States has long had one of the highest rates of unintended pregnancy in the industrialized world. It has declined 23 percent in the last three decades, and 46 percent of pregnancies are now unintended. In Western Europe, by comparison, 36 percent are unintended, and the rate has not changed much.

> **Research has shown a big increase in the share of women using more effective long-acting reversible contraceptives like IUDs.**

The new analysis suggests that during the period of the study, American women rapidly gained more autonomy over their family planning, and had fewer abortions because of it.

The data indicates that "far fewer individuals were becoming pregnant in 2015 than in 2009, and that abortion incidence went down because individuals did not get pregnant, not because their pregnancies continued to a birth instead of an abortion," wrote the paper's authors, the Guttmacher researchers Kathryn Kost, Mia Zolna and Rachel Murro.

In 2015, just under a quarter of women said their pregnancy came too soon, a decline of 18 percent from 2009. There was also a slight decline of 5 percent, to 17 percent, in the share of pregnant women who said they did not want a baby at all. These declines were driven by younger women having significantly fewer unwanted pregnancies.

During this period, birth control became more easily accessible, largely because of a provision in the Affordable Care Act requiring it to be free for patients. Research has shown a big increase in the share of women using more effective long-acting reversible contraceptives like IUDs. A program in Colorado to provide free long-acting birth control led to a 40 percent decline in births to teenagers and young adults.

There is also data showing that young people are having less sex, perhaps because they are socializing online more and engaging in fewer risky behaviors overall.

. . .

The fertility rate has been increasing among the oldest childbearing women, ages 35 to 44, and in one sense, researchers said, this indicates that women are exercising more control over the timing of their pregnancies. Highly educated women have been delaying pregnancies until they complete their educations and start their careers, and more recently, that has become true of women of all educational backgrounds.

Yet the analysis also shows something new—that for many women over 35, their pregnancies are coming later than they want. The share who said so increased 84 percent, while the share who said they occurred at about the right time dropped 26 percent. (The new data does not include women who never became pregnant.)

This could be because they run into fertility troubles at older ages, the researchers wrote, and suggests a "substantial, and growing, unmet need for fertility treatment services."

It could also indicate, researchers said, that for some, family planning was driven by financial uncertainty—they may have waited to get pregnant until they found their financial footing but wished it had been earlier. It could suggest that, in hindsight, they regretted having waited. Or it could signal that more women are having difficulty finding suitable partners.

"To see it increasing, we started thinking this isn't just about difficulty becoming pregnant at an older age," said Ms. Kost, who has a Ph.D. in sociology and is director of domestic research at Guttmacher. "We are also wondering to what extent is this a reflection of economic constraints and realities people are living through, and the increasing burdens people are feeling in the ability to have families on the timeline they want."

Print Citations

CMS: Miller, Claire Cain. "More U.S. Women Are Avoiding Unwanted or Mistimed Pregnancies." In *The Reference Shelf: Reproductive Rights,* edited by Micah L. Issitt, 170-172. Amenia, NY: Grey House Publishing, 2024.

MLA: Miller, Claire Cain. "More U.S. Women Are Avoiding Unwanted or Mistimed Pregnancies." *The Reference Shelf: Reproductive Rights,* edited by Micah L. Issitt, Grey House Publishing, 2024, pp. 170-172.

APA: Miller, C. C. (2024). More U.S. women are avoiding unwanted or mistimed pregnancies. In M. L. Issitt (Ed.), *The reference shelf: Reproductive rights* (pp. 170-172). Amenia, NY: Grey House Publishing. (Original work published 2023)

Bibliography

"14th Amendment." Legal Information Institute (LII). *Cornell Law School*, www.law.cornell.edu/constitution/amendmentxiv.

"Abortion Policy in the Absence of Roe." *Guttmacher Institute,* 24 Apr. 2023, www.guttmacher.org/state-policy/explore/abortion-policy-absence-roe.

"Abortion Viewed in Moral Terms: Fewer See Stem Cell Research and IVF as Moral Issues." *Pew Research Center*, 15 Aug. 2013, www.pewresearch.org/religion/2013/08/15/abortion-viewed-in-moral-terms/#:~:text=is%20morally%20acceptabl[...]tion,-https://www.pewresearch.org/short-reads/2024/05/13/americans-overwhelmingly-say-access-to-ivf-is-a-good-thing/For%20comparison%20purposes.

Abrams, Abigail. "No, Birth Control Doesn't Make You Have Riskier Sex, Researchers Say." *Time Magazine*, 12 Oct. 2017, time.com/4975951/donald-trump-birth-control-mandate-sexual-behavior/.

Badger, Emily, Margot Sanger-Katz, and Claire Cain Miller. "States with Abortion Bans Are Among Least Supportive for Mothers and Children." *New York Times*. 28 July 2022.

Barr, Beth Alison. *The Making of Biblical Womanhood: How the Subjugation of Women Became Gospel.* Brazos Press, 2021.

Borelli, Gabriel. "Americans Overwhelmingly Say Access to IVF Is a Good Thing." *Pew Research Center*, 13 May 2024, www.pewresearch.org/short-reads/2024/05/13/americans-overwhelmingly-say-access-to-ivf-is-a-good-thing/.

Brenan, Megan, and Sydia Saad. "Record Share of U.S. Electorate Is Pro-Choice and Voting on It." *Gallup*, 13 June 2024, news.gallup.com/poll/645836/record-share-electorate-pro-choice-voting.aspx.

Caldwell, Noah, Katia Riddle, and Ailsa Chang. "The Family Politics Behind J. D. Vance's 'Childless Cat Ladies' Comment." *NPR*, 25 July 2024, www.npr.org/2024/07/25/nx-s1-5051873/the-family-politics-behind-j-d-vances-childless-cat-ladies-comment.

Citron, Danielle K. "Sexual Privacy." *Yale Law Journal*, 2019.

Clark, Simon. "How White Supremacy Returned to Mainstream Politics." *CAP*, 1 July 2020, www.americanprogress.org/article/white-supremacy-returned-mainstream-politics/.

"Crisis Pregnancy Centers." *ACOG*, www.acog.org/advocacy/abortion-is-essential/trending-issues/issue-brief-crisis-pregnancy-centers.

"Declaration of Independence: A Transcription." *National Archives*, www.archives.gov/founding-docs/declaration-transcript.

DeRose, Jason. "Despite Church Prohibitions, Catholics Still Choose IVF to Have Children." *NPR*, 22 Mar. 2024, www.npr.org/2024/03/22/1239879602/despite-church-prohibitions-catholics-still-choose-ivf-to-have-children.

Dessalegn, Banchiamlack. "Gender Equality Isn't Possible Without Abortion and Contraception." *Al Jazeera*, 18 Mar. 2023, www.aljazeera.com/opinions/2023/3/18/gender-equality-isnt-possible-without-abortion-and-contraception.

Farrar, Lauren. "Sex Education in America: The Good, the Bad, the Ugly." *KQED*, 16 Sept. 2020, www.kqed.org/education/534518/sex-education-in-america-the-good-the-bad-the-ugly.

Forouzan, Kimya. "Midyear 2024 State Policy Trends: Many US States Attack Reproductive Health Care, as Other States Fight Back." *Guttmacher Institute,* June 2024, www.guttmacher.org/2024/06/midyear-2024-state-policy-trends-many-us-states-attack-reproductive-health-care-other.

"Freedom of Religion, Speech, Press, Assembly, and Petition." *Constitution Center*, constitutioncenter.org/the-constitution/amendments/amendment-i.

"Grand Jury, Double Jeopardy, Self-Incrimination, Due Process, Takings." *Constitution Center*, constitutioncenter.org/the-constitution/amendments/amendment-v.

Haas, John M. "Begotten Not Made: A Catholic View of Reproductive Technology." *United States Conference of Catholic Bishops*, www.usccb.org/issues-and-action/human-life-and-dignity/reproductive-technology/begotten-not-made-a-catholic-view-of-reproductive-technology.

Hesse, Monica. "Embryos Are Vessels of Hope, Pain and Love: But They Are Not Children." *Washington Post*, 21 Feb. 2024, www.washingtonpost.com/style/power/2024/02/21/embryos-alabama-supreme-court-ruling/.

Horowitch, Rose. "*Dobb's* Confounding Effect on Abortion Rates." *The Atlantic*, 26 Oct. 2023, www.theatlantic.com/politics/archive/2023/10/post-roe-national-abortion-rates/675778/.

Hubbard, Kaia. "The Link Between Abortion Rights and Gender Equality." *U.S. News and World Report,* 25 Aug. 2022, www.usnews.com/news/best-states/articles/how-abortion-rights-are-linked-to-gender-equality.

Iannacci, Nicandro. "Recalling the Supreme Court's Historic Statement on Contraception and Privacy." *Constitution Center*, 7 June 2019, constitutioncenter.org/blog/contraception-marriage-and-the-right-to-privacy.

Janfaza, Rachel. "The Nuanced Push for American Sex Education." *Harvard Political Review*, 24 Jan. 2020, harvardpolitics.com/american-sex-education/.

Ma, Adrian, and Wailin Wong. "Abortion Access Tends to Lower Child Poverty Rates, Economists Say." *NPR*, 26 May 2022.

Maddow-Zimet, Isaac, and Kathryn Kost. "Even Before Roe Was Overturned, Nearly One in 10 People Obtaining an Abortion Traveled Across State Lines for Care." *Guttmacher Institute,* July 2022, www.guttmacher.org/article/2022/07/even-roe-was-overturned-nearly-one-10-people-obtaining-abortion-traveled-across.

Martin, Jennifer. "50 Surprising Things Americans Actually Agree On." *CBS News*, 27 Sept. 2022, www.cbsnews.com/pictures/surprising-things-americans-actually-agree-on/.

Mies, Maria. *Patriarchy and Accumulation on a World Scale: Women in the International Division of Labor*. Zed Books, 1998.

"Modeling the Future of Religion in America." *Pew Research Center*, 13 Sept. 2022, www.pewresearch.org/religion/2022/09/13/modeling-the-future-of-religion-in-america/.

"Moral Case Against Contraception." *BBC*, 2014, Ethics Guide, www.bbc.co.uk/ethics/contraception/against_1.shtml.

Morrison, Alan B. "Selective Judicial Activism in the Roberts Court." *American Constitution Society*, www.acslaw.org/analysis/acs-journal/acs-supreme-court-review-sixth-edition/selective-judicial-activism-in-the-roberts-court/#_ftnref1=.

Mulvihill, Geoff, and Linley Sanders. "Few Adults Support Full Abortion Bans, Even in States That Have Them, an AP-NORC Poll Finds." *Associated Press*, 11 July 2023, https://apnews.com/article/abortion-poll-roe-dobbs-ban-opinion-fcfdfc5a799ac3be617d99999e92eabe.

"Non-Enumerated Rights Retained by People." *Constitution Center*, constitutioncenter.org/the-constitution/amendments/amendment-ix.

Ollove, Michael. "Some States Already Are Targeting Birth Control." *Stateline*, 19 May 2022, stateline.org/2022/05/19/some-states-already-are-targeting-birth-control/.

Petchesky, Rosalind Pollack. *Abortion and Women's Choice: The State, Sexuality, and Reproductive Freedom*. Verso, 1989.

Popovich, Nadja. "Explainer: US Abortion Rates Drop, but Data and Reasons Behind It Are Complex." *The Guardian*, 8 June 2015, https://www.theguardian.com/world/2015/jun/08/us-abortion-down-new-survey.

Pratasava, Veleryia. "Unwanted Pregnancies: Outcomes for Children." *Drexel University*, 18 Feb. 2022, drexel.edu/medicine/academics/womens-health-and-leadership/womens-health-education-program/whep-blog/unwanted-pregnancies-outcomes-for-children/.

"Premarital Sex Is Nearly Universal Among Americans and Has Been for Decades." *Guttmacher Institute*, 19 Dec. 2006, www.guttmacher.org/news-release/2006/premarital-sex-nearly-universal-among-americans-and-has-been-decades.

"Privacy." Legal Information Institute (LII). *Cornell Law School*, www.law.cornell.edu/wex/privacy.

"Public Opinion on Abortion." *Pew Research Center*, 13 May 2024, www.pewresearch.org/religion/fact-sheet/public-opinion-on-abortion/.

"Public Opinion on Privacy." *Electronic Privacy Information Center (EPIC)*, archive.epic.org/privacy/survey/.

"Quartering of Soldiers." *Constitution Center*, constitutioncenter.org/the-constitution/amendments/amendment-iii.

Rice, Andrea. "Self-Managed Abortions Rose Sharply After Roe's Reversal, Study Finds." *Healthline*, 25 Mar. 2024, www.healthline.com/health-news/self-managed-abortions-increasing-post-roe.

Robertson, Rachael. "Why Discarding Embryos Is Inherent to the IVF Process." *Medpage Today*, 28 Feb. 2024, www.medpagetoday.com/obgyn/infertility/108932.

"Search and Seizure." *Constitution Center*, constitutioncenter.org/the-constitution/amendments/amendment-iv.

Skelley, Geoffrey, and Holly Fuong. "How Americans Feel About Contraception." *FiveThirtyEight*, 12 July 2022, fivethirtyeight.com/features/abortion-birth-control-poll/.

"A Step-By-Step Look at the IVF Process." *Penn Medicine*, 20 Apr. 2020, www.pennmedicine.org/updates/blogs/fertility-blog/2020/april/how-does-the-ivf-process-work.

"Survey Shows Strong Support for Increased Access to Fertility Treatments." *American Society for Reproductive Medicine (ASRM)*, 23 Apr. 2024, www.asrm.org/news-and-events/asrm-news/press-releasesbulletins/survey-shows-strong-support-fertility/.

Treisman, Rachel. "States with the Toughest Abortion Laws Have the Weakest Maternal Supports, Data Shows." *NPR*, 18 Aug. 2022, www.npr.org/2022/08/18/1111344810/abortion-ban-states-social-safety-net-health-outcomes.

"Turnout in the United States." *Fairvote*, fairvote.org/resources/voter-turnout/.

"US Adolescents' Receipt of Formal Sex Education." *Guttmacher Institute*, Feb. 2022, www.guttmacher.org/fact-sheet/adolescents-teens-receipt-sex-education-united-states?gad_source=1&gclid=CjwKCAjwnqK1BhBvEiwAi7o0Xw-8jEk2O-R7g1cB4l8eeHKy9nM0e8SwFEjdnmk64TYx_i5DZ5TgDRoCPP4QAvD_BwE#gad_source=1.

"U.S. Pregnancy Rates Drop During Last Decade." *CDC*, 12 Apr. 2023, www.cdc.gov/nchs/pressroom/nchs_press_releases/2023/20230412.htm.

"Views of the U.S. Political System, the Federal Government and Federal-State Relations." *Pew Research Center*, 19 Sept. 2023.

"Voter Turnout, 2018–2022." *Pew Research Center*, 12 July 2023, www.pewresearch.org/politics/2023/07/12/voter-turnout-2018-2022/.

Waldman, Michael. *The Supermajority: How the Supreme Court Divided America*. Simon & Schuster, 2023.

Wamhoff, Steve. "Trio of GOP Tax Bills Would Expand Corporate Tax Breaks While Doing Little for Americans Who Most Need Help." *ITEP*, 11 June 2023, itep.org/gop-tax-bills-expand-corporate-tax-breaks/.

Websites

Americans United for Life (AUL)
www.americansunitedforlife.org

Established in 1971, Americans United for Life (AUL) is the second-oldest political antiabortion organization in the United States. AUL opposes all forms of abortion and recommends complete abortion bans, and also opposes physician assisted suicide, euthanasia, embryonic stem cell research, and in vitro fertilization (IVF). The organization has campaigned against all of these medical technologies and methods in judicial cases and also has worked on the implementation of antiabortion and restrictive reproductive legislation. Founded by a Unitarian minister, the organization promotes a conservative Christian perspective on abortion and related issues.

Center for Reproductive Rights (CRR)
www.reproductiverights.org

The Center for Reproductive Rights (CRR) is a global health advocacy organization that supports research and funds political efforts to oppose laws restricting reproductive rights and access to services. Founded in the 1990s, the CRR produces a wide variety of research reports, surveys, and analyses of reproductive laws in the United States and abroad. In 2016, the CRR took the lead in the first ever case involving abortion tried in front of the United Nations.

Guttmacher Institute
www.guttmacher.org

The Guttmacher Institute is a research and policy think tank and advocacy organization focused on expanding access to reproductive health care and protecting reproductive rights worldwide. The Guttmacher Institute supports and funds research into reproductive rights issues and makes much of this research available to researchers and students at no charge. Founded in 1968, as an outgrowth of Planned Parenthood, the Guttmacher institute also operates as an educational institute, providing training for citizens and health-care professionals in addressing reproductive health and rights issues.

National Organization for Women (NOW)
www.now.org

The National Organization of Women (NOW), started in 1966, is not solely focused on reproductive rights but is a feminist social welfare organization, operating in all fifty states, and with satellite connections around the world, that advocates for the rights of women and opposes limitations on civil liberties and individual rights affecting women and members of lesbian, gay, bisexual, transgender, queer or questioning, intersex, asexual, and more (LGBTQIA+) communities, and racial minorities. Because reproductive rights are closely related to women's rights, NOW also supports efforts to protect reproductive freedoms, and opposes laws banning abortions or restricting access to contraception, in vitro fertilization (IVF), while also promoting policies that enhance women's health and welfare.

National Right to Life Committee (NRLC)
www.nrlc.org

The National Right to Life Committee (NRLC), started in 1966 by the National Conference of Catholic Bishops, is the nation's oldest and largest antiabortion organization. The NRLC gathers funding from citizens and uses this to promote antiabortion legislation at the local, state, and national level. The organization has produced documentaries and public information campaigns designed to reduce public support for abortions and abortion-related health care. Information on their beliefs and views can be found in a number of informational pamphlets produced by the organization explaining moral objections to abortion.

Planned Parenthood Federation of America (PFFA)
www.plannedparenthood.org

Planned Parenthood is one of the oldest and most controversial reproductive health clinics in the United States. Started in New York by reproductive rights pioneer Margaret Sanger, Planned Parenthood clinics provide treatment and information about abortion, sexually transmitted disease, pregnancy, and birth control. They are the most targeted American health clinic by antiabortion extremists and currently fund efforts to help pregnant people find and obtain abortions and related care. The PFFA website contains a variety of information about the reproductive rights debate and current challenges, as well as medical information about pregnancy, abortion, contraception, and other reproductive issues.

Reproductive Freedom for All (NARAL)
www.reproductivefreedomforall.org

Established in 1969, as the National Association to Repeal Abortion Laws, or NARAL, Reproductive Freedom for All is a US lobbyist and political action organization that opposes restrictions on abortion-related care and birth control and also campaigns on related issues involving maternal care and welfare. NARAL provides a variety of research reports and studies, most available to the public at no charge, and also supports legal efforts to challenge restrictive abortion laws or to defend individuals accused of abortion related offenses.

Index

Abortion and Woman's Choice, 143
abortion law, 6, 23, 24, 37, 39, 59, 147, 148
abortion-rights, xvi, 4, 5, 6, 16, 17, 34, 35, 36, 37, 59, 64, 69, 71, 72, 76, 102, 103, 104, 143, 147, 148, 150, 158, 166
Abrahamic faiths, 81
Access to Family Building Act, 129, 138
Adelson, Miriam, 63
Affordable Care Act, 92, 171
African Americans, xii
Alito, Samuel, 3, 74
Al Jazeera, 144, 147
Alliance Defending Freedom, 61
Alliance for Hippocratic Medicine, 11, 28, 70
American Academy of Child and Adolescent Psychiatry (AACAP), 167
American Academy of Pediatrics (AAP), 168
American Civil Liberties Union, 17
American College of Obstetricians and Gynecologists (ACOG), 92, 134, 153, 160
American Communities Project (ACP), 53
American Constitution Society, 3, 7
American Foundation for Suicide Prevention, 168
American Journal of Obstetrics & Gynecology, 153
American Medical Association, 92
American Pharmacists Association, 93
American Psychological Association (APA), 166
American rights, 143
American Society for Reproductive Medicine (ASRM), 113, 126, 134
Anderson, Robert, 156

antiabortion activists, xvi, xvii, 3, 4, 5, 7

Bacon, Don, 137
Barnes, Stan, 104
Becerra, Xavier, 19
Beltsos, Angeline, 131
Beussink, Deb, 31
Biden, Joe, 17, 18, 19, 20, 22, 53, 57, 58, 59, 60, 61, 66, 67, 68, 73, 74, 77, 102, 103, 104, 136, 138
Bill of Rights, xi, 43
birth control pills, 50, 81, 91
Birthright of Cape Girardeau, 31
Bixby Center for Global Reproductive Health, 92
Blouin, Amy, 31
Breyer, Stephen, 73
Britt, Katie, 115, 136
Buttigieg, Pete, 108

Cedars, Marcelle, 132
Center for American Progress, 144
Center for Reproductive Rights, 17, 132
Centers for Disease Control and Prevention, 126, 153, 159
childbirth, 4, 107, 144, 153, 154, 156
Citron, Danielle K., xiii
Civil War, xii
Colinvaux, Roger, 62
Collins, Francis, 127
Collura, Barbara, 138
Comstock Act, 19, 22, 23
Connors, Kate, 160
conservative fundamentalism, xv
COVID-19 pandemic, 11
Cox, Kate, 58
crisis pregnancy centers (CPCs), 6, 7, 8, 30, 31, 32, 33
Crux, Ted, 115

Dannenfelser, Marjorie, 18, 77
Declaration of Independence, xii, xvii, xviii
Department of Health and Human Services, 69, 71, 93
Depo-Provera injection, 88, 89, 90
Dessalegn, Banchiamlack, 144
Dickey-Wicker Amendment, 128
Digital Age, xiii
Dobbs v. Jackson Women's Health Organization, 3, 12, 18, 39, 91
Donalds, Byron, 122
Duckworth, Tammy, 122, 123, 129, 131, 138

Ehlers-Danlos Society, 158, 159
Ehlers-Danlos Syndrome, 158, 159, 160
emergency contraceptive pills (EC), 97
Emergency Medical Treatment and Active Labor Act (EMTALA), 18, 71
Emergency Medical Treatment and Labor Act (EMTLA), 13
Ethics and Religious Liberty Commission, 114, 115
evangelical Christians, xv, 115

Faculty of Reproductive and Sexual Health (FSRH), 89
Faith and Freedom Coalition, 68, 77
Family Research Council, 77, 123, 129
FDA v. Alliance for Hippocratic Medicine, 11, 70
Fertility Clinic Success Rate and Certification Act of 1992, 126
Fifth Amendment, xi, xii
First Amendment, x, xi, xv
Food and Drug Administration (FDA), 5, 27, 69, 91
Fourteenth Amendment, xii, 12
Free the Pill, 92, 93

Gersen, Jeannie Suk, 123
Graham, Lindsey, 57

Griswold v. Connecticut, ix, 73
Gupta, Sarah, 166

Haas, John M., 107
Harris, Kamala, 102, 104, 108
Health Insurance Portability and Accountability Act (HIPAA), 6
Heritage Foundation, 137, 138
Hesse, Monica, 110
Hilton, Ebony Jade, 93
Human Fertilisation and Embryology Authority, 128
Human Life Amendment, 123
Hunt, Megan, 104
Hyde Amendment, 12
Hyde-Smith, Cindy, 122, 129

infertility, 88, 89, 90, 107, 109, 113, 126, 132, 138
Instagram, 88
intrauterine devices (IUDs), 4, 50, 81, 82, 85, 86, 89, 90, 97, 99, 100, 101, 171
in vitro fertilization (IVF), xvi, xvii, 18, 21, 77, 105, 107, 109, 110, 111, 112, 113, 114, 115, 116, 117, 118, 119, 120, 121, 122, 123, 124, 125, 126, 127, 128, 129, 130, 131, 132, 133, 134, 136, 137, 138, 139, 147

Jackson-Bey, Tia, 132
Johnson, Alexis McGill, 163
Johnson, Mike, 116, 123, 138
Joseph, K.S., 154
Judaism, 81, 82

Kacsmaryk, Matthew, 27, 28
Kagan, Elena, 72, 73
Kavanaugh, Brett, 27, 74
KFF Women's Health Survey, 95
Kirk, Charlie, 65
Klein, Jennifer, 18
Kost, Kathryn, 7, 171

Lake, Kari, 57
Lawrence v. Texas, 73
Leatherwood, Brent, 114
Leo, Leonard, 63
levonorgestrel, 99, 100
LGBTQIA+, 71, 147, 167, 168
Life at Conception Act, 122, 123, 136, 137
Living Infants Fairness and Equality Act (LIFE Act), 23
Loper Bright Enterprises v. Raimondo, 69
Luna, Anna Paulina, 138

Mace, Nancy, 122, 138
Marshall, Roger, 128, 136
Marsh, Margaret, 128
maternal death, 153, 155, 156, 168
Medicare, 19, 48, 77
miscarriage, 14, 27, 58, 131, 133, 134, 164
Mohler, Albert, 115
Molinaro, Marc, 138
Moore, Wes, 35
Morrison, Alan B., 3
Moyle v. United States, 13
MSI Reproductive Choices, 144
Murray, Patty, 131, 138
Murro, Rachel, 171

National Center for Health Statistics, 155, 170
National Institutes of Health, 127
National Suicide Prevention, 168
National Women's Law Center, 17
Native American, 54, 55, 92
New York Times, 39, 76, 122, 128, 144, 147, 170
Ninth Amendment, xii
nonreproductive sex, x, xiv, 81, 82, 83
NPR, 34, 38, 112, 136, 147
Nussbaum, Martin, 62

Obergefell v. Hodges, 73

Ocasio-Cortez, Alexandria, 108
Old Testament, 81
Orrell, Mandolyn, 160

PAC Women Speak Out, 18
parental rights, 62, 67, 147
parenthood, 15, 107, 108, 112
Parker, Tom, 120
Parson, Mike, 30
Pearce, Russell, 92
Perkins, Tony, 77, 123, 129
personhood rights, 115
Petchesky, Rosalind Pollack, 143
Pew Research Center, xvii, xviii, 8, 19, 52, 111, 112, 113
Pezaro, Sally, 159
Planned Parenthood, 12, 36, 143, 161, 163, 168
Planned Parenthood v. Casey, 12
Plotz, David, 127
political action committees (PACs), 48
Politico, 73, 102, 103, 114, 129, 163
pregnancy complications, 132, 158, 168
Preimplantation genetic testing (or PGT), 133
Prelogar, Elizabeth, 18, 28
ProPublica, 30, 32, 61, 62, 123, 153, 154

Reed, Ralph, 68, 77
Reproductive Health Center, 168
Republican Party, ix, xv, xvi, 3, 7, 48, 76, 77, 78, 107, 145
RESOLVE: The National Infertility Foundation, 138
Rieman, Kyle, 32
rights to adopt, 147
Right to Build Families Act, 131
Right to Privacy, ix, x, xi, xiii, 12, 37, 74
Roe v. Wade, ix, x, 3, 4, 5, 6, 7, 8, 9, 10, 12, 13, 14, 15, 16, 18, 22, 23, 24, 27, 30, 34, 35, 37, 39, 45, 57, 58, 61, 73, 74, 76, 91, 97, 102, 103,

114, 123, 125, 129, 131, 132, 133, 134, 135, 149, 150, 151, 153, 158, 160, 161, 163, 164, 165, 166, 167, 168, 169
Roman Catholics, xv, 83
Royce, Katie, 115
Rubio, Marco, 137

Schmidt, Renee, 158
Schupp, Jill, 33
Seid, Barre, 63
Sekhon, Lucky, 132
Senderowicz, Leigh, 92
sex education, 47, 49, 50, 51, 83, 84
sexual identity, xiii, xiv
sexually transmitted disease (STD), 50, 84
sexually transmitted infection (STI), 95, 100
sexual privacy, xiii, xiv, xvii, xviii
Slotkin, Elissa, 138
Social Security, 77
Society for Assisted Reproductive Technology, 126, 130
Sotomayor, Sonia, 73
Southern Baptist Convention, 114
Southern Baptist Theological Seminary, 115, 116
Steel, Michelle, 137
Supermajority, 3, 8
Susan B. Anthony Pro-Life America, 18, 77, 103, 138

telehealth, 11, 14, 22, 28
Texas v. Becerra, 71
Third Amendment, xi
Thomas, Clarence, 27, 73, 91
TikTok, 88, 90, 164
Time Magazine, 84, 86
Tipton, Sean, 126
Torres, Karla, 132
Trevor Project, The, 167, 168
Trump, Donald J., 10, 12, 17, 20, 22, 23, 28, 53, 57, 59, 61, 62, 63, 65, 66, 67, 68, 76, 77, 78, 84, 85, 86, 102, 112, 114, 115
Turning Point USA, 61, 65, 68

ulipristal, 99, 100
United States Conference of Catholic Bishops, 107, 112
unwanted pregnancy, 50, 168
U.S. Circuit Court of Appeals, 27, 71
U.S. Department of Health, 49, 69, 71, 93
U.S. health care, ix, x, xvi, 9, 14, 19, 35, 43, 51, 57, 62, 69, 91, 92, 93, 94, 95, 97, 125, 126, 127, 131, 132, 150, 151, 160, 163, 164, 166, 167, 168
U.S. Supreme Court, 3, 17, 27, 29, 30, 34, 35, 39, 40, 47, 55, 153

Vance, J. D., 109, 112, 113

Waldman, Michael, 3
Walker, Andrew, 116
Wallnau, Lance, 65
Wall Street Journal, 57
Washington Post, 110, 113, 122, 127, 168
White, Byron R., 3
Wiemann, John, 33
Wild, Susan, 138
World Health Organization, 126, 156
Worrell, Frank C., 166
Wrongful Death of a Minor Act, 21, 119

Yale Law Journal, xiii, xvii
Youngkin, Glenn, 57

Zahn, Christopher, 153
Zielke, Christina, 58
Ziklag, 61, 62, 63, 64, 65, 66, 67, 68
Zolna, Mia, 171
Zurawski, Amanda, 58